Praise for Horton Foote and *The Orphans' Home Cycle*

"These gentle plays, with their unswerving human truths, are formidable creations. Horton Foote works with the warp and woof of unalterable proven fact, and surprise. The result can make your hair stand on end."

—EUDORA WELTY

"I'm confident that *The Orphans' Home Cycle* will take its rightful place near the center of our largest American dramatic achievements—a slowly generated, slowly won, apparently effortless, surprisingly wide vision of human life that flowers before our patient, incredulous eyes with an opulent richness of fully communicated pleasure, comprehension, and usable knowledge: a permanent gift."

—REYNOLDS PRICE

"Horton Foote is a national treasure. His contributions to American literature and theater and film are in the treasures he mines and shares in plays like these. The words and the people who speak them are real. So are the tears and the laughs, the frowns and the grins."

—JIM LEHRER

"[In these plays,] Horton Foote remembers his own parents. I very much like his memories. In them, family *is* history, and marriage *is* philosophy. I believe every syllable of Horton Foote, and envy him."

—JOHN LEONARD, *New York*

"The work of an artist who knows just what he wants to do and how he wants to do it, *The Widow Claire* has the lucid details and buried poignancy of a naturalistic American short story from the era in which it is set. [Foote's] Texans open just enough for attentive onlookers to discover the hard compromises, devastating losses and unshakeable faith in familial love that have forged their spirit."

—FRANK RICH, *The New York Times*

"[*Lily Dale*] has a shimmering sense of a world remembered . . . what is distinctive is the manner in which its atmosphere, texture and construction are merged into one dramatic artifact. The play is one to be remembered."

—CLIVE BARNES, *New York Post*

"One of the most intimately monumental dramatic ventures of the decade. . . . There's no question that the plays gather cumulative and associative impact."

—JAY CARR, *The Boston Globe*

"Foote has assessed American character, American myth, and American ambience more accurately than has just about any other figure in the American theater."

—MARIAN BURKHART, *Commonweal*

"Horton Foote is the very definition of a modern American playwright. His plays are as fascinating to read as they are thrilling to see."

—GARSON KANIN

Roots in a Parched Ground, Convicts, Lily Dale, The Widow Claire

HORTON FOOTE

The First Four Plays of The Orphans' Home Cycle

With an Introduction by the Author

Grove Press
New York

Published by Grove Press
a division of Wheatland Corporation
920 Broadway
New York, N.Y. 10010

Library of Congress Cataloging-in-Publication Data
Foote, Horton.
[Plays. Selections]
Roots in a parched ground; Convicts; Lily Dale; The Widow
Claire; the first four plays of the orphans' home cycle/Horton
Foote; with an introduction by the author.—1st ed.
p.   cm.
ISBN 0–8021–1055–X   ISBN 0–8021–3081–X (pbk.)
I. Title.   II. Title: Roots in a parched ground.
PS3511. 0344A6   1988   87-35058
812 .54—dc19   CIP

The author gratefully acknowledges the permission of Harcourt Brace Jovanovich to reprint *Roots in a Parched Ground*.

Grateful acknowledgement is made for permission to reprint from the following works: "Raleigh Was Right" from *Collected Later Poems* by William Carlos Williams, copyright © 1944 by William Carlos Williams, reprinted by permission of New Directions Publishing Corp.; "In Distrust of Merits" from *The Complete Poems of Marianne Moore*, copyright renewed © 1986, Lawrence E. Brinn and Louise Crane, Executors of the Estate of Marianne Moore.

Designed by Irving Perkins Associates, Inc.
Manufactured in the United States of America
First Edition 1988
10   9   8   7   6   5   4   3   2   1

For Lillian

The world's an orphans' home.

—Marianne Moore, from
"In Distrust of Merits"

Contents

Introduction

THE ACTUAL WRITING of these plays began after my mother's death in 1974. My father had died the year before in the very room and on the bed my brothers had been born in.

After my mother's death, I was alone in our house in Wharton, Texas for a week, sorting letters and personal papers, making decisions about what to do with the accumulations of fifty-nine years of life in that house.

After I returned to my then home in the New Hampshire woods, I began making notes for these plays. I don't remember if at the time I thought there would eventually be nine plays, but I am sure that the writing of these first notes was prompted by my thinking over my parents' lives and the world of the town that had surrounded them from birth to death.

Some two years later I had finished first drafts of eight of the plays: *Roots In a Parched Ground, Convicts, Lily Dale, Courtship, Valentine's Day, 1918, Cousins* and *The Death of Papa. The Widow Claire*, the last to be written, was finished some time later.

On a trip to New York, I bought all the records of Charles Ives I could find, playing his music over and over while resting from my work on the plays. It was a time of fuel shortages and exorbitantly high fuel prices, and my family and I kept warm in the New Hampshire winter by burning wood in the fireplaces and stoves. In the spring and summer I would write in a screen house overlooking the woods and a large stone wall. My surroundings couldn't have been more different from the place and time in Texas I was writing about.

I don't remember now, either, the sequence in which I wrote the plays, but I believe *1918* was the first completed, although an earlier version of *Roots In a Parched Ground* had been written years before and done on the *Du Pont Play of the Month* television series, long before I thought of the possibility of there being nine plays or could have imagined the changes that would lead to my living and working in New Hampshire.

Change, however, was an early acquaintance in my life. My grandfather, who seemed impervious to all mortal ends, died when I was nine, and the reverberations and changes from that death continued for many years. It was soon after that I was to see a quiet, serene street (in front of my grandparents' house) begin its slow but steady descent into a metaphor for all the ugly, trashy highways that scar a great deal of small-town America. And these plays, I feel, are about change, unexpected, unasked for, unwanted, but to be faced and dealt with or else we sink into despair or a hopeless longing for a life that is gone.

My first memory was of stories about the past—a past that, according to the storytellers, was superior in every way to the life then being lived. It didn't take me long, however, to understand that the present was all we had, for the past was gone and nothing could be done about it.

I learned, too, how unreliable memory can be, for when members of my family would recount a story from their collective past, I would early on marvel how subtly it would change from storyteller to storyteller.

The time of the plays is a harsh time. They begin in 1902, a time of far-reaching social and economic change in

Texas. The aftermath of Reconstruction and its passions had brought about a white man's union to prevent blacks from voting in local and state elections. But in spite of political and social acts to hold onto the past, a way of life was over, and the practical, the pragmatic were scrambling to form a new economic order. Black men and women were alive who knew the agony of slavery, and white men and women were alive who had owned them. I remember the first time slavery had a concrete face for me. I was on a fourteen-mile hike to complete some phase of becoming a Boy Scout. I stopped in a country store for a bottle of soda water and on the gallery of the store was an elderly black man. As I drank my soda water we got to talking and he asked me my name, and when I told him he said he had been a slave on my great-great-grandfather's plantation. I have never forgotten the impact that made on me. Slavery up until then was merely an abstract statistic that I'd heard older people talking about. "Our family had one hundred sixty slaves, one hundred twenty . . ." or whatever, but as I looked into that man's tired, sorrowing face, I was shocked to realize that this abstraction spoken of so lightly ("we were good to them," "we never mistreated them") was a living, suffering human being. The tales of the past had a new reality for me after that.

And so with the 1918 influenza epidemic, which causes such havoc in the play *1918.* I was raised on stories of the terror of the flu, what it did to my family and to the families of the town, but it seemed only a local phenomenon to me until I read Katherine Anne Porter's "Pale Horse, Pale Rider" and I began to understand how far-reaching it was. Since the productions of *1918,* I have heard from many people telling me how it affected their lives or the lives of their families.

All the plays are based on family stories—stories

often of dislocation, sibling rivalries, elopements, family estrangements, family reconciliations, and all the minutiae that make family life at once so interesting and yet at times so burdening, causing a reaction described by Katherine Anne Porter in "Old Mortality":

> Her mind closed stubbornly against remembering, not the past, but the legends of the past, other people's memory of the past, at which she had spent her life peering in wonder like a child at a magic lantern show. Oh, but there is my own life to come yet, she thought, my own life now and beyond. I don't want any promises, I won't have false hopes, I won't be romantic about myself, I can't live in this world any longer, she told herself listening to the voices back of her. Let them tell their stories to each other. Let them go on exploring how things happened. I don't care. At least I can know the truth about what happened to me, she assured herself, silently making a promise to herself in her hopefulness, in her ignorance.

But many of us do care, of course, and we do continue to remember, and we give to our children and their children our versions of what has gone before, remembering always how unreliable a thing memory is and how our versions of what has gone before can only be what we have come to perceive the past and its people and stories to be. To quote Miss Porter again:

> By the time the writer has reached the end of a story, he has lived it at least three times—first, in a series of actual events that, directly or indirectly, have continued to set up the condition in his mind and senses that causes him to write the story; second, in memory; and third, on re-creation of this chaotic stuff.

I have worked on the plays for about ten years, from the first drafts to the forms found here, during various readings, staged readings, and theater productions, in and out of New York. But essentially the plays have remained the same, some with no revisions whatsoever.

Here, then, are the first four of the plays, their stories and characters, I hope, true to their place and time—true at least to my memory of what I was told or have seen

—HORTON FOOTE
March 1988

Roots in a
Parched Ground

Love itself a flower
with roots in a parched ground.

—William Carlos Williams, from
"Raleigh Was Right"

Characters

CORELLA THORNTON ROBEDAUX
LILY DALE ROBEDAUX
MARY THORNTON
ROBERT THORNTON
HORACE ROBEDAUX
ALBERT THORNTON
MINNIE CURTIS
MR. RITTER
ELIZABETH HILL ROBEDAUX
SALLY ROBEDAUX CURTIS
TERRENCE ROBEDAUX
PAUL HORACE ROBEDAUX
JOHN HOWARD
VIRGIE THORNTON
INEZ THORNTON
GLADYS THORNTON
MARY THORNTON DAVIS
GEORGE TYLER
LLOYD CARPENTER
THURMAN
LARRY
PETE DAVENPORT
FIRST MAN

Act One

Place: Harrison, Texas
Time: 1902–1903

During the action of the play, we visit sections of the ROBEDAUX *and* THORNTON *houses, a section of a riverbank, and an alley in town. The action of the play should be as fluid as possible, and the various sections should be defined by the lights and a few furnishings and props. This was not an affluent time in the lives of these people, and the furnishings and the props used should reflect that.*

The area right stage will be used for all the actions involving the THORNTONS, *and the area left stage will be given to the* ROBEDAUXS. *The area center stage will be used for the riverbank and town alley.*

The lights are brought up right stage on the THORNTON *area. Seated down right is* CORELLA ROBEDAUX, *thirty-one, and at her feet is her daughter,* LILY DALE, *ten. To her left are her mother and father:* MRS. THORNTON, *fifty-two, and* MR. THORNTON, *fifty-six.*

Offstage we hear girls singing "Meet Me Tonight In Dreamland," accompanied by piano, banjo, guitar, and mandolin. CORELLA *sews as she listens to the music, and during the song she motions* LILY DALE *to stand up and holds the half-completed dress up against her daughter.*

5

CORELLA (*whispering*): Go try the dress on, sweetheart.

(*She takes it and goes out. The singing continues.* MRS. THORNTON *turns to her husband.*)

MRS. THORNTON (whispering): It's like old times, isn't it, having the girls together playing and singing?

MR. THORNTON: Yes.

(HORACE ROBEDAUX, *twelve, enters. He sits near his grandfather. The singing continues.* LILY DALE *comes back in wearing the dress her mother was working on.* CORELLA *begins to pin the hem.*)

MRS. THORNTON: It's going to be beautiful.

CORELLA: I think I have a talent for sewing.

MRS. THORNTON: You certainly do.

(ALBERT THORNTON, *twenty-five, enters.*)

MRS. THORNTON: Bring a chair and sit by me, Son.

(*He gets a chair and sits by his mother.*)

Now, we're all together . . . the whole family. The first time in five months.

ALBERT: How do you like Houston, Sis?

CORELLA: Fine.

ALBERT: I love the shirt you brought me.

CORELLA: I'm glad you like it.

LILY DALE: Is that one of the shirts you made, Mama?

CORELLA: Yes.

ALBERT: Big Horace is very low.

CORELLA: Oh?

ALBERT: I just saw Sally. She said they were very concerned for him. I thought you should know, Sister.

(She continues working on the dress as her sisters continue singing. After a moment HORACE *gets up and goes out as the lights fade.)*

(The lights are brought up left stage on the ROBEDAUX *area.* MINNIE, *seventeen, is seated at the edge of the area downstage. She is a plain girl, brusque in her speech and lacking all graciousness.* HORACE *comes in as the singing continues in the distance.)*

HORACE: Cousin Minnie . . . *(She looks up at him, turns away without answering.)* What's the matter with you?

MINNIE: I think it's disgusting.

HORACE: What is?

MINNIE: The music going on over at the Thornton's while your father is so sick.

HORACE: Do you think he can hear it?

MINNIE: Certainly he can hear it. Can't you?

HORACE: Yes, I can.

MINNIE: What's the singing all about?—if you call it singing.

HORACE: My mother and my Aunt Mary came home on visits.

MINNIE: Your mother still in Houston?

HORACE: Yes.

MINNIE: Is she still making men's shirts?

HORACE: Yes.

(MR. RITTER, *seventy-four, comes by*.)

MR. RITTER: Good afternoon.

HORACE: Hello, Mr. Ritter.

MR. RITTER: How are you, Horace?

HORACE: Pretty well, thank you.

(MR. RITTER *looks at* MINNIE.)

MR. RITTER: You're Minnie, aren't you?

MINNIE: Yes.

MR. RITTER: You are a grown young lady now. (*To* HORACE): How is your father today, son?

HORACE: He's all right.

MINNIE: He's not all right at all. He's very low.

MR. RITTER: I'm sorry to hear it. Yes, indeed.

HORACE: My mother came home on a visit.

MR. RITTER: That's nice. How does she like Houston?

HORACE: She likes it well enough.

MR. RITTER: How long will she be here?

HORACE: For three days. My Aunt Mary's here too.

MR. RITTER: Is she? She's married now, isn't she?

HORACE: Yes Sir.

MR. RITTER: And lives in West Texas?

HORACE: Yes Sir.

MR. RITTER: Well, they're all at home now. I bet your grandfather and grandmother are glad.

HORACE: Yes Sir. They sure are.

MR. RITTER: I've always enjoyed being in their home, you know. There was always music while you visited. Are you as fond of music as your aunts and uncles?

HORACE: Yes Sir.

MINNIE: Do you call what's going on over there now music?

MR. RITTER: Why, yes, I do.

MINNIE: I don't. I call it a public nuisance. My grand-mother almost called the sheriff. You know, we have a sick man in this house.

(MRS. ROBEDAUX, *sixty, comes out.*)

MRS. ROBEDAUX: Horace, will you please go over there and ask in heaven's name they cut out that noise? Your father is in there fighting for his very life and the least noise is a torture to him.

HORACE: Yes Ma'am. (*He goes out.*)

MRS. ROBEDAUX: You don't know, Mr. Ritter, how sick my boy is. I'm afraid now we can't save him. (*She cries.*)

MINNIE: Now Grandma. . . .

MRS. ROBEDAUX: I'm afraid he is going to be taken from me. (*She wipes her eyes. The music has continued.*) Just listen to that noise. (*She calls out.*) Be quiet over there!

MINNIE: She came home on a visit.

MRS. ROBEDAUX: Who?

MINNIE: You know . . . and her sister Mary too.

MRS. ROBEDAUX: Oh, she's as frivolous and lightheaded as the rest of them. All any of them think about are parties and dances. Not a brain in their heads, any of them. I hope Horace don't take after the Thorntons. I hope and pray the Robedaux blood fights and overcomes all the silliness he's bound to inherit from them. Lily Dale, of course, is clearly a Thornton: silly, flighty, vain, self-centered.

(*The singing stops.*)

MR. RITTER: There. The singing has stopped.

MRS. ROBEDAUX: Yes.

MR. RITTER: I'll stop by tomorrow. I hope there will be better news tomorrow.

MRS. ROBEDAUX: I hope so, but I fear not, Mr. Ritter.

(*He goes on off.*)

MINNIE: How does he live?

MRS. ROBEDAUX: I don't know. People invite him in for a meal now and then. He has a little garden over there. The whole time he boarded with Corella and Gladys he never paid them a cent, you know. No wonder they couldn't make a success of their boardinghouse. They had every deadbeat in town living over there.

MINNIE: Did the boardinghouse belong to them?

MRS. ROBEDAUX: No. They rented it from someone. Mr. Ritter just lives on over there.

MINNIE: Does he pay rent?

MRS. ROBEDAUX: No.

MINNIE: Who does the house belong to?

MRS. ROBEDAUX: I don't know. I don't expect that he does. It's a funny thing about men. They don't have money for food or rent, but they can always find the money to buy whiskey. Mr. Ritter has been drunk half his life, but it hasn't affected his health. He just goes on.

(SALLY, MINNIE'S *mother and* MRS. ROBEDAUX'S *daughter, comes out.* MRS. ROBEDAUX *turns to her.*)

Does he need me?

SALLY: He's asleep.

MRS. ROBEDAUX: I'm glad. I don't think he slept more than five minutes last night, and neither did I.

SALLY: Go and get some rest now, Mama.

MRS. ROBEDAUX: No.

SALLY: You'll wear yourself out, Mama.

MRS. ROBEDAUX: What does it matter? (*Pause. She cries.*) I worship him above all earthly things. When I lost your other two brothers, I never complained once. I just bowed to God's will. But I can't bear the loss of Horace. Why, if the Lord takes him, he will be taking my right arm, my rod and my staff, my eyes and my ears. (*A boy walks by with schoolbooks.*) There's the Lewis boy coming home from school.

SALLY: I guess school is just out. He's such a good boy—he never has to stay after school.

MRS. ROBEDAUX: That means little Horace didn't go to school again today.

MINNIE: He didn't go yesterday either.

SALLY: Or the day before that. I saw him uptown at eleven o'clock looking for empty whiskey bottles in the alley behind the saloon day before yesterday. We should speak to his Grandfather Thornton.

MRS. ROBEDAUX: He doesn't care. And Corella doesn't care. None of them went to school. Mr. Thornton doesn't have any education to speak of, and certainly none of his children have. Why should they worry or concern themselves about Horace? Where is Terrence?

SALLY: He's reading. He was talking this morning about looking for a job, but he doesn't know where to turn. It's too bad they sold the newspaper, he said. Of course, he couldn't have run it alone after Brother Carl died. I didn't want to hurt his feelings, but you know he couldn't have, Mama. Why, no one could understand the editorials when he wrote them. If you don't know Latin and Greek, you're lost trying to read what he writes. People just laughed at his editorials, Mama—you know that.

MRS. ROBEDAUX: Well, don't ever tell him that.

SALLY: Oh, I wouldn't, but you know it's true.

MRS. ROBEDAUX: They laugh at everything but the common and vulgar here—everything.

(HORACE *comes in.*)

HORACE: I told them. They were sorry. They're worried, though, because they are going to have a dance at Grandpa's tonight and they hope that won't disturb him.

MRS. ROBEDAUX: Of course it will disturb him.

SALLY: Why are they having a dance?

HORACE: I don't know. They are always having dances. It's not going to be a big dance—just a few couples, they said. It will be over by eleven.

MRS. ROBEDAUX: Well, if it gets too noisy, I'll just have to call the sheriff. You tell them that for me.

HORACE: Yes Ma'am.

MRS. ROBEDAUX: Why weren't you in school today?

HORACE: I didn't want to go.

MRS. ROBEDAUX: You just don't go when you don't want to?

HORACE: No Ma'am.

MRS. ROBEDAUX: Doesn't your Grandfather Thornton make you go?

HORACE: No Ma'am.

SALLY: What does your mother say?

HORACE: She doesn't care.

SALLY: Does Lily Dale go?

HORACE: No Ma'am. Not too much.

SALLY: I think it's terrible, Mama. I think it's just terrible.

(TERRENCE *comes out. He has a book in his hand.*)

TERRENCE: Brother is awake.

MRS. ROBEDAUX: Thank you. (*She gets up and goes inside.*)

TERRENCE: Hello, Horace.

HORACE: Hello, Uncle Terrence.

TERRENCE: How's the fishing?

HORACE: Pretty good.

TERRENCE: How many customers do you have?

HORACE: Let's see . . . Mrs. Lewis, Mrs. Henry, Mrs. Theile, Mrs. Howard, for regular customers. And then there are a few others that aren't so regular.

(MRS. ROBEDAUX *comes out.*)

MRS. ROBEDAUX: Horace, your father heard you out here. He wants to see you. Don't stay long.

HORACE: No Ma'am.

(*He starts into the area. The light has widened and we see far upstage a single bed. PAUL HORACE is there. HORACE goes over to the bed.*)

Hello, Papa. How do you feel?

ROBEDAUX: Pretty well, thank you. How are you, Son?

HORACE: I'm just fine, Papa.

ROBEDAUX: Is it a pretty day out?

HORACE: Yes Sir.

ROBEDAUX: Have you been fishing this afternoon?

HORACE: No Sir. I'll go down later on and check on my lines.

ROBEDAUX: How's Lily Dale?

HORACE: She's fine.

ROBEDAUX: And your mother?

HORACE: She's fine.

ROBEDAUX: Is she still in Houston?

HORACE: Yes Sir. She's come home now on a visit, though. Aunt Mary is here too. They were all over there this afternoon together, singing, but Grandma said it was disturbing you so I asked them to stop it.

ROBEDAUX: It certainly wasn't disturbing me. You tell them to sing all they want to.

HORACE: Yes Sir.

ROBEDAUX: Does your mother like Houston?

HORACE: Yes Sir. I guess so.

ROBEDAUX: Do you think you and Lily Dale will ever go live with her in Houston?

HORACE: I don't know, Sir. Mama thinks I should live with Grandpa because he can make me behave.

ROBEDAUX: Did you go to school today?

HORACE: No Sir.

ROBEDAUX: Did you go any this week?

HORACE: No Sir.

ROBEDAUX: You don't like school?

HORACE: No Sir.

ROBEDAUX: Why?

HORACE: I just don't. I'm not smart.

ROBEDAUX: Do you study?

HORACE: Sometimes.

ROBEDAUX: Bring your books over here tomorrow.

HORACE: Yes Sir. (*Pause.*) What for?

ROBEDAUX: I just want to see what you know.

HORACE: I don't know anything.

ROBEDAUX: Yes, you do.

HORACE: No, I don't. I'm dumb.

ROBEDAUX: You're not dumb, Horace. You don't study.

HORACE: I'm dumb.

ROBEDAUX: Who says so?

HORACE: My teacher.

ROBEDAUX: Who is your teacher?

HORACE: Miss Philips.

ROBEDAUX: Well, you're not dumb.

HORACE: Yes, I am.

(ROBEDAUX *closes his eyes. Pause.*)

ROBEDAUX: I want you to bring your books over here every day. If I can't work with you, your Uncle Terrence can.

HORACE: He reads Latin and Greek, don't he?

ROBEDAUX: Doesn't he.

HORACE: Doesn't he?

ROBEDAUX: Yes.

HORACE: Are you a lawyer?

ROBEDAUX: Yes.

HORACE: You and Mr. John Howard are partners? His two children were burned up in a fire, weren't they?

ROBEDAUX: Yes.

HORACE: They say that has affected his wife's mind. She never leaves the house. Did you ever see her?

ROBEDAUX: Yes.

HORACE: Was she pretty?

ROBEDAUX: Yes.

HORACE: Did you ever know his children?

ROBEDAUX: Yes.

HORACE: How long ago was the fire?

ROBEDAUX: Ten years ago.

(MRS. ROBEDAUX *comes in.*)

MRS. ROBEDAUX: John Howard is here to see you.

ROBEDAUX: All right. (*She starts to get* JOHN HOWARD.) Mama, that singing over at the Thorntons didn't bother me. You shouldn't have stopped it. I told Horace to tell them to sing all they want to.

MRS. ROBEDAUX: All right.

HORACE: They're having a dance tonight.

MRS. ROBEDAUX: It's all a lot of foolishness.

(*She goes out.* ROBEDAUX *closes his eyes.* JOHN HOWARD *comes in.*)

JOHN HOWARD: How is the patient today?

ROBEDAUX: I'm still here. How's the weather?

JOHN HOWARD: It's a lovely day.

ROBEDAUX: Have you been keeping busy?

JOHN HOWARD: It's kind of quiet. You're not missing much.

ROBEDAUX: I talked to Harris Martin yesterday afternoon. He wants to buy my law books.

JOHN HOWARD: Do you want to sell them?

ROBEDAUX: Yes.

JOHN HOWARD: Why?

ROBEDAUX: I need the money. We have no money. None.

(*He closes his eyes.* MRS. ROBEDAUX *comes in.*)

MRS. ROBEDAUX: Anything happening uptown of interest, John Howard?

JOHN HOWARD: No Ma'am, nothing. It's very quiet. And I was telling Paul Horace there is no law practice whatsoever. He's missing nothing.

MRS. ROBEDAUX (*looking over at her son*): I think he's tired. I think we'd all better go and let him have some sleep.

(JOHN HOWARD *and* HORACE *get up. They go outside.* MRS. ROBEDAUX *puts a sheet over her son and then leaves as the lights fade.*)

(*The lights are brought up right stage on the* THORNTON *area. A dance is in progress in the house offstage. Someone plays a piano, and from time to time couples dance into the area and out. They are* VIRGIE, INEZ, GLADYS, ALBERT *and his date, and another couple.* CORELLA, MARY, LILY DALE, *and* MR. *and* MRS. THORNTON *sit at the edge of the area watching.* HORACE *enters and sits beside them.*)

MRS. THORNTON: Mary, do you and Jim go to many dances out in West Texas?

MARY: Once in a while. Jim isn't so fond of dancing.

MRS. THORNTON: Do you still like to dance?

MARY: Oh, yes, I do.

MRS. THORNTON: The young married couples all go to the dances in the Opera House here, which I think is nice. I swear, I don't think Virgie would get married if they didn't. She does love to dance.

MARY: When is she marrying?

MRS. THORNTON: In a month. She and Gladys plan a double wedding. Inez will be married soon after.

MARY: They all three should get married at the same time.

MRS. THORNTON: Inez didn't want to.

LILY DALE: I'm going to be the flower girl.

(ALBERT *comes up.*)

ALBERT: Come on, Mary. You dance with me.

MARY: What about your date?

ALBERT: She wants us to have a dance together. Then I'll come and get Corrie.

CORELLA: No. Don't bother about me. My dancing days are over.

MARY: Oh, come on now, Sis.

CORELLA: I just like to watch.

(ALBERT *and* MARY *dance off.* LILY DALE *gets in her mother's lap.*)

LILY DALE: When are you leaving again for Houston?

CORELLA: I swear, honey, I've told you a thousand times. I go back in two days.

LILY DALE: Take me with you.

CORELLA: I can't, honey.

LILY DALE: Why?

CORELLA: Because it's not practical right now. You and Horace will have to live on with your grandfather for awhile.

(LILY DALE *cries*.)

MRS. THORNTON: Lily Dale, what's the matter with you?

LILY DALE: Nothing.

MRS. THORNTON: What are you crying for then?

LILY DALE: Nothing.

MRS. THORNTON: Then stop crying. Heavens . . . your mother has enough on her mind without you carrying on that way. Look at your brother. He's not crying.

LILY DALE: He likes it here. He likes to fish in the river.

CORELLA: You like it here, honey . . .

LILY DALE: No, I don't. I want to be with you in Houston.

CORELLA: We'll see.

LILY DALE: Can I go with you and live in Houston?

CORELLA: We'll see.

LILY DALE: June Dale Robinson said you and Daddy were divorced. And I said you were not—you were separated. And she said, "That's the same thing." Is it?

CORELLA: No.

LILY DALE: What's the difference?

CORELLA: Well, when you are separated, you are still married, even if you don't live in the same house or the same town together. And when you're divorced, you are no longer married.

LILY DALE: If you were divorced, would he still be my father?

CORELLA: Yes.

LILY DALE: Why?

CORELLA: Because he is your father. He will always be. (*Pause.*) Horace, would you mind if Lily Dale went and lived with me for a little while in Houston? (*Pause. He doesn't answer.*) Horace?

HORACE: What?

CORELLA: Did you hear what I said?

HORACE: Yes.

MR. THORNTON: Horace, what do you have in your mouth?

HORACE: Chewing tobacco.

MR. THORNTON: Where did you get it?

HORACE: Bought it uptown.

MR. THORNTON: Spit it out. You're too young to chew tobacco.

(*He spits it out.* MINNIE *comes in.*)

MINNIE: Grandma said would you mind stopping the music now. Uncle Horace is very low. She thinks he might not last until morning.

MR. THORNTON: I'll stop them at once.

MINNIE: Thank you.

(*She goes.* MR. THORNTON *goes. The music stops.* HORACE *gets up.*)

MRS. THORNTON: Where are you going, Horace?

HORACE: I'm going over to Papa's.

MRS. THORNTON: Don't get in the way over there, Horace. Your Grandmother Robedaux has enough on her mind without worrying about you. (HORACE *leaves*.) Your father is crazy about him, you know. We're glad to have him here with us. He's strict with him, but that's good for the boy.

CORELLA: I'm glad he makes him mind.

MRS. THORNTON: He's such a manly little fellow. And he works hard. Your grandfather talked to him plain about that. He said he had all he could do putting food on the table and that if Horace wanted anything to spend, or clothes, he would have to work for it.

CORELLA: That won't hurt him.

MRS. THORNTON: No. He has regular customers for his fish, you know. Of course, Mrs. Lewis takes terrible advantage of him. She's always telling him the fish he left for her was spoiled and she refuses to pay him. I said, "It seems mighty funny to me no one else's fish is spoiled." Doesn't that strike you funny? She's just trying to get out of paying him. He won't take money from me for fish. He says he wants to do his part. Of course, he doesn't go to school half the time, but your papa and I see no sense in making him go if he doesn't want to do it. He will just play hookey anyway. We couldn't keep Albert in school even when we tried. Of course, I think there is a thing of too much education. I think that's part of the Robedauxs' trouble. They are all overeducated.

LILY DALE: Can I go to Houston with you, Mama?

CORELLA: I guess so.

LILY DALE: When are we going to leave?

CORELLA: In two days.

LILY DALE: Can't we leave tomorrow?

CORELLA: No, honey, we can't. I'm here on a little vacation.

(*The lights fade as the lights are brought up left stage on the* ROBEDAUX *area. They have brought chairs into the area.* JOHN HOWARD *and* GEORGE TYLER *are there.*)

JOHN HOWARD: I think it is very serious this time.

GEORGE TYLER: Do they have any money at all?

JOHN HOWARD: I don't think so. He asked me to sell his law books today. I don't know what I can get for them. What do you think?

GEORGE TYLER: I wouldn't know.

JOHN HOWARD: I'll get as much as I can.

GEORGE TYLER: Do you have a customer?

JOHN HOWARD: Yes.

GEORGE TYLER: Who?

JOHN HOWARD: Harris Martin.

GEORGE TYLER: That skinflint! You'll get nothing from him. Paul Horace used to have quite a library.

JOHN HOWARD: Yes, he did.

GEORGE TYLER: Full sets of Thackeray, Dickens, Wilkie Collins, Bulwer-Lytton, Milton, Shakespeare, George Eliot . . .

JOHN HOWARD: Mark Twain, Emerson, Washington Irving . . .

GEORGE TYLER: He had a fine library. (*Pause.*) The last time I was in the house, I saw none of it left.

JOHN HOWARD: There are no books now, except for a few Latin, Greek volumes that belong to Terrence.

GEORGE TYLER: He's some kind of a fool, isn't he? Sitting in the house reading Latin and Greek all day. What happened to the books?

JOHN HOWARD: Whiskey . . . whiskey . . . whiskey. He gave them to Mr. Dawdy to pay off some saloon debts.

GEORGE TYLER: He worries, you know, about his family and what's to become of them. My wife is distantly kin to the Thorntons and she's very loyal to them in all this, and she says it's too bad he don't worry about his children like he does his mother, his sister, and his brother. And I said, "How come you think he doesn't?"

JOHN HOWARD: He does worry about them.

GEORGE TYLER: Of course he does. I know he does.

JOHN HOWARD: He had his mother call me over here right after breakfast the other morning and he wanted me to go and talk to Mr. Thornton about Horace not going to school. I said, "I can't do that." And he said he wanted me, if anything ever happened to him, to try and see that Horace stayed in school. "How can I do that?" I said. "By talking to Horace," he said, "reasoning with him, telling him how important it is to stay in school. And if he's interested at all in law later on," he said, "will you promise me he can read law in your office?" he asked. "Why, yes," I said, "certainly I can promise you that much."

GEORGE TYLER: He's called for me twice. He said, "I know you have children of your own to worry about, but promise me if anything ever happens to Mr. Thornton, you'll see that Horace and Lily Dale always have enough to eat and a home." (*Pause.*) Of course, you have to be careful the kind of promises you make, as I have four children of my own and Lily Dale and Horace have aunts and uncles, and they are the ones that should really take the responsibility. And, of course, his mother . . . (*He whispers.*) My wife has heard she has been seeing a gentleman in Houston. He works for the railroads.

JOHN HOWARD: Do you think if anything happens to Horace she'll marry again?

GEORGE TYLER: My wife has been told he's asked her. He even wanted her to get a divorce, but she wouldn't.

JOHN HOWARD: Then I'm sure the children will live with them if she marries him.

GEORGE TYLER: I don't know. (*He looks around, whispering.*) I do know, too. That's part of why she won't get a divorce. He doesn't want the children. He says he can't afford to keep them in Houston. He said he would consider taking the girl but never the boy. Evidently, he had to work to support his family at ten or twelve; he thinks boys should all work. He thinks Horace should quit school and go to work.

JOHN HOWARD: Do the Robedauxs know any of this?

GEORGE TYLER: God forbid!

JOHN HOWARD: Do they own their house?

GEORGE TYLER: I think so. I believe it's clear, too.

JOHN HOWARD: What could they get for it if they have to sell it?

GEORGE TYLER: God knows. You can't give houses away here now. That house Corrie and Gladys used for a boardinghouse is vacant. They're trying to sell it. They can't even get $500 for it.

JOHN HOWARD: If anything happens to him, I told Mrs. Robedaux that you and I would see to all the burial expenses.

GEORGE TYLER: I told her that too. They have their own lot in the cemetery, she said.

JOHN HOWARD That's right. Two of his brothers are buried there.

(HORACE *comes in.*)

JOHN HOWARD: Hello, son.

HORACE: Hello.

GEORGE TYLER: How are you, son?

HORACE: I'm all right.

JOHN HOWARD: The doctor is with your daddy now. He's very low.

HORACE: Yes Sir.

GEORGE TYLER: We haven't given up hope yet, though, have we, John Howard?

JOHN HOWARD: No Sir.

GEORGE TYLER: He's fooled us before. Hasn't he?

JOHN HOWARD: Yes Sir.

GEORGE TYLER: Remember about four months ago Mrs. Robedaux told us to hurry and get over here if we wanted to see him alive; but he's still here . . .

(*The doctor comes out. He walks to the edge of the stage and the two men follow after him.* HORACE *watches them. The doctor leaves. The two men come over to* HORACE.)

GEORGE TYLER: It doesn't look good, son. (*Pause.*) Does it to you, John Howard?

JOHN HOWARD: No.

(*Pause.*)

GEORGE TYLER: Why don't you go on home, son? It could be six or seven hours before anything happens. We'll call you when the time comes. (*Pause.*) There is nothing you can do. (*Pause.*) Don't you think he'd be better off at home getting his rest, John Howard?

JOHN HOWARD: Yes, I do. (HORACE *doesn't budge.*) How's your mother?

HORACE: She's well.

JOHN HOWARD: I heard she was home on a visit.

GEORGE TYLER: Your Aunt Mary too?

HORACE: Yes Sir.

GEORGE TYLER: Did her husband come too?

HORACE: No Sir.

GEORGE TYLER: I used to go with your Aunt Mary.

HORACE: Did you?

GEORGE TYLER: Yes, I did. I think I was her first beau. She has one of the loveliest alto voices I've ever heard. How long will she be here?

HORACE: I don't know.

GEORGE TYLER: How long will your mother be here?

HORACE: Until day after tomorrow.

JOHN HOWARD: What kind of work does she do in Houston?

GEORGE TYLER: She makes men's shirts.

(*Pause.*)

JOHN HOWARD: She makes shirts? What have we come to? Her grandfather was governor and his plantation ran from here to the coast.

GEORGE TYLER: What about the Robedauxs? They owned a shipping fleet in Galveston.

JOHN HOWARD: The Thorntons shouldn't have lost their land. They were cheated out of it.

(MR. RITTER *comes up.*)

MR. RITTER: I hear he's very low.

GEORGE TYLER: Yes.

(*He takes out some whiskey and has a swig. He passes it to* JOHN HOWARD, *who has a swig.*)

Mr. Ritter?

MR. RITTER: I don't mind if I do.

(JOHN HOWARD *passes it to* MR. RITTER *who takes a swig and passes it back to* GEORGE.)

JOHN HOWARD: What are they asking for that house you stay in?

MR. RITTER: Five hundred dollars.

JOHN HOWARD: That's what I'd been told.

MR. RITTER: I hope to buy it in time. I've been expecting a little check of late which as yet hasn't arrived. (*He looks at* HORACE.) This boy, gentlemen, is a remarkable boy. He's always working. I see him early every morning and late in the afternoon going to the river and checking his fishing lines; and he combs the alleys behind the saloons looking for empty whiskey bottles to sell. Sometimes I see him sweeping out stores, collecting bills for the merchants, delivering newspapers and groceries; he's always busy.

JOHN HOWARD: It's all very well if he doesn't neglect his schooling.

GEORGE TYLER: We think you miss school too much, son.

MR. RITTER: I recall the time you got lost, Little Horace. That was a terrible two weeks. We didn't know if you were alive or dead. Your mother and aunt had the boarding-house then, remember?

HORACE: Yes Sir.

MR. RITTER: It will be two years ago this fall. Do you gentlemen remember?

JOHN HOWARD: Of course we remember. We helped search the river bottoms for a week.

MR. RITTER: And there he was all the time, up at the Brodler's plantation, safe and sound. The two Brodler brothers were on a drunk, you know. That's why he couldn't get back home.

GEORGE TYLER: How come you went out in that storm in the first place?

HORACE: I didn't know it was going to be a storm. I went up the river to fish. I had a little boat and where I first went, the fishing wasn't too good so I decided to spend the night, and then the next day I went further and further and somehow I got lost, and I thought I was heading home and instead I was going all the time towards the gulf.

MR. RITTER: And then the hurricane struck and he did the wise thing. He abandoned the boat and headed for the

woods and he ended up at the Brodler plantation, and
then the river began to rise and you couldn't get anyplace
at all in that part of the county without a boat, and by that
time the Brodler brothers were drunk and they wouldn't
give him a boat, and it was two weeks before they sobered
up and let him come back home.

GEORGE TYLER: And by that time we all thought you were
dead . . . drowned.

JOHN HOWARD: There's no one like those Brodler brothers.
Mr. Comstock says Clarence Brodler invited him out to
the plantation once to have supper with him. He went, he
said, and they sat down at the table and the cook brought
a huge platter of fried chicken. Clarence was drunk by
this time and when they sat at the table, Clarence took out
his gun and pointed it at Comstock and said, "Now, you
sonofabitch, I want you to eat every piece of that chicken
or I'll blow your brains out." Well, Comstock said, he
knew drunk as he was, he meant it, too. So he began to
eat. There were at least four chickens there, and finally he
said he thought he would die if he had to eat another
piece, but every time he'd try to slow up, old Clarence
would nudge him with his gun and tell him to go on
eating. He said he doesn't know what would have happened if the cook hadn't taken pity on him and made an
excuse to get Clarence back into the kitchen. And Comstock said he jumped out the dining room window then
and he didn't stop running until he got back to Harrison.

(*The men all laugh.* MINNIE *comes out.*)

MINNIE: Grandma says to please not talk. My uncle is
very low.

(*She goes back into the house. The men are silent. They light
pipes.* TERRENCE *comes outside.*)

TERRENCE: Gentlemen . . .

JOHN HOWARD: Terrence . . .

TERRENCE: Brother is very sick. Very sick.

(*He sits down near the men as the lights fade.*)

(*The lights are brought up. It is early morning. The men are dozing.* HORACE *is stretched out on the ground asleep.* MINNIE *comes out. She is crying.* TERRENCE *goes to her.*)

MINNIE: He's dying, Uncle Terrence. He is dying for sure.

(HORACE *stirs in his sleep.* MRS. ROBEDAUX *comes out.* TERRENCE *goes to her. She goes to* HORACE *and shakes him.*)

MRS. ROBEDAUX: Horace, wake up . . . (*The boy opens his eyes.*) Run home and get your sister and get right back here if you all want to see your daddy alive one last time. (*He stares at her.*) Do you hear me, boy? Your daddy is dying. Hurry and get your sister. (HORACE *gets up and goes running out.*) Gentlemen, come with me now if you want to tell him goodbye.

(*She starts back into the area; the men follow as the lights fade.*)

(*The lights are brought up upper right.* GLADYS, VIRGIE, INEZ, *and* MARY *are playing cards.* CORELLA *is sewing* LILY DALE's *dress.* LILY DALE *is near her mother.* HORACE *comes in.*)

CORELLA: Did you spend the night down at the river?

HORACE: No, over to Papa's. Lily Dale, Grandma Robedaux said if we want to see Papa alive, we'd better hurry.

LILY DALE: Are you coming, Mama?

CORELLA: I can't, honey.

LILY DALE: Why?

CORELLA: Now, you know why.

LILY DALE: Why?

CORELLA: It would be embarrassing to everyone concerned, that's why.

LILY DALE: Then I'm not going.

CORELLA: Oh, yes, you have to.

LILY DALE: Why do I have to?

CORELLA: For your father's sake.

LILY DALE: Aunt Virgie says Papa is a drunkard and a cigarette fiend. Is he?

CORELLA: Don't you dare repeat things like that. For heaven sakes!

LILY DALE: And she says Grandma Robedaux runs him. Does she?

CORELLA: It's not for me to say, and your aunt shouldn't be talking that way either. Now run on.

(HORACE *starts out. She follows after him as the lights fade. The lights are brought up down left.* HORACE *and* LILY DALE *enter.* MR. RITTER, GEORGE TYLER, *and* JOHN HOWARD *come into the area from the house. They see* HORACE *and* LILY DALE. *They go to them.*)

JOHN HOWARD: It's very sad, children. It's very sad. You have our sympathy.

GEORGE TYLER: Now, he is not dead yet, John Howard. None of us must give up hope. We're going off to work now, son. Your grandmother knows where to call us if we're needed.

(*They leave. HORACE and LILY DALE start into the area up left. She pauses and pulls back.*)

LILY DALE: Horace . . .

HORACE: What?

LILY DALE: I'm scared.

HORACE: What are you scared of?

LILY DALE: I'm scared of seeing Papa. Aunt Virgie says he looks like a ghost. (HORACE *starts on.*) Horace . . . (*He pauses.*) Is he gonna die?

(*He doesn't answer her. He starts again towards the upper left area as MINNIE appears.*)

MINNIE: What took you so long?

HORACE: We got here as fast as we could.

MINNIE: I'm his favorite. I guess you know that.

LILY DALE: You're not his daughter. You're just his niece.

MINNIE: Yes, but I'm smart and he admires that in anyone, he told me once.

LILY DALE: Can you read Latin and Greek?

MINNIE: No, but I'm learning.

LILY DALE: Who's teaching you?

MINNIE: Uncle Terrence. That's all he will read.

LILY DALE: I'm going to learn to play the piano.

MINNIE: What good is that?

LILY DALE: Don't you like music?

MINNIE: Not very much. Not the kind you hear coming from where you live.

LILY DALE: Can you dance?

MINNIE: Good heavens, no! And I have no interest in learning.

LILY DALE: My aunts are going to teach me. My Aunt Virgie has won nine prizes for dancing: five for waltzing, two for the turkey trot, and two for the cakewalk.

MINNIE: Do you always brag so much?

LILY DALE: I don't brag.

MINNIE: What do you call what you've just been doing? Where did you get that dress?

LILY DALE: My mama made it.

(*The light has widened and we see far upstage the single bed. HORACE and LILY DALE's father is dying. MRS. ROBEDAUX, his sister, and his brother are with him.*)

MINNIE: Come on. Grandma said I was to take you back to the room.

HORACE: Where is Grandma?

MINNIE: She's with Uncle. (LILY DALE *begins to cry.*) What's the matter with you?

LILY DALE: Nothing.

MINNIE: What are you crying about?

HORACE: She's scared.

MINNIE: What's she scared of?

HORACE: She's scared of seeing Papa.

MINNIE: He's not going to hurt you.

(They cross the lighted area slowly to their father's bed. His eyes are closed; his breathing is irregular and comes now only in gasps. MRS. ROBEDAUX is so near the bed of her son, she is not aware of the children's entrance. His brother and sister are huddled together at the side of the area. MINNIE comes in closer to the bed, followed by LILY DALE and HORACE. MINNIE finally goes over to her grandmother and tugs at her dress sleeve, and the grandmother looks up and sees the children. She motions them to come over to her, but they don't move. MINNIE goes to them.)

MINNIE: Come on . . .

(HORACE takes LILY DALE by the hand and they slowly go over to their father's bedside. The grandmother looks up again and sees them and motions them even closer to their father. HORACE leads LILY DALE to the bed. There is silence in the room except for their father's breathing.)

MRS. ROBEDAUX: Come closer, children. Look long and hard at his sweet, dear face. Oh, he has suffered so. I hope you children will never know the suffering your dear, sweet father has known. *(She takes a cloth and gently wipes his brow.)* Dear Lord, why have you brought this suffering on this precious child of mine? Spare him, I pray you, for the sake of these two innocent children who so need a father's love and guidance.

(She puts away the cloth. Again there is silence except for the breathing of the sick man. MRS. ROBEDAUX puts her arm around

HORACE *and* LILY DALE. LILY DALE *has had her eyes closed since entering the area.*)

MRS. ROBEDAUX: Pray with me, children. Close your sweet eyes and pray with me for the life of your father. Pray with me to God to spare his precious life.

(*She closes her eyes.* HORACE *closes his.*)

MINNIE: Grandma . . . look . . . his lips moved.

(MRS. ROBEDAUX *opens her eyes.*)

MRS. ROBEDAUX: Son? What are you trying to tell us? Son? Open your eyes. Look at Little Horace. Look at sweet Lily Dale. (MRS. ROBEDAUX *again pulls the children to her.*) Speak to him, children.

HORACE: What shall I say?

MRS. ROBEDAUX: Say hello to him, sugar.

HORACE: Hello, Papa.

MRS. ROBEDAUX: Son, did you know who that was? That was Little Horace, your precious little boy. (*To* LILY DALE:) Now, Lily Dale, you speak to your father.

MINNIE: She has her eyes closed. She's had them closed ever since she came in here. Why do you have your eyes closed?

MRS. ROBEDAUX: Darling, why do you have your eyes closed? Are you praying? Is that why you have your eyes closed?

LILY DALE: No Ma'am.

MRS. ROBEDAUX: Then why do you have them closed?

LILY DALE: Because I'm scared.

MRS. ROBEDAUX: Of what, honey?

(HORACE *points to his father.*)

HORACE: Of him.

MRS. ROBEDAUX: Of her own sweet father? Oh, surely not. That's not so, is it, precious?

LILY DALE: Yes Ma'am, it is.

MRS. ROBEDAUX: Well, shame on you. Open your eyes and speak to your father.

(LILY DALE *opens her eyes and tries to speak, but she begins to cry instead. Her aunt quickly comes over to her and holds her.*)

LILY DALE: I want to go home.

(SALLY *looks up at* MRS. ROBEDAUX *to see what her mother thinks she should do*).

MRS. ROBEDAUX: Let her go home. I don't want that crying in here.

(*The aunt leads* LILY DALE *out of the area.* MRS. ROBEDAUX *looks toward* HORACE.)

You'd better go, too. We don't want to tire him. (HORACE *starts away.*) Tell him goodbye before you leave.

HORACE: Goodbye, Papa.

(*Silence.*)

MRS. ROBEDAUX: All right, son. You can go now.

(*He leaves. He joins* LILY DALE *and the aunt. When the aunt sees him, she goes back into the area.*)

LILY DALE: Horace, what's wrong with him?

HORACE: I don't know.

LILY DALE: I don't want to ever go in there again. I'm going to tell Mama. Everytime I see him I have bad dreams.

(MINNIE *comes out to them.*)

MINNIE: What are you hanging around for? You can't do him any good now. It's too late to help him now. Your mama is to blame for it, you know. She deserted him when he needed her. All she was ever interested in was money. When he got sick and couldn't work, she left him.

(*She goes inside.*)

LILY DALE: Do you believe that? Aunt Virgie says it isn't true. She says Papa is being killed by whiskey and cigarettes and worry. Worry because he has to feed and clothe his relatives. She says his family are all shiftless and lazy. (*Pause.*) Brother, how did it all happen? I won't ever forget it. Walking down the street at two in the morning in our nightgowns with the neighbors all watching from their windows, Minnie screaming at Mama, Grandma Robedaux crying, Mama crying . . . Uncle Terrence calling to everybody to be calm.

(*The lights are brought up upper right in the* THORNTON *area.* CORELLA *is there sewing.* LILY DALE *and* HORACE *come in.*)

LILY DALE: When can I start taking music?

CORELLA: As soon as I can afford it.

LILY DALE: Why can't Aunt Virgie teach me?

CORELLA: Because she's never learned. She plays by ear.

LILY DALE: She plays everything by ear?

CORELLA: Yes. Everything she plays. Did you get to see your papa?

HORACE: Yes Ma'am.

LILY DALE: I don't want to ever go back there again. He breathes so funny. Why does he breathe that way?

(MINNIE *comes in. She stands at the edge of the area.*)

MINNIE (*calling*): Miss Corrie . . . (*She is crying now, sobbing loudly.*) Miss Corrie . . . Miss Corrie . . . Miss Corrie . . .

(CORELLA, *followed by* HORACE *and* LILY DALE, *comes to the edge of the area.*)

CORELLA: Minnie . . . Minnie, what is it?

(MINNIE *is sobbing so she can't speak.* CORELLA *gathers the children to her.* MR. *and* MRS. THORNTON *come out.*)

MR. THORNTON: What is it, Corella?

CORELLA: I don't know. Minnie hasn't been able to tell me.

(MR. THORNTON *goes to* MINNIE.)

MR. THORNTON: Minnie . . . is he dead?

(MINNIE *nods her head yes.* MRS. THORNTON *goes to her.*)

MRS. THORNTON: There, there, Minnie . . . you were very good to him. Poor thing. Maybe it's for the best—he suffered so.

(MINNIE *controls her sobs and wipes her eyes.*)

MINNIE: He died a peaceful death.

MRS. THORNTON: Did he?

MINNIE: Oh, yes. I was in the room with him and saw the whole thing. Grandma was holding him in her arms.

MRS. THORNTON: Was he conscious before he died?

MINNIE: No Ma'am.

(*The children look up at their mother to see how she is taking the news. She is not crying.* MINNIE, *too, looks up at* CORELLA.)

Don't you have any feeling for him at all? Can't you shed even one tear?

CORELLA: I did all my crying a long time ago, Minnie.

MINNIE: I wouldn't want to have on my conscience what you have on yours.

MRS. THORNTON: Now, Minnie, be careful how you speak. You're saying things you'll surely be sorry for later.

MINNIE: She knows what I think about her.

MRS. THORNTON: Minnie, you will not speak to my daughter that way in my presence.

MINNIE: She's selfish and hateful and mean . . .

MRS. THORNTON: Minnie, I will have to ask you to leave my yard—at once.

(MINNIE *goes.* MRS. THORNTON *goes to her daughter.*)

MRS. THORNTON (*to* CORELLA): Pay no attention to anything she says. She's just very emotional.

LILY DALE: She's always talking that way.

MRS. THORNTON: Be quiet, Lily Dale.

LILY DALE: I hate the old, ugly thing.

MRS. THORNTON: Just be quiet, Lily Dale.

(INEZ *comes out.*)

INEZ: What is it, Mama?

MRS. THORNTON: Big Horace is dead.

INEZ: Oh, goodness!

(MARY *comes out.*)

Big Horace is dead!

MARY: Oh, I'm sorry. Did he just die?

MRS. THORNTON: Yes.

MARY: Did you children get to see him when you went over there?

CORELLA: Yes, they did.

LILY DALE: I didn't see him . . . I closed my eyes. I was scared to look at him.

CORELLA: Shh, Lily Dale.

HORACE: I saw him and I spoke to him. Grandma Robedaux told me to.

MARY: What did you say?

HORACE: I said, "Hello, Papa."

MARY: Is that all?

HORACE: Yes. First, Grandma Robedaux said who I was.

INEZ: Didn't he recognize you?

HORACE: No Ma'am. I don't think so.

MRS. THORNTON: I wonder if any of us should call to pay our respects or send food?

CORELLA: I'm not going near them. I'll not put my foot in that house.

MARY: Will you go to the cemetery?

CORELLA: No. I couldn't stand being near them and if I went and stayed apart from them . . . (*Pause.*) Well, you know. Oh, don't look at me that way, Sis. I am very bitter still and I can't help it.

MRS. THORNTON: The children certainly have to go and pay their respects.

CORELLA: I think they should too.

LILY DALE: I'm not going to go anywhere that I'll have to see that ugly Minnie.

CORELLA: Shh, Lily Dale. I think they should go over to the house before the funeral and afterwards for awhile.

(HORACE *starts away.*)

CORELLA: Where are you going?

HORACE: I didn't get to check on my lines at the river before.

CORELLA: You'd better stay home now. We'll be having dinner soon.

HORACE: I don't want any dinner.

CORELLA: You have to eat something.

HORACE: I'm not hungry.

CORELLA: You better stay here now.

LILY DALE: He smokes cigarettes down at the river and chews tobacco. I've seen him.

(MR. THORNTON *grabs him.*)

MR. THORNTON: Is that true?

HORACE: No, she's a liar.

MR. THORNTON. Don't use language like that.

HORACE: Well, she is.

(MR. THORNTON *shakes him.*)

MR. THORNTON: Well, just stop talking that way. And you'd better not be smoking or chewing tobacco. I'll skin you alive if I ever catch you doing anything like that at your age.

(*He lets the boy go. Pause.*)

HORACE: I have to see to my fishing lines.

MR. THORNTON: Then go see to your fishing lines.

(HORACE *leaves.*)

MRS. THORNTON (*to her husband*): I wonder when the funeral will be?

CORELLA: They have relatives all over the state, so I expect it will be later in the week.

MRS. THORNTON: I wonder if they'll bury him here or in Galveston?

CORELLA: I don't know, but I would guess here. I don't think they can afford to take his body back to Galveston.

MRS. THORNTON: Poor things. What's to become of them? I don't know how they've managed since he's been sick and had to give up his law practice. Do you?

CORELLA: No Ma'am.

(*The lights are brought up center stage.* HORACE *is there wrapping up his fishing lines.* LLOYD, *a boy his age, comes in.*)

LLOYD: Did you have any luck?

HORACE: No . . .

LLOYD: Are you gonna fish any more?

HORACE: No, I've got to go on home now.

LLOYD: Did you go to school today?

HORACE: No.

LLOYD: Did you quit school?

HORACE: No, I just didn't feel like going.

LLOYD: If I didn't go to school every day, I'd get it. You got any chewing tobacco?

HORACE: No.

LLOYD: Let's go down to the alley and get some empty whiskey bottles to sell so we can buy some tobacco.

HORACE: I can't.

LLOYD: Why?

HORACE: I have to go home.

LLOYD: Why?

HORACE: My papa died.

LLOYD: He died? When?

HORACE: Just awhile ago.

LLOYD: I bet my father is going to be one of the pallbearers, don't you? They're good friends. They always ask your good friends to be your pallbearers.

(THURMAN *comes in. He has a pole.*)

LLOYD: Horace's papa died.

THURMAN: When did he die?

LLOYD: Just awhile ago.

THURMAN: Aren't your mama and papa divorced?

HORACE: No.

THURMAN: How come they don't live in the same house?

HORACE: They're separated.

THURMAN: What's the difference?

(HORACE *doesn't answer.*)

LLOYD: You got any chewing tobacco?

THURMAN: Yes, I do.

(*He takes out a plug. He bites off a chew; he hands it to* LLOYD, *who bites a chew and then hands it to* HORACE, *who takes a chew and hands it back to* THURMAN.)

THURMAN: I bet you feel sad about your papa dying.

(HORACE *doesn't answer. He takes his fishing line and leaves.*)

When they going to bury his father?

LLOYD: I don't know.

THURMAN: Do you think they'll close school for the funeral?

LLOYD: I hope so, but I doubt it.

THURMAN: What's the difference in being separated and divorced?

LLOYD: I don't know.

(*They start out as the lights fade.*)

(*The lights are brought up upper right on the* THORNTON *area. The aunts are there with the grandmother and grandfather playing cards.* HORACE *comes in.* LILY DALE *goes to him.*)

LILY DALE: Mama is sick.

HORACE: What is wrong with her?

LILY DALE: I don't know. I went into our room just now and she was lying on the bed and she said she was sick.

(HORACE *starts out.*)

Where are you going?

HORACE: Downtown.

LILY DALE: Why?

HORACE: To look for empty whiskey bottles.

LILY DALE: I'm going to Houston to live with Mama. Don't you wish you could?

HORACE: No.

(*He leaves. The lights are brought up center stage.* MR. RITTER *lies on the ground. He is drunk and has fallen asleep.* HORACE *comes in. He goes over to him; he shakes him.*)

HORACE: Mr. Ritter . . . Mr. Ritter . . . are you all right?

(MR. RITTER *looks up at* HORACE.)

MR. RITTER: Who is that?

HORACE: It's Horace Robedaux.

MR. RITTER: Where am I?

HORACE: You're in the alley behind Dawdy's Saloon.

MR. RITTER: How did I get here?

HORACE: I don't know, Sir.

MR. RITTER: Am I drunk?

HORACE: I don't know, Sir. I just found you.

(*He tries to get up. He can't.*)

MR. RITTER: I'm very drunk. You say you're Horace Robedaux?

HORACE: Yes Sir.

MR. RITTER: I live in your old house. I was your mother's and your aunt's last boarder.

HORACE: Yes Sir.

MR. RITTER: She told me I could stay in the house until somebody else rented it. Nobody has.

HORACE: No Sir.

MR. RITTER: I owe your mother a board bill. I haven't forgotten that. You tell her for me.

HORACE: Yes Sir.

MR. RITTER: How is your mother?

HORACE: She's not too well today.

MR. RITTER: I'm sorry. You tell her I was asking for her.

HORACE: Yes Sir.

MR. RITTER: How is your father?

HORACE: He died.

MR. RITTER: Did he? I'm sorry to hear that. When did he die?

HORACE: Late this morning.

MR. RITTER: Well . . . you have my sympathy.

HORACE: Yes Sir.

MR. RITTER: It's terrible to lose a father.

HORACE: Yes Sir.

MR. RITTER: I well remember losing mine. How old are you?

HORACE: Twelve.

MR. RITTER: I was thirty-nine when I lost mine. Life was never the same again. Is there a whiskey bottle over there?

HORACE: Yes Sir.

MR. RITTER: Is there any whiskey left in it?

(HORACE *takes it*.)

HORACE: No Sir.

MR. RITTER: Well, I guess I drank it all. What time is it?

HORACE: Five.

MR. RITTER: Why are you here?

HORACE: I was looking for empty whiskey bottles. I wanted to get a little tobacco for myself.

MR. RITTER: What kind of tobacco did you want?

HORACE: Chewing tobacco.

MR. RITTER: I don't have any of that. I have some cigarette tobacco and some . . . (*Pause*) in my coat pocket. Help yourself.

HORACE: Thank you. (*He looks inside the pockets.*)

MR. RITTER: Did you find it?

HORACE: No Sir.

MR. RITTER: I guess I smoked it all. When did you start using tobacco?

HORACE: Last year.

(MR. RITTER *tries to get up again. He can't.*)

MR. RITTER: Will you help me up, son? (HORACE *reaches out to him, but* MR. RITTER *can't manage.*) That's all right. Thank you. I'll sleep on here.

(ALBERT *comes in.*)

ALBERT: Horace, what are you doing back here?

HORACE: Looking for empty whiskey bottles.

ALBERT: Did you hear about your father?

HORACE: Yes Sir.

ALBERT: Don't you think you'd better go home?

HORACE: I'm going in a little while.

MR. RITTER: Who is that, son?

HORACE: It's my Uncle Albert.

ALBERT: Albert Thornton, Mr. Ritter. Are you a little under the weather?

MR. RITTER: Yes Sir. I believe I am. Could you help me up, Albert? The boy couldn't manage. (ALBERT *extends his hand to* MR. RITTER *and helps him up to his feet. He is very unsteady.*) I wonder if someone could help me to the house. I'm very unsteady, it seems.

ALBERT: You help him, Horace. I'm going into the saloon to play cards.

HORACE: Yes Sir. Have you got any chewing tobacco?

ALBERT: Yes.

HORACE: Would you give me some?

ALBERT: What do you want with it?

HORACE: I want to chew.

ALBERT: Well, all right—this once. But don't you ever tell Papa I gave you any.

HORACE: No Sir.

(ALBERT *gives him a plug.* HORACE *takes a chew.*)

ALBERT: Can I offer you a chew, Mr. Ritter?

MR. RITTER: What is it you're offering, son?

ALBERT: Chewing tobacco.

MR. RITTER: No, thank you. I don't use it. If you have a little whiskey, I would appreciate a drink of that.

ALBERT: Here. . . .

(*He takes a bottle from his coat and passes it to* MR. RITTER, *who has a swig and then hands the bottle back to* ALBERT.)

MR. RITTER: Thank you. Thank you so much.

ALBERT: Papa doesn't know you chew tobacco, does he?

HORACE: No Sir.

ALBERT: Does Sister?

HORACE: No Sir.

ALBERT: Well, see you spit it out before you go into the house.

HORACE: Yes Sir. (ALBERT *continues into the saloon.*) Are you ready, Mr. Ritter?

MR. RITTER: Where are we going?

HORACE: You said you wanted to go home.

MR. RITTER: Oh, yes. Do you know where I live, young man?

HORACE: Yes Sir. My mother used to have a boarding-house there, remember? You boarded with us.

MR. RITTER: Oh, yes. Of course. How is your mother? Is she well?

HORACE: Yes Sir. Thank you.

MR. RITTER: And your father?

HORACE: He's dead.

MR. RITTER: Is he? I'm sorry to hear that. (*Pause.*) When did he die, son?

HORACE: This morning. Right before noon.

MR. RITTER: Is that so? My father is dead, you know. He was a remarkable man. I'm afraid I was always a disappointment to him. Your mother and father were separated, weren't they?

HORACE: Yes Sir.

MR. RITTER: Were you with your father when he died, son?

HORACE: No Sir.

MR. RITTER: Was anybody with him?

HORACE: My grandmother.

MR. RITTER: Not your mother?

HORACE: No Sir.

MR. RITTER: That's right—they were separated.

HORACE: Yes Sir.

MR. RITTER: Any hope for a reconciliation?

HORACE: No Sir.

MR. RITTER: Why not? There's always hope, I think.

HORACE: He's dead.

MR. RITTER: Oh, of course. When is the funeral?

HORACE: I don't know.

(They continue on. The lights are brought up upper right on the THORNTON *area.* LILY DALE *is there dressed in a new dress.* VIRGIE *comes in.)*

LILY DALE: Aunt Virgie . . .

VIRGIE: Yes?

LILY DALE: Play a piece on the piano.

VIRGIE: I can't.

LILY DALE: Why?

VIRGIE: Because today is your father's funeral. People would think we were very disrespectful if they heard music over here today.

LILY DALE: Why?

VIRGIE. They just would.

LILY DALE: When did you know you could play the piano by ear?

VIRGIE: I don't remember. I just remember that one day I went over to the piano and started to play.

LILY DALE: I'm going to have music lessons when Mama starts making money sewing in Houston.

VIRGIE: That's what I hear.

LILY DALE: Why didn't you ever have music lessons?

VIRGIE: What did I need them for? I already knew how to play. Anyway, we never had the money. When I was your age we lived on an island and no one was around to teach music—if we could have afforded it.

LILY DALE: Why did you live on an island?

VIRGIE: Because Mama's people were there. Times were so hard here after the war. Papa got a job running a lighthouse.

LILY DALE: How long were you there?

VIRGIE: A year or two. I don't remember. A hurricane came up unexpectedly and Papa was at the lighthouse and there was a tidal wave and we were in our house across the island from the lighthouse, and by the time Papa got a boat and got to us the water was up to the second story of our house. As soon as we could get away we left the island and never went back. We are a very close family . . . we always have been. I hope we always will be.

It won't be as easy now with Mary married and living in West Texas and your mother living in Houston. If Papa and Mama had their way, they would build houses for us all when we marry right around their house. (*She puts her arms around* LILY DALE.) You and Horace are the first grandchildren and all of us love you like you were our own. But I love everything that has a drop of Thornton blood in it and so do my sisters and my brother.

(MARY *comes in.*)

MARY: Where is Horace?

LILY DALE: I don't know. Where is Mama?

MARY: Resting. She's not feeling well. (LILY DALE *gets up.*) Where are you going?

LILY DALE: Outside.

MARY: I think you'd better stay in the parlor. You want to keep your dress fresh and clean. We're taking you over to see your father's body in awhile.

LILY DALE: I don't want to go.

MARY: You have to go, honey.

LILY DALE: Is Mama going?

MARY: No.

LILY DALE: Why?

MARY: It wouldn't be proper under the circumstances.

LILY DALE: I don't want to go.

MARY: You have to go, honey.

LILY DALE: Why?

MARY: Because you're his daughter, honey, and it's the

respectful thing to do. It will be your last chance to see him. They are burying him this afternoon.

LILY DALE: Am I going to the funeral?

MARY: No. We feel you're too young to go to funerals. So does your father's family.

LILY DALE: Are you going?

MARY: No.

LILY DALE: Is Mama?

MARY: No.

LILY DALE: Is Horace?

MARY: No, he's too young to go too.

(GLADYS *comes in.*)

GLADYS: Today would have been his birthday, Corrie told me. He would have been thirty-three years old.

LILY DALE: Who would have been?

GLADYS: Your father.

LILY DALE: Am I an orphan now?

GLADYS: No. Heavens! How could you be an orphan?

LILY DALE: Jess Ray Pickard told me I was because my father died.

GLADYS: Well, you're not. You have a mother, a grand-mother, a grandfather, aunts, and an uncle to take care of you.

LILY DALE: Jess Ray Pickard says Mama is going to Houston and Grandma and Grandpa are old now and will die soon, and you will get married before long and have

children of your own and won't want to fool with me and
Horace.

GLADYS: Well, she's crazy. Mama and Papa have no intention of dying anytime soon, and I don't care how many
husbands and children any of us have, we would never
neglect you or Horace.

LILY DALE: Do you think Mama will ever let Horace come
live with her in Houston?

GLADYS: You know she will. As soon as she can.

(HORACE *enters. He has on a suit and tie.*)

MARY: I'm taking the children over to the Robedaux
house now.

(LILY DALE *leaves the area.*)

VIRGIE: Are you going into the house?

MARY: No.

VIRGIE: Then let them walk over by themselves.

MARY: I just thought under the circumstances it would be
the proper thing to walk over with them.

VIRGIE: I don't agree. I think it will look ridiculous walking
over with two half-grown children.

MARY (*to* HORACE): Do you mind going by yourself,
Horace?

HORACE: No Ma'am.

MARY: Do you think your sister will mind?

HORACE: No Ma'am.

VIRGIE: Certainly they won't mind, Mary. I would think

they would be embarrassed to death if you walked with them and then, when they got to the edge of the yard, turned around and came home. I never heard of such a thing.

MARY: I was only doing what I thought was best and proper under the circumstances.

(MRS. THORNTON *comes in.*)

MRS. THORNTON: Horace, your mother said you'll have to go to your father's without your sister. She's come down with a fever, she thinks.

INEZ: Poor little thing.

GLADYS: How's Sis, Mama?

MRS. THORNTON: She's not well either.

(*The lights are brought up upper left on the* ROBEDAUX *area.* MR. RITTER, JOHN HOWARD, *and* GEORGE TYLER *are there. They are dressed for the funeral.* TERRENCE *comes out. He sits beside them.*)

GEORGE TYLER: What are your plans, Terrence? Will you live on here?

TERRENCE: No Sir. As soon as we can dispose of the house, we'll leave. Mama says losing Paul Horace has broken her heart and it will never mend here where there are so many memories of him.

JOHN HOWARD: George Tyler and I are taking care of all the funeral expenses.

TERRENCE: Mama told me. We appreciate it.

(MR. RITTER *takes his watch out.*)

What time is it, Mr. Ritter?

MR. RITTER: Two.

TERRENCE: Well, the hour approaches. (*He cries.*) It's going to be hard saying goodbye to him, gentlemen.

(HORACE *has entered the area.*)

GEORGE TYLER: Of course it is.

JOHN HOWARD: But he was suffering, Terrence. This is an end to that. You wouldn't want his suffering to continue.

TERRENCE: I know . . . I know. I told Mama that's what should console us: his suffering is ended. But she said it didn't console her at all. Mama thought the sun rose and set around my brother. She worshipped him, you know. She literally worshipped him. Poor Brother. (*He looks up and sees* HORACE.) Hello, son.

HORACE: Hello, Uncle Terrence.

TERRENCE: How are you on this sad, bleak day?

MR. RITTER: I know what it is to lose a father. I was thirty-nine when I lost mine. Life was never the same again.

(TERRENCE *gets up.*)

TERRENCE: Come on with me, son. I know you want to see your father before we take him away.

(TERRENCE *takes him to the far edge of the area where the coffin is. The coffin is surrounded by* MINNIE, SALLY, MRS. ROBEDAUX, *and several other women. They make way for* TERRENCE *and* HORACE.)

JOHN HOWARD: I'm going to be as close to that boy as I can, for Paul Horace's sake.

GEORGE TYLER: We all will want to look out for him. My wife has been told that Lily Dale is going to live with Corrie in Houston. My wife feels Corrie might marry again now for sure.

JOHN HOWARD: Albert Thornton lost over a hundred dollars last night in a poker game.

GEORGE TYLER: My God!

JOHN HOWARD: He's a good merchant. He could prosper if he kept his mind on his business.

GEORGE TYLER: He doesn't, though. You can't stay up all night gambling and tend to your business the next day.

(TERRENCE *and* HORACE *rejoin them.*)

MR. RITTER: Your father looks well, doesn't he? So peaceful.

GEORGE TYLER: Son, John Howard and I are giving him the best funeral money can buy.

TERRENCE: We'll never forget it. None of us. We will always be in your debt.

JOHN HOWARD (*to* HORACE): Your father was a brilliant man, son. A great lawyer. Always be proud of him.

GEORGE TYLER (*to* HORACE): And you must go to school and keep on with your studies. That's what he wanted you to do, you know.

TERRENCE: Horace doesn't like school. He's discouraged and has gotten behind. His father and I told him he shouldn't be. I'll help him as long as I'm here. . . .

JOHN HOWARD (*to* HORACE): We'll all help you, son.

MR. RITTER: Except me. I did poorly in school, myself. My father was a brilliant man, but he soon saw he was wasting his money trying to give me an education. I just couldn't seem to learn . . .

GEORGE TYLER: Nonsense, Mr. Ritter. Anybody can learn . . . anybody.

TERRENCE (*to* HORACE): John Howard and George Tyler were your father's best friends, son. They are paying for the funeral out of their own pockets.

JOHN HOWARD: We told him that, Terrence.

GEORGE TYLER: We didn't spare a nickel on the funeral. I'll tell you that.

MR. RITTER: No, you didn't.

GEORGE TYLER (*to* HORACE): Always be proud of your father, son.

HORACE: I'm proud of him.

GEORGE TYLER (*to* HORACE): And keep on with school like he wanted you to.

HORACE: Yes Sir.

(*The boy is silent. The men are silent. The lights fade.*)

Act Two

The lights are brought up upper right on the THORNTON *area.*
MR. THORNTON *is there reading a paper.* HORACE *comes in.*
MR. THORNTON *continues reading for a beat.*

MR. THORNTON: Want part of the Houston paper?

HORACE: Thank you.

MR. THORNTON (*handing the paper to him*): I have the Harrison paper here too, if you care to see it.

HORACE: Thank you.

MR. THORNTON (*handing the other paper to him*): I swear the Harrison paper hasn't improved since your uncle sold it. It has gone steadily downhill. (*Pause.*) Get your fish delivered?

HORACE: Yes Sir.

MR. THORNTON: Go to school today?

HORACE: No Sir.

MR. THORNTON: Mr. Wiley came by to see me yesterday. He says if you miss any more school they will just have to keep you back. I said I didn't think you were too interested in school and I wasn't of the opinion that you could force anyone to take an interest in something like that. I used your Uncle Albert as an example. I said I had even whipped him once or twice to make him go, but it did no

61

good. And he's making a living for himself. I said, "I see to it that Horace works."

HORACE: Mr. John Howard said if I wanted to read law, I could use his law books. He said my father was anxious for me to study law.

MR. THORNTON: Well, if you want to read law, you had better go on with school. But you're not going to get anywhere in school unless you attend. Now, your grand-mother and I are happy to have you go to school, but I don't see any sense in just dragging it out.

HORACE: Yes Sir.

MR. THORNTON: Either go, or quit and get yourself a regular job. (*Pause.*) How are your grades?

HORACE: Not so good.

MR. THORNTON: Well, you don't study.

HORACE: No Sir.

MR. THORNTON: Why don't you study?

HORACE: I don't know, Sir. I get sleepy when I try to study.

MR. THORNTON: Well, you have to study, you know. I don't know a whole lot about school, but I know that much.

HORACE: Yes Sir. When Papa died, Mr. John Howard said he or Uncle Terrence or Mr. George Tyler would help me catch up with my studies.

MR. THORNTON: Well, maybe they will.

HORACE: Uncle Terrence hasn't been feeling so well lately himself, so he can't help me. Mr. George Tyler is never home, and Mr. John Howard helped me twice . . . but lately he has been too busy. I wonder if you or Uncle Albert could maybe help me sometime?

MR. THORNTON: I can't son. I know nothing about all that. You'll have to do that on your own. Your Uncle Albert knows nothing about it either. He quit in the fourth grade, you know.

(MRS. THORNTON *comes in. She has a letter.*)

Here's a letter from your sister, son. Read it to us.

(HORACE *takes the letter.*)

HORACE (*reading*): "Dear Family: How are you all? I trust well. We are well. Mama has taken me to see two plays. I am going to be an actress. How are you? Do you miss me? Mama has a beau. Ha-ha! He is nice. She may marry him. Write soon. Lily Dale." (*He puts the letter down.*) Who's her beau?

MRS. THORNTON: A gentleman from Atlanta. He works for the railroad. He wants your mama to marry him. We hope she does. She can't make a living for herself working as hard as she has to. Lily Dale ought to be here with us.

MR. THORNTON: Well, you'll never get her back now.

MRS. THORNTON: Sis says Mr. Davenport has just fallen in love with Lily Dale. He just worships her.

HORACE: Who is Mr. Davenport?

MRS. THORNTON: He's the man your mama is going with.

(HORACE *gets up. He gives the letter to his grandmother. He leaves.*)

MR. THORNTON: Albert says he liked Mr. Davenport when he met him. He says he thinks he will make Corella a good husband. He has no bad habits.

MRS. THORNTON: I know he said so. I'm glad for that.

(*The lights fade*).

(*The lights are brought up down left on the* ROBEDAUX *area.* MINNIE *is there.* HORACE *comes in.*)

MINNIE: We sold the house.

HORACE: Who bought it?

MINNIE: Mr. George Tyler. We leave day after tomorrow. Grandma says she hopes never to see this place again. She said she wished she could take the bodies of her three sons with her and bring them where she's going.

HORACE: Where is she going?

MINNIE: Marshall.

HORACE: Where is that?

MINNIE: Don't you know anything? That's in East Texas. Nothing but pine trees all around you. Grandma says her heart was broken in this place and it may never mend. She regrets the day she left Galveston.

(TERRENCE *comes out.*)

TERRENCE: Well, Horace, have you heard our news?

HORACE: Yes Sir. Where's Grandma?

TERRENCE: She's not well, son. Your Aunt Sally is nursing her. She held up so long, all the time your father needed her, and now she has just collapsed.

HORACE: Yes Sir.

(*In the distance we can hear "Beautiful Dreamer" sung by the* THORNTON *girls.*)

TERRENCE: They're singing at your house again. Hasn't been much singing over there since your aunts' marriages.

HORACE: No Sir.

TERRENCE: How's your mama?

HORACE: All right.

TERRENCE: How's Lily Dale?

HORACE: She's all right.

MINNIE: How does she like Houston?

HORACE: All right.

(GEORGE TYLER *enters*.)

GEORGE TYLER: I brought your check over for your mama, Terrence.

TERRENCE: Thank you.

GEORGE TYLER: How is she today?

TERRENCE: Still weak as a kitten. I figure once we get her away from here, she'll get her strength back.

GEORGE TYLER: I'm sure. (*He sees* HORACE *and speaks to him*.) My wife tells me you've been by the house a couple of times. I'm sorry, I've been away. I've had to spend a lot of time out at the farms these days. I feel bad about neglecting you.

HORACE: That's all right.

GEORGE TYLER: John Howard and I had a long talk about you the other day. Did he tell you that?

HORACE: No Sir.

GEORGE TYLER: Well, we did. A long talk. (*To* TERRENCE:) He's not going to school half the time, you know.

TERRENCE: Yes, I know. I've been wanting to help him with his schoolwork, but I've been so preoccupied.

GEORGE TYLER: We're all busy. That's the trouble. John Howard said the same thing. He says every time the boy has come around to him for help he has been in the midst of something, and then when he has the time, he's gone looking for Horace and he can't find him. I tell you, if he lived with me or John Howard, we could keep more of an eye on him—see he got to school and did his homework. Of course, we have four children and so we really don't have the time for the boy. John Howard has no children, but he has that peculiar wife and he says he can't get anywhere with her. She says to take in another child would be disloyal to their two dead children. Anyway, his health isn't all that good either, you know. Of course, my wife says Corrie is thinking of marrying again. Have you all heard that?

TERRENCE: No.

GEORGE TYLER (*to* HORACE): Have you heard that, son?

HORACE: Yes Sir.

GEORGE TYLER: Well, if she does marry, like I told John Howard, they will probably want him with them.

(MRS. ROBEDAUX *and* SALLY *come out. She leans on her daughter's arm.*)

MRS. ROBEDAUX: I thought I heard you out here, George Tyler.

GEORGE TYLER: I brought you your check by.

MRS. ROBEDAUX: Thank you.

GEORGE TYLER: Lovely day, isn't it?

MRS. ROBEDAUX: Oh, yes. Oh, yes. (*She hears the singing as it continues*.) Those Thornton girls are at it again. I thought since they married they'd given up that kind of foolishness. They tell me they were the first at the dance at the courthouse the other night and the last to leave. What will they do when they have children? Take them along to the dances, I suppose. Mercy!

MINNIE: She's getting married again.

MRS. ROBEDAUX: Who is "she"?

MINNIE (*pointing to* HORACE): You know.

MRS. ROBEDAUX: Oh, mercy! Yes, I know. Yes, I know all too well.

MINNIE: I'm never going to marry.

SALLY: Don't talk foolishness, Minnie.

MINNIE: I'm never going to marry. I'm going to college and teach school.

SALLY: Of course you'll want to marry, honey.

MINNIE: Not me. Marriage means nothing but kids and trouble. You'll not catch me marrying.

MRS. ROBEDAUX: Did you go to school today, Horace?

HORACE: No Ma'am.

MRS. ROBEDAUX: Don't you ever go to school anymore?

HORACE: Not much.

MINNIE: And he chews tobacco too. I've seen him.

MRS. ROBEDAUX: No, he doesn't.

MINNIE: Yes, he does too. I've seen him twice chewing away down at the river while he was fishing.

MRS. ROBEDAUX: I can see it all now. Plain as day. He'll not go back to school. Next, he'll be drinking and gambling like his Uncle Albert. Well, I'm glad I'm not going to be here to witness it. (*Pause.*) George, I hoped to have a tombstone put up on my son's grave before I left, but I haven't been able to manage it. When we get settled in Marshall, I'll send you the money and you can attend to it for me, if you will.

GEORGE TYLER: I'll be happy to.

MRS. ROBEDAUX: The other thing I want is a magnolia tree planted in the lot.

TERRENCE: Why? Horace never cared for magnolias.

MRS. ROBEDAUX: He did too.

TERRENCE: No Ma'am, he didn't. It was Cape jasmines he loved. I heard him say many a time he wanted one day to live near a sandy soil on the coast so he could have Cape jasmines growing again. He said—

MRS. ROBEDAUX (*interrupting*): Don't tell me what he said. I know what Horace liked and didn't like.

SALLY: Brother is right, Mother. He did prefer Cape jasmines. He really did.

MRS. ROBEDAUX: Well then, he'll have to go without. The soil here is too rich for Cape jasmines. I've tried many a time to grow them. Do you remember the Cape jasmines we had in our home in Galveston, children? Cape jasmines and camellias and oleanders . . . (SALLY *gets up and goes into the house.*) Poor Sally. She is so sensitive. Our being poor is so hard on her. She can't bear to have me mention Galveston and our life there.

MINNIE: Were you really rich?

MRS. ROBEDAUX: Yes, we were.

MINNIE: Very rich?

MRS. ROBEDAUX: Yes, we were. Your grandfather's ships sailed around the world. And we were educated people: ministers, lawyers, and doctors, and scholars—Latin scholars and Greek scholars. We lived then in a world that valued those things.

(*Pause.*)

GEORGE TYLER: John Howard and I were talking the other day about Little Horace. We were saying if he lived with one of us, we could see he at least finished school. Of course, I have four children of my own, so I can't take him at present, and John Howard has this peculiar wife. . . .

MRS. ROBEDAUX: I don't think the Thorntons would let you take him.

GEORGE TYLER: I don't know. John Howard could try talking to them if his wife weren't so peculiar.

MRS. ROBEDAUX: She is peculiar, poor thing. (*Pause. Again the singing is heard.*) Horace, would you mind asking your aunts to stop their singing? Tell them I'm not well and it makes me extremely nervous. Tell them I'll be gone in a week and they can sing their hearts out, if they care to.

HORACE: Yes Ma'am.

(*He goes.*)

GEORGE TYLER: I didn't want to discuss it too much in front of the boy, but my wife tells me Corella will be married before the month is out.

MRS. ROBEDAUX: Does he have anything?

GEORGE TYLER: He's just a working man. He works for the railroads.

MRS. ROBEDAUX: Is he educated?

GEORGE TYLER: No. I don't think he can do much more than read and write.

MRS. ROBEDAUX: Well, that's about what she deserves. I think she always resented my son's education, you know. His brother's too. The sight of Terrence reading used to drive her into a fury.

MINNIE: She once took some of his Greek and Latin books and burned them out of meanness.

TERRENCE: You're not sure of her motive, now, Minnie.

MINNIE: Grandma saw her and said it was meanness that made her do it.

TERRENCE: But she claims she did it out of ignorance. That she didn't know what they were or that I wanted them.

MRS. ROBEDAUX: She claimed many things.

(HORACE *comes in.*)

HORACE: I told them you were nervous. They said they were sorry. My mama is getting married again. She is marrying a man from Atlanta, Georgia. And I'm going to live with them and go to school in Houston and read law there one day.

MRS. ROBEDAUX: When did you hear all this?

HORACE: Just now. They wrote my Grandmother Thornton of their plans. They are planning to educate me in law and Lily Dale in music.

GEORGE TYLER: Well, John Howard will be relieved to hear it. I know I am. We didn't like to feel we let Paul Horace down. You know how we felt about Paul Horace.

MRS. ROBEDAUX: You were his good friends.

GEORGE TYLER: We tried to be.

MINNIE: When are you going to Houston, Little Horace?

HORACE: Before too long. Anyway, I may not be a lawyer. I may turn out to be a railroad man and work for the railroad. (*Pause.*) How much does a tombstone cost?

MRS. ROBEDAUX: Why, I have no idea. What do you think it costs, George Tyler?

GEORGE TYLER: They're expensive. John Howard and I were talking about it the other day. We want to put one on Paul Horace's grave.

MRS. ROBEDAUX: No, I'm going to manage that someway, someday. You've done enough for us, paying for the funeral. We'll never forget that . . . any of us. (*To* HORACE:) Always remember, Son, these were your daddy's two best friends. They came to see him every night when he was so sick, and they paid all his funeral expenses when he was buried.

(JOHN HOWARD *and* MR. RITTER *come in.*)

GEORGE TYLER: Our worries are over about Horace, John Howard. Corrie is marrying again and they are going to take him to Houston to live and he'll go to school there and read law, in time.

MINNIE: Or work for the railroad.

GEORGE TYLER: I know he's going to study law. It was his father's dying wish that he be a lawyer.

MR. RITTER: All my life I wanted to be a train conductor. I once applied for the job of butcher boy, but they said I was too old.

GEORGE TYLER: I bought the house you're living in too, Mr. Ritter.

MR. RITTER: Did you?

GEORGE TYLER: Yes, this morning.

MR. RITTER: What are you going to do with it, Sir?

GEORGE TYLER: I intend to rent it.

MR. RITTER: I see. By the room or the whole house?

GEORGE TYLER: The whole house.

MRS. RITTER: I see. What will you be asking for it?

GEORGE TYLER: Thirty-five a month. I'll be glad to give you first refusal.

MR. RITTER: I thank you. That's very kind and courteous of you, but it so happens I'm leaving in a week or so too.

MRS. ROBEDAUX: Where are you going, Mr. Ritter?

MR. RITTER: My plans are not definite yet.

MINNIE: What is the name of your stepfather, Horace?

HORACE: Davenport.

MINNIE: What's his first name?

HORACE: I don't know.

MINNIE: What are you going to call him? Stepdaddy?

HORACE: I don't know what I'll call him.

MINNIE: What do you call your stepdaddy?

MR. RITTER: My cousin had a stepfather. He called him "Uncle" until he had lived with him a year or two, and then he called him "Daddy."

MRS. ROBEDAUX: I better never hear of you calling anyone but your own daddy "Daddy."

HORACE: I didn't call him "Daddy." I called him "Papa."

MRS. ROBEDAUX: I know what you called him. But don't you call anybody else "Daddy" either.

MINNIE: My daddy ran away.

MRS. ROBEDAUX: Minnie, he did not run away. Don't you talk that way.

MINNIE: Where is he then?

MRS. ROBEDAUX: I don't know. I'm of the opinion, myself, that he's been the victim of some strange tragic accident that has prevented his return to you and your mother.

MINNIE: I think he's run away and I don't think he's ever coming back. But that's all right with me. There was nothing but fighting when he was here. Anyway, I'm glad Mama never married again. There are two things I never wanted: one was a stepmama, and the other was a stepdaddy. They are always mean and hateful and cruel to the poor orphaned stepchildren.

HORACE: Lily Dale is crazy about Mr. Davenport.

MINNIE: How do you know?

HORACE: She wrote me and told me. He is crazy about her too.

(SALLY *comes out.*)

MINNIE: She's getting married again for sure. He's going to live with them in Houston and go to school.

SALLY: I heard the whole thing from the house.

(HORACE *gets up.*)

HORACE: I'm going to check on my fishing lines.

(*He starts out.*)

SALLY: Bring me by a couple of pounds of fish if you have anything. I need it for our supper.

HORACE: Yes Ma'am.

(*He continues on as the lights fade.*)

(*The lights are brought up center stage.* HORACE *comes in with a fishing pole.* LARRY *is there fishing.* THURMAN *is next to him.*)

HORACE: Have you had any luck?

LARRY: No. Have you?

HORACE: I did earlier. I was down here around daybreak.

LARRY: Why do you fish so early these days?

HORACE: So I can get to school.

LARRY: How come you started going to school so regularly?

HORACE: Because my mother has married again—a man that works for the L & N Railroad in Houston. They're coming here tomorrow and I'm going back to live with them and go to school in Houston. I wanted to learn all I could before then so I wouldn't be too far behind in Houston.

(THURMAN *takes out a plug of tobacco and hands it to* LARRY, *who has a bite and then hands the plug to* HORACE.)

HORACE: No, thank you. I don't chew it anymore.

LARRY: How come?

HORACE: Because my stepfather doesn't. He doesn't chew, he doesn't drink, he doesn't smoke. As a matter of fact, he doesn't have any bad habits at all.

LARRY: What do you call your stepdaddy?

HORACE: I don't know. I'll call him what he wants me to call him.

LARRY: What does Lily Dale call him?

HORACE: I don't know. But he's nice, I know that. Lily Dale says he is and she's hard to please. And my Uncle Albert went down to meet him. That's why I know he has no bad habits. That's the first thing my Uncle Albert told us.

(*The lights fade and are brought up upper right.* MR. *and* MRS. THORNTON *are there. A small upright piano is far upstage.* ALBERT *comes in.*)

ALBERT: Who is going to the station to meet Sis and her new husband?

MRS. THORNTON: Virgie.

ALBERT: I heard the train whistle.

MRS. THORNTON: So did we.

MR. THORNTON: When do you start out at the Gautier plantation?

ALBERT: Next week. Do you think Horace will go and live with Sis and her husband now?

MR. THORNTON: I don't know what their plans are.

ALBERT: I can give him a job this summer when he's out of school, out at the plantation store. I'll need someone to help me. I can't stay in the store all the time.

MRS. THORNTON: Would he live out there with you?

ALBERT: He'd have to. He could come home on a visit every month or so. I'd bring him in on a Sunday for dinner.

MRS. THORNTON: Any other white children out there?

ALBERT: No. There are no other children of any kind—white or black. There is a Negro couple out there—she does cooking for Mr. Gautier. And then there are the convicts that work the plantation, and the overseer and the guards. There is a lot of good fishing out that way, though, and he loves to fish.

MRS. THORNTON: Yes, he does.

ALBERT: And he'd be learning something useful. I could train him how to run a store.

MRS. THORNTON: Where is he?

MR. THORNTON: I think he's getting dressed to meet his stepfather. Tell him to hurry, Albert.

ALBERT: Yes Sir.

(*He goes.*)

MR. THORNTON: George Tyler came by this morning to tell me John Howard died last night.

MRS. THORNTON: Did he?

MR. THORNTON: He died in his sleep. His wife found him when she went to call him for breakfast.

MRS. THORNTON: Where will the funeral be?

MR. THORNTON: Not here, I understand. She's taking him back to her home to bury him. And George Tyler says Mr. Ritter has been missing for a few days. He said the neighbors report he hasn't been seen around his home since last Wednesday. He was last seen walking towards the river woods.

MRS. THORNTON: I declare.

MR. THORNTON: If he doesn't show up by evening, they're sending a search party out looking for him.

MRS. THORNTON: Does he have any people?

MR. THORNTON: Not that anyone knows of.

MRS. THORNTON: Isn't that sad? I tell Albert and the girls we may not have much, but we have each other. We can always help each other out some way.

MR. THORNTON: I think they're loyal to each other.

MRS. THORNTON: Oh, I think so.

MR. THORNTON: I'll be glad when Albert's married. I think it will settle him down.

MRS. THORNTON: I'm sure it will.

(LILY DALE *comes running in.*)

LILY DALE: Hello, Grandma. Hello, Grandpa.

(*She embraces each of them.*)

MRS. THORNTON: Well, my goodness, you've grown. And you're so pretty, too. Did you have a nice trip?

LILY DALE: Oh, yes Ma'am. I love the train. I could ride the train day and night. Mr. Davenport says someday he is going to take me to Atlanta to visit his people. He works for the railroad and so naturally he gets a pass to anywhere in the world he wants to go.

(CORELLA *and her new husband,* PETE DAVENPORT, *enter.* PETE *is* CORELLA's *age. He is a handsome man, but shy and withdrawn.* MR. *and* MRS. THORNTON *go to* CORELLA *and embrace her.*)

MRS. THORNTON: We're so glad for you, Corrie.

MR. THORNTON: You're looking well, Sister.

CORELLA: Thank you, Papa. Papa . . . Mama . . . this is Pete.

MR. THORNTON: How do you do?

MRS. THORNTON: It's nice to meet you.

PETE: Thank you.

(HORACE *comes in.* CORELLA *goes to him. She hugs him.*)

CORELLA: Hello, honey.

HORACE: Hello, Mama.

CORELLA: Horace, this is my new husband. This is Mr. Davenport.

(PETE *goes to him and extends his hand.*)

PETE: Hello, Horace.

HORACE: Hello, Mr. Davenport.

PETE: I've heard a lot about you.

HORACE: Yes Sir.

LILY DALE: Mr. Davenport didn't have to pay a nickel for our tickets. He gets a pass to anywhere in the world.

MRS. THORNTON: Sit down, won't you? (*They take chairs.*) Are you in your new place yet, Sister?

CORELLA: Yes Ma' am. We got everything moved in before we were married. We went to Galveston for two days on our honeymoon. We took Lily Dale with us. I was going to send her here to stay with you, but Pete wouldn't hear of it. He thinks the sun rises and sets on Lily Dale. He just worships her. And she's crazy about him. (*She looks over at* HORACE.) You look well, Son.

HORACE: Thank you.

CORELLA: I think you've grown.

MRS. THORNTON: I think he has too. Albert wants him to come with him this summer and work at the plantation store. He says he can make a merchant out of him.

CORELLA: That's nice of Albert.

MRS. THORNTON: We thought so. John Howard died.

CORELLA: Oh, I'm sorry.

MRS. THORNTON: Died in his sleep. His wife found him this morning. Had you heard that, Horace?

HORACE: No Ma'am.

MRS. THORNTON: He came over to talk to us about a month ago. It worried him that Horace has lost interest in school. He said he was hoping to be able to help him with his lessons in time, if he'd just stick it out. Well, I said, "John Howard, I can't promise you he will. You know how boys are—they don't care a thing in the world about school. I've never seen one yet that did." Of course, none of you girls liked it either. You couldn't wait to get out. I always thought the problem with the Robedauxs was too much education.

CORELLA: Pete only went to the third grade.

HORACE: I've been going to school lately, Grandma. I haven't missed a day in three weeks.

PETE: I went to work when I was ten. I worked twelve hours a day at my first job. Seven days a week.

CORELLA: His father died two months before. His mother had four other children. He went to work and supported them all.

HORACE: I've been to school every day for three weeks and got my lessons all done.

PETE: Of course, we didn't have too much to eat, but we got by. Hard work never hurt nobody.

MRS. THORNTON: I believe that. Especially a boy.

PETE: I wouldn't let a boy of mine go to school. I would put him to work as soon as he was able. I think work makes a man out of anybody.

MRS. THORNTON: Horace works. He has customers he sells fish to. He does odd jobs. Would you like to go to the country this summer and work with your Uncle Albert, Son?

HORACE: Well . . .

LILY DALE: I have started piano lessons. Can I play a piece for you?

MRS. THORNTON: Certainly.

(LILY DALE *goes to the piano.*)

Too bad you're not like your Aunt Virgie. She plays piano by ear.

LILY DALE: It ruins you to play by ear, my teacher says.

(*She starts to play a very simple piece.*)

HORACE (*almost mumbling*): I kind of want to go to Houston and live with you, Mama.

CORELLA: What, Son? I didn't hear you. I was listening to Lily Dale.

HORACE: I said—

PETE (*interrupting*): Shh . . . shh. . . .

CORELLA: Tell me later, Son, when she's finished.

(*There is silence.* LILY DALE *finishes. They clap.*)

MRS. THORNTON: Well, that's just fine.

LILY DALE: That's a classical piece.

MRS. THORNTON: Is it?

LILY DALE: My teacher says the kind of music my aunts play and sing is junk.

CORELLA: Now, Lily Dale, don't be forward. You've always liked to hear them play and sing. I hope myself we have a concert tonight, for old times' sake.

MRS. THORNTON: I'm sure we will.

(CORELLA *turns to* HORACE.)

CORELLA: What did you say to me, Son, before?

HORACE: I said I kind of wanted to come and live with you in Houston and maybe go to school. You see—

LILY DALE: Go to school in Houston? Why, they wouldn't even let you in the first grade in Houston. I went for two weeks and it gave me such headaches, Mama told me I never had to go again.

CORELLA: You just never have liked school, honey— that's all.

HORACE: You see, I promised my daddy . . . (*Pause.*)

CORELLA: What did you promise him?

HORACE: That I would study law, and Mr. John Howard talked to me last week again and I told him it was my intention.

MRS. THORNTON: John Howard is dead. Did we tell you that?

HORACE: Yes Ma'am. Anyway, he said last week if I wanted to study law, I would have to keep on with my schooling.

CORELLA: Well, you can keep on with it here. This is the only schooling a lot of lawyers here have had.

HORACE: Yes Ma'am.

CORELLA: And we don't have the room for you in Houston, Son. Our place is very small. Pete doesn't make a whole lot and he has Lily Dale now to take care of, and he doesn't want me working full time.

PETE: I want her home taking care of her daughter. I don't want Lily Dale growing up on the streets of Houston. Every girl needs a mother's supervision.

CORELLA: I want you to come visit us, though, sometimes; and we'll be coming down here often because Pete has a pass, you see.

PETE: Lawyers are a dime a dozen, you know. All the lawyers I know are starving to death. I wouldn't let a son of mine study for the law.

LILY DALE: Can I play you another piece?

CORELLA: Not now, Lily Dale. We're talking.

PETE: Let her play it, Corrie. She just loves to play the piano, you know.

(LILY DALE *goes to the piano. She begins to play.*)

(*The lights fade and are brought up center stage* [*the river-bank*]. HORACE *is there stretched out on his back, smoking a pipe.* LLOYD *comes in. In the distance we can hear the aunts singing.*)

LLOYD: There's singing over at your house. (*He takes out a pipe too, and begins to smoke*.) Why aren't you up there with the rest?

HORACE: Too noisy. Too many people. I like it down here where it's quiet.

LLOYD: Did you meet your new daddy? (HORACE *nods his head yes*.) What's his name?

HORACE: Mr. Davenport.

LLOYD: What's his first name?

HORACE: Pete.

LLOYD: What do you call him?

HORACE: Mr. Davenport.

LLOYD: Mr. Davenport?

HORACE: Yes.

LLOYD: I guess that's because you're not used to him. (*Pause*.) Do you think you'll ever call him anything else?

HORACE: Nope.

LLOYD: My mama says she bets you'll go live with them now.

HORACE: Nope. They want me to, but I won't go.

LLOYD: Why? I'd like to live in Houston.

HORACE: I wouldn't. They say if I do go, I'd have to go to school, and I'm through with school.

LLOYD: You're not going back to school?

HORACE: Nope.

LLOYD: What are you going to do?

HORACE: Going out to the Gautier plantation with my uncle and work in the store.

LLOYD: How much will he pay you?

HORACE: My grub, all the tobacco I want, and four bits a week.

LLOYD: You're on your own now.

HORACE: I'm on my own.

LLOYD: See the lanterns down at the bottom? They're looking for Mr. Ritter. They think he may have died down there. Mr. John Howard died.

HORACE: I know.

LLOYD: They're not going to bury him here.

HORACE: I heard.

LLOYD: Did you go to your daddy's funeral?

HORACE: No. I've never been to a funeral.

LLOYD: Neither have I. Maybe we can go to Mr. Ritter's funeral, if they find him.

(*Pause. They listen to the music.*)

Do all your aunts sing?

HORACE: Yes.

LLOYD: And they all play musical instruments?

HORACE: Yes.

LLOYD: Do you play anything?

HORACE: No.

LLOYD: Last time I talked to you, you were going on about studying law in Houston.

HORACE: I've changed my mind. I wouldn't care for a city, I decided. I'd miss my fishing.

LLOYD: Aren't you going to study law here?

HORACE: No.

LLOYD: You change your mind a lot. Two months ago you were going on about studying law in Mr. John Howard's law office.

HORACE: Mr. John Howard is dead.

LLOYD: I know that. What do you think we were talking about just a minute ago? He's not the only lawyer in the world, you know. Mr. George Tyler is a lawyer. You could study law in his office.

HORACE: Mr. George Tyler has a son. He'll be studying law in his office. Anyway, I've changed my mind about all that.

LLOYD: You have?

HORACE: I certainly have. Lawyers are a dime a dozen, you know. There's no future in it.

LLOYD: I reckon not.

HORACE: No future at all. How much do tombstones cost? Do you know?

LLOYD: About a hundred dollars, I reckon. Why?

HORACE: I thought I might save my money and buy one.

LLOYD: What for?

HORACE: To put on my daddy's grave.

LLOYD: Take you a long time to save a hundred dollars.

(*Two men come in.*)

FIRST MAN: Boys, you all haven't seen anything strange while you've been back here?

LLOYD: What you mean, strange?

FIRST MAN: You haven't seen an old man's body of any kind?

LLOYD: No Sir. If we had, we would have reported it.

FIRST MAN: Keep your eyes open. Old man Ritter's lost or dead down here, we're afraid.

(*They leave.*)

LLOYD: I'm going home. Are you coming?

HORACE: I guess so.

(*They start out as the lights are brought up left on the* ROBEDAUX *area.* GEORGE TYLER *is there.* HORACE *comes in.*)

GEORGE TYLER: Hello, son. When do you leave for Houston?

HORACE: I changed my mind. I'm not going. I'm giving up law. I'm going to be a merchant.

GEORGE TYLER: Well, I tell you, now that you've decided, I think it's a wise decision for a boy in your circumstances. Of course, being the good friend of your daddy's I was, I would have done all in my power to help you, but I think you are doing the right thing. How do you like your new stepdaddy?

HORACE: He's all right. How much does a tombstone cost?

GEORGE TYLER: Well, I'm not exactly sure. John Howard and I were talking about getting one for your daddy's grave before he died; now it'll be up to me. I know poor old Mrs. Robedaux will never have the money for it. I'll get around to it one of these days. (*They hear the music in the distance.*) There's music over there at the Thorntons again. There's been some changes, haven't there? Your daddy's dead, the Robedauxs moved, your mama married again—a lot of changes. Well, we have to get used to change, son. All of us. I try to teach my children that.

(HORACE *turns his head away. He has begun to cry. He doesn't want* GEORGE TYLER *to know it.*)

Are you crying, son? Now, you mustn't cry. You've been mighty brave up till now. (*He puts his arm around the boy.*) Would you like to come inside and see how I've changed the house around? You wouldn't know it now.

HORACE: No Sir. Thank you.

(HORACE *moves away.*)

GEORGE TYLER: Where are you off to?

HORACE: Going uptown to look for empty whiskey bottles.

GEORGE TYLER: Well, you always keep busy. That's a good thing. (*He reaches in his pocket.*) Here's a dime for you. Buy yourself something.

HORACE: Thank you.

(*He takes it. He continues on as* GEORGE TYLER *goes on into the house and the singing continues in the distance as the lights fade.*)

Convicts

Characters

MARTHA JOHNSON
BILLY VAUGHN
ASA VAUGHN
HORACE ROBEDAUX
BEN JOHNSON
LEROY KENDRICKS
SOLL GAUTIER
SHERIFF
JACKSON HALL

Act One

Place: Floyd's Lane, Texas
Time: 1904

December 24. The lights are brought up upper right on part of the Gautier *plantation store. It has only the most rudimentary items.* Martha Johnson, *a black woman in her late forties, is seated by a potbellied stove, half asleep.* Billy Vaughn, *white, thirty-five, comes into the area.*

Billy: Martha, where is Horace?

Martha: He's gone fishing.

Billy: Where is Mr. Soll?

Martha: He's in Harrison. He went for the sheriff. One of them convicts kilt another one and tried to run away, but he and the overseer caught him before he got away and they chained him to a tree at the edge of the pasture while Mr. Soll rode into Harrison to get the sheriff. He didn't think he could make it back before early afternoon, he said. He has Ben down guarding the convict chained to the tree. They got the rest all locked up in their quarters to keep them from fighting amongst themselves.

Billy: Is that why it's so quiet around here and no one out in the fields? I thought he was maybe giving the convicts the day off because of Christmas Eve.

MARTHA: You know Mr. Soll don't give nobody any time off. He'll work them Christmas Day too. Always has. Only reason he don't have them out in the fields now is so trouble won't spread.

BILLY: My God, I don't know what Horace's people are thinking of, letting him work out here in this Godforsaken place. Do you know where Horace fishes?

MARTHA: Yes Sir.

BILLY: Would you go see if you can find him?

MARTHA: Yes Sir.

(*She goes out.* BILLY *stands by the stove warming himself.* ASA, *his wife, thirty-four, comes in. She is drunk.*)

ASA: Sonofabitch, it's cold out in that buggy, Billy. What the hell was Martha trying to tell me about Horace?

BILLY: He's off fishing.

ASA: Then let him stay fishing. I want to get on back to town.

BILLY: I'm going to wait for him. I'm going to bring him back with us. What are his people thinking about, letting him stay out here surrounded by convicts? There's only two white families between here and Harrison.

ASA: I was raised out here. I survived.

BILLY: Not too well.

ASA: Thank you.

BILLY: Anyway, most of the time you were off at school. Wonder where he stays out here. His uncle is no good. He's in town gambling while the boy looks after his job.

ASA: What's it to you, Billy?

BILLY: It sickens me. It sickens me to see a boy abandoned this way.

ASA: He'll survive. Give me a drink.

(He hands her the flask.)

BILLY: I wish we could raise the boy.

ASA: Don't be a sentimental fool. What would we do with him? You have a child. Take care of your own child. *(Pause. She lights a cigarette.)* Oh, the questions I'm asked. Where is Billy's first wife now? And his little girl? Was she having an affair? Or was Henry Vaughn making trouble?

BILLY: My God, Asa. Don't you have any decency? You're a slut, Asa. You think like one, you act like one, you talk like one.

ASA: Yes, indeed. But I'm a rich slut. My daddy owns three thousand acres. My Uncle Soll owns four thousand acres. And even though my uncle and my daddy don't speak, my uncle's childless, and who is to get all this but me and my sister Velma? *(Pause. She has a drink.)* Anyway, you married me because I was a slut. You need a slut. Only a slut becomes you.

(MARTHA comes back in.)

MARTHA: I can't find him. Ben hasn't seen him either.

ASA: Let's go. It will be dark now before we make it back to town.

BILLY: Where does the boy live, Martha? Up at the big house with Mr. Soll?

MARTHA: No Sir. He didn't like it over there. He sleeps here on the floor. When it's cold me and Ben sleep in here too, by the fire to keep warm.

ASA: Give me some more whiskey.

BILLY: That's all I have. (*He points to the flask.*)

ASA: I'm going up to Uncle Soll's to get me some more.

(*She starts out.*)

BILLY: If he comes back anytime soon, tell him to wait here until I come back.

(*He leaves.* MARTHA *goes behind the counter.* HORACE *enters through the door at the back.*)

MARTHA: Where you been?

HORACE: I been down to the field where they found the dead convict.

MARTHA: Mr. Billy wants to take you into Harrison for Christmas.

HORACE: I won't leave until Mr. Soll gets back. He told me yesterday he'd pay me today.

MARTHA: And he told you the day before that he'd pay you yesterday. Did he do it?

HORACE: No.

MARTHA: And I wouldn't hold my breath waitin' for him to pay you today.

HORACE: I don't want to go until I get my money. There's no tombstone on my daddy's grave and I want to make a down payment on one. It worries me to death there is still no tombstone on my daddy's grave. What do you think a tombstone would cost me?

MARTHA: I don't know. Ain't your folks gonna be mad with you if you don't get home for Christmas Day?

HORACE: My folks don't care what I do.

MARTHA: Yes, they do. Sure they do.

HORACE: No, they don't. My daddy cared about me, but he's dead. (*Pause.*) I saw the grave they buried the murdered convict in. They got no marker on it. What was his name?

MARTHA: I don't know what his name was. I don't study them convicts.

HORACE: I wonder if Ben knew his name?

MARTHA: I don't know.

HORACE: If we knew his name we could put his name on a board and put it over his grave. I wonder if anybody said a prayer over him when they buried him?

MARTHA: What do you think? The only prayers said on this place is right in here.

HORACE: Maybe we should go say a prayer over his grave.

MARTHA: I'm going to do nothing of the kind. I'm going to stay right here and mind my own business. I want nothing to do with convicts, dead or alive. It's bad enough I have to live out here where they can get loose and sneak in here and cut your throat, without going out amongst them. The happiest day I'll have is the day me and Ben leave here.

(*We hear a man's voice out in the yard calling "Horace . . . Horace."*)

HORACE: I'm coming, Ben.

(*He goes outside as the lights are brought up down left where* BEN JOHNSON, *a black man, forty-five, waits with a gun. Near him, chained, is* LEROY KENDRICKS, *a black man, thirty, in*

convict workclothes, stretched across the ground. HORACE
comes up to them.)

BEN: I'm cold waiting out here. You take the gun and
watch him for a spell while I go in and get warm by the
stove. I won't be long. Now, you stay way over here out of
the reach of his chain. Whatever you do, don't let him get
holt of that gun.

HORACE: I won't. (BEN *hands him the gun.*) What was the
name of the convict that was kilt?

BEN: I don't know.

HORACE: Do you think he knows?

BEN: I don't know.

HORACE: Was there any prayer said over his grave?

BEN: No. Now, you know Mr. Soll is not gonna have any
prayer said over a dead convict's grave. Who's going to say
it? Mr. Soll? There's no preacher out here—nobody but Mr.
Soll and the overseer and the guards and you and me and
the convicts.

HORACE: You've been here a long time, haven't you?

BEN: I was born out here. Right at the end of slavery time.
My mama and daddy are buried out here. Our cabin was
right over yonder. Mama and Papa worked on here for
wages after slavery time—a lot of the old folks did. When
they began to die off, Mr. Soll brought in convicts to work
the place.

(*He goes on his way.* HORACE *sits down on the ground, watching the* CONVICT. *After a moment he calls after* BEN.)

HORACE: Ben . . . (BEN *turns and comes back to him.*) Can I
talk to the convict?

BEN: I guess you can. He may not want to talk to you.

(*He goes into the store. There is silence.* HORACE *studies the man for a beat. He takes out a plug of tobacco and cuts off a piece and puts it in his mouth and starts to chew.*)

HORACE: Hey, convict . . . you want a chew of tobacco? (*The* CONVICT *doesn't move.* HORACE *chews silently for a beat and then . . .*) Convict, are you asleep? If you're asleep, I won't bother you.

CONVICT: I ain't asleep. It's too cold on this ground to sleep.

HORACE: Why don't you get up?

CONVICT: I get tired of standing.

HORACE: Can you stand, chained like that?

CONVICT: Sure, I can stand.

HORACE: You want a chew of tobacco?

CONVICT: Pass it along.

(*He throws it to him. The* CONVICT *catches it. He sits up.*)

CONVICT: Throw me a knife—I've got nothing to cut it with.

HORACE: You'll have to bite it off. I can't give you a knife.

(*The* CONVICT *doesn't argue. He bites the tobacco off and throws it back to* HORACE.)

HORACE: I came out here from Harrison in June when the hands that work the plantations around here had money to buy groceries from the store. I came out to help out my uncle, but I ended up doing all the work because he spent all his time up at Mr. Soll's house gambling. I hope to earn enough money out here to put a tombstone on my daddy's grave.

(*Pause. In the distance a convict sings "Ain't No More Cane On the Brazos."*)

HORACE: I was out this way once before—during a storm, a terrible one. I ran away from home when the storm was just starting, and I got lost and ended up on the Brodler brothers' plantation, a little way up the river from here. They got drunk during the storm and stayed on a drunk for a month afterwards. They were two old bachelor brothers: Clarence and Murray Brodler. They're both dead now. About two months ago, after I left there, they were in Harrison drinking in Dawdy's Saloon, and they got into an argument with Jessie Shatther, and he got his gun and killed Murray and wounded Clarence, but Clarence got away before he could kill him too. He left there and went back to some place in Tennessee where he came from, and he let his hair grow long and he grew a beard and he came back here and no one recognized him, and he went into Dawdy's Saloon and got a friend to watch out for Jessie Shatther, and when he walked into the saloon, he pulled out a pistol and killed him. A month later he got into a fight with William Jenkins and he got killed. The Brodler brothers were terrors. (*Pause.*) My name is Horace. (*Pause.*) What's your name?

CONVICT: Leroy.

HORACE: Leroy what?

CONVICT: Leroy Kendricks.

HORACE: There are a lot of Kendricks out around Kendelton. Are you kin to them?

CONVICT: No.

HORACE: Everybody that lives there is colored.

CONVICT: I still never been there. I come from Louisiana.

HORACE: How did you get down here?

CONVICT: I was working in the cane fields over in Brazoria County and I got into a fight and I cut a man.

HORACE: What did you cut him for?

CONVICT: What do you mean, what I cut him for?

HORACE: Were you mad at him?

CONVICT: Sure, I was mad at him. I was drunk, but I was mad at him too.

HORACE: Did you cut him bad?

CONVICT: No. He hollered like I kilt him, but I only cut him across the face. Anyway, they sentenced me to the Retrieve Prison Plantation on the coast. That's the worst place I was ever in in my life. I heard you could hire out to work on plantations around here until you paid off your fine, so I asked if I could go work out my fine and they sent me here.

HORACE: What's your fine?

CONVICT: Five hundred dollars. They pay me seven dollars a month, or they pay the state for me to pay off my fine.

HORACE: How long have you been here?

CONVICT: About a year.

HORACE: Twelve months?

CONVICT: I think so. No, not quite—I'd say nearer ten months. Tomorrow is Christmas, isn't it?

HORACE: Yes.

CONVICT: It was quite a spell after Christmas. They were planting when I got here.

HORACE: How long will you have to work at seven dollars a month to pay off your fine?

CONVICT: I don't know. They didn't tell me.

HORACE: Didn't you figure it out?

CONVICT: How am I going to figure it out?

HORACE: Just figure it out.

CONVICT: I don't know how.

HORACE: Did you go to school?

CONVICT: No.

HORACE: Never?

CONVICT: No.

HORACE: I went to the sixth grade, then I came out here to work with my uncle. Let's see—seven dollars a month at twelve months is eighty-four dollars. Eighty-four dollars into five hundred is . . . (*pause*) I can't do that in my head. I'll have to go back to the store and get a pencil to do that. I get four bits a week. Plus my room and board. I know how much I'll earn after I been here a year—twenty-four dollars. Of course, I ain't seen any of it yet. I go to Mr. Soll every other day and ask him to pay me and he always says he'll pay me tomorrow. But tomorrow never comes. (*Pause.*) You got any folks?

CONVICT: Sure.

HORACE: Where?

CONVICT: I don't know now. Used to be around New Iberia, Louisiana, last I heard.

HORACE: Do they know where you are?

CONVICT: No.

HORACE: Didn't you get word to them?

CONVICT: How am I going to do that? I can't write and they can't read.

HORACE: I been doing some figuring in my head. It comes to almost six years to pay off five hundred dollars.

CONVICT: It's going to be more than that now . . . (*pause*) because I kilt a man now.

HORACE: How come you kilt him?

CONVICT: Because he was always bothering me.

HORACE: How was he bothering you?

CONVICT: Just like I say. I told him to stop and he wouldn't. I told him if he didn't stop I was going to kill him first chance I got. I reckon he knew I meant what I said now.

HORACE: What was his name?

CONVICT: Jessie.

HORACE: Jessie what?

CONVICT: Jessie Wilkes.

HORACE: How old was he?

CONVICT: He was young.

HORACE: How old?

CONVICT: Twenty-two or so, I reckon. He has a brother here too. Brother say he gonna kill me if the white sheriff don't kill me.

HORACE: You scared of him?

CONVICT: No. His name is Sherman. Sherman Edwards.

HORACE: How come they are brothers if one is named Wilkes and one's named Edwards?

CONVICT: They had the same mama but a different daddy. He had a white man for a daddy.

HORACE: Who did?

CONVICT: Sherman Edwards. That's why he's so mean. It's the white blood in him. He'd kill you too, if he got a chance . . . mean as he is. He don't like white people. He says he'd kill them all if he got the chance. "How come you don't like white people," I asked him, "when you're half white?" He didn't answer that. He just cussed me. (*Pause.*) After I killed Jessie, I thought I might run for the brush and try to get away, but they're devils around here and they'd catch you sooner or later. I heard they caught one colored man who was a convict and stealing cattle to keep alive. And they caught him as he was butchering one of the cows he stole, and they grabbed him and sewed him up alive in the carcass of that cow as an example to all the cattle thieves.

HORACE: What do you think happened to him?

CONVICT: I think he died. That's what I think happened to him. (*Pause.*) If you give me that knife I might just cut my own throat and save somebody else the trouble. (*Pause.*) Would you give me the knife?

HORACE: No.

CONVICT: Would you give me another chew of tobacco?

HORACE: Sure. (*He chucks it to him.*) Keep it.

(*The* CONVICT *tears off a piece and begins to chew. He puts the rest in his pocket.*)

CONVICT: Overseer say they going to take me to the county jail. What's the name of the town that's at?

HORACE: Harrison. That's where I come from.

CONVICT: You born there?

HORACE: Yes.

CONVICT: You got people there?

HORACE: I told you—an uncle and some aunts.

CONVICT: You didn't tell me nothing.

HORACE: I thought I did. My daddy is dead. My mama and my baby sister live in Houston.

CONVICT: How come you're not with your mama?

HORACE: She lives in a small house. She's got no room for me. How did you get to Texas from New Iberia?

CONVICT: I ran away.

HORACE: I ran away too, once. Did I tell you that?

CONVICT: Yes, you did.

HORACE: I could run forever now and nobody would even know I was gone.

CONVICT: If you were running away from here, which way would you go?

HORACE: Depends on where I was running to. If you want to get to Houston, it's one way—

CONVICT: How far is Houston?

HORACE: Sixty miles. That's where my mama lives. Did I tell you that?

CONVICT: Yes, you did.

HORACE: Galveston is ninety. Corpus Christi is ninety. The gulf is thirty-five.

CONVICT: All in the same direction?

HORACE: No.

CONVICT: If you was heading for Corpus, how would you go?

HORACE: I never been there, but I would head for the river and follow that to the gulf and then head south.

CONVICT: How far is the river?

HORACE: About a quarter of a mile.

CONVICT: Which direction?

HORACE (*pointing*): That way. Can you swim?

CONVICT: A little bit.

HORACE: Stay away from the river if you can't swim. There are alligators and suckholes down there. People are always drowning in the river. I'm a good swimmer.

CONVICT: How did you learn?

HORACE: I taught myself. I was raised by the river. I'm going to ask Mr. Soll for my money I've earned so far when he gets back from Harrison today. It's Christmas Eve, so I figure he'll be in a good humor and he'll give it to me. Did I tell you what I was gonna do with my money?

CONVICT: Yes, you did.

HORACE: I don't know how big a tombstone I can get for twenty-four dollars, but I guess I can get some kind. If I give you this knife, would you really try to kill yourself?

CONVICT: Give it to me and see.

HORACE: I couldn't do that.

CONVICT: You're not in chains waitin' for a sheriff.

HORACE: I couldn't do it. I'm afraid of dying. You're not afraid of dying?

CONVICT: No.

(HORACE *starts away.*)

CONVICT: Where are you going?

HORACE: I'm going to say a prayer over Jessie's grave. (*Pause.*) Is it Jessie or Sherman?

CONVICT: Jessie. Why are you doing that?

HORACE: Because I feel bad he was just dumped into the ground and no prayer was said.

CONVICT: How come you feel bad about it? You didn't know him.

HORACE: I just do. Did you ever go to a funeral?

CONVICT: No.

HORACE: Neither have I. So I don't know what they do. When my daddy was buried I didn't get to go to his funeral because they said I was too young; and Mr. John Howard's wife took his body back to Waxahachie because she hated Harrison and all its people, she said; and Mr. Ritter wandered off into the woods one winter day and they never have found his body, only his gun, and some people think he's still alive. Excuse me, I'm just going over there and say the Lord's Prayer.

(*He goes off. The* CONVICT *lies down on the ground again and closes his eyes.* HORACE *comes back in.*)

Do you know the Lord's Prayer?

CONVICT: No.

HORACE: I've forgotten the last part of it.

(BEN *comes out from the store.*)

Ben, do you know the Lord's Prayer?

BEN: Yes, I do.

HORACE: What comes after . . . "forgive us our tres-passes . . ."?

BEN: What?

HORACE: What comes after—

BEN (*interrupting*): I can't say it that way. I have to start from the beginning: "Our Father, which art in heaven, Hallowed be Thy name. Thy kingdom come. Thy will be done on earth, as it is in heaven. . . ."

(SOLL, *a white man, seventy-eight, and the* SHERIFF, *a white man, fifty, come in.* SOLL *is very drunk.*)

SOLL: There he is, Sheriff.

(*The* SHERIFF *goes over to the* CONVICT.)

SHERIFF: Are you the one?

(*The* CONVICT *doesn't answer. He lies on the ground with his eyes closed. The* SHERIFF *gives him a kick.*)

SHERIFF: Answer me when I speak to you.

(*The* CONVICT *still doesn't move. The* SHERIFF *kicks him again and again.* HORACE *starts away.*)

Who has the keys?

(SOLL *takes a key out of his pocket and hands it to the* SHERIFF. HORACE *continues offstage. The* SHERIFF *unlocks the* CONVICT'S *chains. He takes a gun and holds it to his head.*)

SHERIFF: Now, move or I'll kill you.

(*The* CONVICT *gets up.*)

SHERIFF: Ben, you're going to have to ride into Harrison with me. This devil is mean. I'll have you drive the buggy while I keep him handcuffed to me.

BEN: Yes Sir.

(*The* SHERIFF *takes the* CONVICT *off.* SOLL *takes a bottle of whiskey and has a swig.* BEN *goes into the store.* HORACE *comes back in.*)

HORACE: Mr. Soll . . .

(SOLL *doesn't answer him if he hears him. In the distance we hear a convict singing "Ain't No More Cane On the Brazos."*)

HORACE: Mr. Soll . . .

(BEN *comes out of the store followed by* MARTHA.)

HORACE: Mr. Soll . . .

(SOLL *slowly turns and looks at the boy.*)

HORACE: You told me yesterday you'd pay me my wages today, Sir. I been working here six months, Sir, and I'd sure appreciate being paid. You see, I may be going into

Harrison, and I want to pay down on a tombstone for my daddy's grave.

SOLL: How much do I owe you?

HORACE: Eleven dollars and fifty cents, Sir.

SOLL: What do I owe you that for?

HORACE: For my wages.

SOLL: You work for me?

HORACE: Here in your store.

MARTHA: You know, Mr. Soll, he works for you.

SOLL: Did I ask you a question?

MARTHA: No Sir.

SOLL: Then you keep quiet until I do.

MARTHA: Shoot.

SOLL: What did you say?

MARTHA: Shoot.

SOLL: Why did you say that?

MARTHA: Because I'm disgusted. This poor boy is out here working to get a tombstone for his daddy's grave. And he's been here six months and you ain't paid him nothin' yet.

SOLL: You come on up to the house in a while and I'll pay you.

(*He leaves.*)

HORACE: Do you think he's going to give it to me?

MARTHA: I wouldn't hold my breath waitin' for it, if I was you.

(*There is a gunshot—then another and another.*)

MARTHA: Oh, Jesus. They're killing each other. Someday all them convicts are gonna get loose and we're all gonna be kilt.

(*The* SHERIFF *comes in.*)

SHERIFF: You won't have to go no place now, Ben. I was waiting for you with him by the buggy and he tried to overpower me and I kilt him. I missed him with the first shot, he was fighting so. It took three shots to kill him. I left him out on the road. You'll have to bury him.

BEN: Yes Sir.

(*He starts away. He sees* HORACE. *He reaches in his pocket and takes out an orange and a sack of hard candy.*)

SHERIFF: Oh, Horace, I almost forgot. Your uncle came by the jail when he heard I was coming out here. He asked me to give this to you . . . for Christmas.

HORACE: Yes Sir. (*He takes the orange and the hard candy.*)

SHERIFF: Merry Christmas.

HORACE: Merry Christmas.

(*The* SHERIFF *leaves.*)

HORACE: His name was Leroy.

BEN: Whose name was Leroy?

HORACE (*pointing in the direction of the dead man*): His. He says he wasn't afraid to die. Do you believe that?

BEN: I don't know.

HORACE: What's it like to die, do you reckon? . . .

BEN: I don't know. How would I know? I ain't never died.

(SOLL *comes in.*)

SOLL: Ben, you get your shovel and dig a grave for him. I'll send Jackson over to help you.

(BEN *goes.* SOLL *sees* HORACE.)

Boy, you go watch the body until we get his grave dug.

HORACE: No Sir. I wouldn't care to see him now.

SOLL: Why?

HORACE: 'Cause he's dead.

SOLL: Ain't you never seen a dead man, boy? Come on . . . nothing to worry your . . . (*He takes him by the arm.*)

HORACE: No Sir. I just don't want to see him.

SOLL: Suppose I told you you had to do it, boy?

MARTHA: He don't have to do it. I'll do it.

SOLL: What the hell are you doing here? You're supposed to be cooking my Christmas dinner.

MARTHA: This ain't Christmas Day yet.

SOLL: What the hell day is it?

MARTHA: Christmas Eve.

SOLL: Oh.

(MARTHA *leaves.*)

SOLL: That convict tried to kill me, you know.

HORACE: Which one?

SOLL: The one the sheriff just shot. (*He calls.*) Martha . . . is he really dead?

MARTHA (*calling from offstage*): Yes Sir.

SOLL: Is he white or colored?

MARTHA (*calling from offstage*): You saw him.

SOLL: I forget.

MARTHA (*calling from offstage*): Come see for yourself.

(*He goes off. We hear a convict singing "Ain't No More Cane On the Brazos." MARTHA comes out.*)

MARTHA: "Is he white or colored?" Crazy old fool.

HORACE: He wasn't afraid of dying. He told me that.

MARTHA: Who did?

HORACE: Leroy. Are you afraid of dying?

MARTHA: Ain't afraid of it. Just not ready to go yet.

(JACKSON HALL, *a black man, fifty-five, comes in.*)

JACKSON: Where is Mr. Soll?

MARTHA: Over there by the body. He says he tried to kill him.

JACKSON: Might have.

HORACE: Jackson, he listens to you. Tell him to give me my money.

JACKSON: He don't listen to me.

SOLL (*calling from offstage*): Jackson, tell Martha to get up to the house and start cooking my Christmas dinner.

JACKSON: You hear that, Martha?

MARTHA: Tell him today ain't Christmas.

(BEN *comes in.*)

JACKSON (*calling*): She says it ain't Christmas yet.

(*He and* BEN *start offstage toward the body.*)

MARTHA (*to* HORACE): You'd better go into the store if you don't want to see the convict. They are going to have to bring him by here.

(HORACE *goes into the store. She follows him.*)

HORACE: Have a piece of my Christmas candy?

MARTHA: Thank you. (*She takes a piece.*)

(*In the distance we hear a convict singing "Ain't No More Cane On the Brazos."* BEN *and* JACKSON *come by with the body of the convict.* BILLY *comes into the yard and into the store. He is very drunk now.*)

BILLY: What was the shootin' about, Martha?

MARTHA: The sheriff shot one of them convicts.

BILLY: Asa is drunk up at the house. As soon as she is sober we're going into Harrison. You want to go with us, boy? You should spend Christmas with your aunts.

HORACE: I'll go if I can collect the money Mr. Soll owes me. He said he would pay me today. He said if I came up to the house in a little, he'd give it to me.

BILLY: How much does he owe you?

HORACE: Eleven dollars and fifty cents.

BILLY: You stay here. I'll see the bastard gives it to you.

(BILLY *goes outside and offstage.*)

HORACE: You think he means that, Martha?

MARTHA: I hope so. He's mighty drunk, though.

(HORACE *goes outside.* BEN *comes in.*)

HORACE: Did you bury him?

BEN: I did. Next to the other convicts' graves. Mr. Soll says all the convicts that die gets buried out there. He don't want them buried near his people, and I don't want them buried near my people in our graveyard. My mama and daddy are buried here, you know. My sister is buried out here, and her baby.

(BILLY *comes in.*)

HORACE: Did you ask him, Mr. Billy?

(BILLY *slumps to the ground.*)

HORACE: Is he dead?

BEN: Dead drunk.

(BEN *goes into the store.* JACKSON *comes in.*)

JACKSON: Who's that on the ground?

HORACE: Mr. Billy Vaughn. He's drunk.

JACKSON: I thought it was another dead convict. (*Pause.*) A lot of them out here now.

HORACE: How many?

JACKSON: God knows. Always room for one more, though, ain't it? (*Pause.*) I'm a convict, you know. They made me a trustee so I can walk about free, but I'm still a convict.

(SOLL *comes in.*)

SOLL: That a convict?

BEN: No.

SOLL: Who the hell is it?

BEN: Who it look like?

(SOLL *peers at him.*)

SOLL: Billy. The sonofabitch is drunk. (BEN *and* JACKSON *pick* BILLY *up.*) Where are you taking him?

BEN: Up to the house.

SOLL: Did the overseer get them convicts back out in the field like I told him to?

JACKSON: All but one.

SOLL: Why isn't he out in the fields?

JACKSON: He's sick.

SOLL: What the hell is wrong with him?

JACKSON: I don't know. You have to ask him.

SOLL: Boy, go tell the damn overseer I said to get that convict out in the fields with the rest of them.

HORACE: Yes Sir.

MARTHA: Don't go over there, Horace.

SOLL: What did you say, woman?

MARTHA: I said for him not to go over to where them convicts live. Let Ben or Jackson go over there.

SOLL: I'll go over there, goddamn it.

MARTHA: Then you go over there.

SOLL: Think I'm scared of any goddamn sick convict? I'm scared of no goddamn convict, sick or well.

(*He goes out.*)

BEN: He ain't going to be sick long now.

HORACE: Which one is it?

JACKSON: The brother to the one that got killed.

(BEN *and* JACKSON *take* BILLY *out.*)

HORACE: Sherman Edwards. His daddy is a white man.

MARTHA: How do you know that?

HORACE: Leroy told me.

MARTHA: Who is Leroy?

HORACE: He is the convict that killed Jessie Wilkes.

MARTHA: Who is Jessie Wilkes?

HORACE: He's the brother of Sherman Edwards, whose father is white.

MARTHA: Uh-huh.

HORACE: What if he is sick?

MARTHA: Who?

HORACE: Sherman Edwards.

MARTHA: Ain't going to help him. He's going to have to

work in the fields just the same. Mr. Soll didn't bring them here to get sick.

HORACE: You know Mr. Billy Vaughn is divorced?

MARTHA: Yes.

HORACE: What happens if you're not divorced, but your first wife dies and you marry again. When you die and go to heaven, which one of the women do you claim as your wife?

MARTHA: I don't know.

HORACE: And take Sherman Edwards . . . he's got a white daddy and a colored mother. Now, when they all go to heaven together, what's going to happen?

MARTHA: How do I know all that, Horace?

HORACE: I worry about things like this because my daddy died and now my mother is married again. I got to wondering last night who was going to be her husband in heaven. Kept me awake half the night.

MARTHA: Read the Bible. All that's in the Bible someplace.

HORACE: Where?

MARTHA: I don't know, but everything is in the Bible, or so they tell me.

HORACE: I hope so. The way it looks to me now is that everything is going to be real mixed up in heaven. Now, my sister calls her stepfather "Daddy," and what's going to happen in heaven when she comes face to face with her real daddy?

MARTHA: I don't know who my daddy is.

HORACE: You don't?

MARTHA: My mama told me once, but I forgot his name.

(BEN *enters the yard.* HORACE *goes out to him.*)

HORACE: Did Mr. Soll see about Sherman Edwards?

BEN: Who?

HORACE: The sick convict.

BEN: No. Mr. Soll is drunk, I tell you. He can't remember his own name half the time when he gets this way. I went up there and told the overseer Mr. Soll wanted him to get him out in the field with the rest of them.

HORACE: Wasn't he sick?

BEN: Naw. Nothing's wrong with him. He just don't want to work. Overseer give him a couple of licks across his back and he got up all right. He got over being sick in a hurry.

HORACE: He's half white.

BEN: He's half something, all right. He can cuss, I know that.

HORACE: He don't like white people, Leroy says.

BEN: I ain't white and he cussed me.

HORACE: Why did he cuss you?

BEN: Because he said he didn't like colored people. (*He takes dice out of his pocket.*) Want to shoot some craps?

HORACE: I don't have any money.

BEN: I don't either. We'll just pretend like we do.

(SOLL *comes in.*)

SOLL: There's a boy out here says I owe him some money. You pay him, Ben.

BEN: What am I gonna pay him with? I've got no money.

SOLL: Take it out of the cash at the store.

BEN: What cash? You know everybody has been buyin' on credit since October.

SOLL: Everybody?

BEN: How else they gonna buy?

SOLL: I got a lot of money, you know.

BEN: I know you do.

SOLL: Where the hell did I put my money?

BEN: I don't know, Sir.

SOLL: Well, tell the boy when I find it, I'll pay him.

BEN: You tell him. There he is right there.

SOLL: Where?

BEN: Right there.

SOLL: Oh. Where is Nancy?

BEN: Nancy is dead. She's been dead fifteen years or more.

SOLL: Where's Julia?

BEN: She's dead too, Sir. Been dead—

(SOLL *looks at him skeptically and then starts away. He stops.*)

SOLL: Where's Sarah?

BEN: She's dead too, Sir.

SOLL: Who the hell is out here?

BEN: Just you and me and Martha and this boy here and the overseer and two guards and the convicts.

SOLL: Ain't Jackson out here?

BEN: Yes Sir. You know he is. Excuse me, I forgot to mention Jackson.

SOLL: Where is my gun?

BEN: I don't know, Sir.

SOLL: Get it for me.

BEN: I don't know where it is, Sir.

SOLL: You got a gun?

BEN: Yes Sir.

SOLL: Get it for me. I'm going hunting.

BEN: Yes Sir. I wouldn't go hunting today, if I were you. It's Christmas Eve.

SOLL: I don't care the hell what day it is. I'm going hunting.

BEN: Yes Sir.

SOLL: Where's Jackson?

BEN: I don't know, Sir.

SOLL: I'll put the lazy sonofabitch back on the chain gang if he ain't careful. (*He sees* HORACE.) Who the hell are you?

HORACE: Horace, Sir.

SOLL: How old are you?

HORACE: Thirteen, Sir.

SOLL: Whose boy are you?

BEN: You know who he is, Mr. Soll. His daddy is dead, Sir, and—

SOLL: Let him answer. Is your daddy dead?

HORACE: Yes Sir.

SOLL: What was his name?

HORACE: Paul Horace Robedaux.

SOLL: I knew the bastard. He wasn't worth killing. He was my brother's lawyer. He helped my brother cheat me. How did you get out here?

BEN: Mr. Albert Thornton is his uncle. He come out here in the fall to help him in the store when the crops were coming in. Now you know all that.

SOLL: Where's Albert?

BEN: He's in town.

SOLL: What the hell is he doin' in town?

BEN: He spoke to you about it. Everything is so quiet at the store. The few customers we have this boy can take care of.

SOLL: I don't want him here. I don't want Paul Horace Robedaux's boy on this place. Take him over to my brother's place. Let him take care of him.

BEN: Your brother is in New Orleans.

SOLL: Then take him back to town.

(*He goes.*)

BEN: He didn't mean that. He knows who you are. He's just drunk. He'll say anything when he's drunk. He'll be all over his drunk tomorrow. Your daddy was a good lawyer. He had to defend his brother. He hired him to do it. Mr. Soll could have hired him same as his brother. He hates his brother and his brother hates him.

HORACE: Who's Sarah?

BEN: She used to live out here. So did Nancy and Julia. They were all three born on this place, and they all died out here.

HORACE: Are they buried out here?

BEN: Yes. They're buried in the colored graveyard. Next to my people. But I couldn't find their graves even if my life depended on it. It's all grown up with weeds and brush out there now. I keep my folks' graves clear of weeds, but I don't have the time to keep the whole graveyard cleared. Mr. Soll makes the convicts keep his people's graveyard clean. Everybody buried in his graveyard has a tombstone.

HORACE: Is there a tombstone on your people's graves?

BEN: No. Just a wooden cross.

HORACE: I want a marble tombstone on my daddy's grave.

(BEN *exits.* HORACE *goes back into the store. He cuts a plug of tobacco and begins to chew as* SOLL *comes in. He has a gun.*)

SOLL: Who the hell are you?

HORACE: Horace, Sir.

SOLL: Horace who?

HORACE: Robedaux, Sir.

SOLL: Oh, yes. What is your daddy's name?

HORACE: Paul Horace. Paul Horace Robedaux.

SOLL: I knew him. He's dead?

HORACE: Yes Sir.

SOLL: I have a brother. Did you ever meet him?

HORACE: No Sir.

SOLL: He has the place next to mine. We don't get along. He's a mean, no-good bastard. You know what my daddy said to me just before he died?

HORACE: No Sir.

SOLL: He called me to his bedside and he sent everybody else out of the room. "Soll," he said, "watch out for that sonofabitch Tyre. He'll steal you blind. He's a rattlesnake and he has venom in his fangs." That's what his own daddy thought about him. (*He takes a bottle out of his pocket.*) You want some whiskey?

HORACE: No Sir.

(SOLL *has a swig.*)

HORACE: I was about to go up to the house looking for you, Sir. You told me to come up there and you would pay me.

SOLL: Pay you for what?

HORACE: For working for you, Sir.

SOLL: You work for me?

HORACE: Yes Sir. Here in the store. I'm watching it while my Uncle Albert is in Harrison for the winter. Things are quiet out here in the country, you all said.

SOLL: How old are you?

HORACE: Thirteen.

SOLL: Then you should pay me for letting you work out here. You should pay me for letting you learn how to run a store.

HORACE: Yes Sir. I suppose so. But you agreed—

SOLL: I agreed to nothin'.

HORACE: Yes Sir, you did. You said you would pay me for working here, fifty cents a week. And I been here six months and you owe me now eleven dollars and fifty cents, and you told me yesterday you would pay me that on Christmas Eve, which is today, and a while ago you said

SOLL: I must have been drunk. I remember you now, boy. You came out here to earn the money for your daddy's tombstone. Your daddy was no good, Albert says. Mistreated your mother. Died a drunkard. "Then why in hell does he want to put a tombstone on the bastard's grave?" I asked him. "That's how the boy is," he says. "He's strange." "He'll get over that," I says. "Some woman will help him get over that." You ever had a woman?

HORACE: No Sir.

SOLL: Well, we're gonna have to do something about that.

HORACE: Yes Sir.

SOLL: You chewing tobacco?

HORACE: Yes Sir.

SOLL: Give me a chew. (HORACE *hands him the plug.* SOLL *cuts off a piece and begins to chew.*) My daddy, God rest his soul in peace, turned out to be a prophet. My brother Tyre is a liar, a thief, a killer. I hope his soul will rot in hell forever. He's got a bitch of a daughter, too. She's up there at my house now. I know what she wants. She wants to know how I've made out my will. Every now and then she says, "Who you gonna leave all this to, Uncle Soll?" (*Pause.*) Can you write?

HORACE: Yes Sir.

SOLL: Get a pencil and a piece of paper and take down what I tell you. (HORACE *does so*.) I, Soll Gautier, on my oath I leave my land, my houses . . . (*Pause*.) Who the hell am I going to leave them to? Everybody that's kin to me is dead except Tyre and his two ugly old daughters. Oh, my Jesus! Do you have a brother?

HORACE: No Sir. I have a sister.

SOLL: Get down on your knees and thank God you've got no brother. They steal everything you've got, cut your heart out, and smile all the while.

(*In the distance a convict sings "The Rock Island Line."*)

I'm going hunting. Come on with me.

(*He hands the gun to* HORACE, *who takes it.* SOLL *starts out.* HORACE *follows after him. They come out into the yard.* SOLL *sees the graves in the distance and points to them.*)

Who the hell is buried out there?

HORACE: Convicts.

SOLL: Sonofabitch. (*Pause*.) Convicts are no good. I work them out here because the state hires them to you cheap, but they're no good. They are more trouble than they are worth. Give me the gun—there's a damn bear over there.

HORACE: No Sir. There is no bear over there.

SOLL: Yes, there is too. An' I'm gonna kill the sonofabitch. (*He takes the gun and shoots*.) Did I kill it?

HORACE: I don't know, Sir.

SOLL: Go see.

HORACE: Well, Sir . . . I . . .

SOLL: Is Sarah Tucker still on the place?

HORACE: Sarah who?

SOLL: Sarah Tucker.

HORACE: Is she the one you asked Ben about earlier?

SOLL: Ben who?

HORACE: Ben Johnson. He works for you. He lives there behind the store.

SOLL: I don't remember if I asked him about her or not. She's a small woman—not more than five feet. Where is her house? It was out this way someplace.

HORACE: It's not out here now.

SOLL: It's not?

HORACE: No Sir. If she's the one you asked Ben about, she's dead.

SOLL: She is?

HORACE: Yes Sir. There's nobody out here now but you and me and Ben and his wife and the overseer and the two guards and the convicts and Jackson.

SOLL: Who is Jackson?

Horace: He's the one who stays up at the house with you.

SOLL: A lot of good-looking women out here, you know. We'll find one you like. I had my first woman by the time I was eleven. What the hell was her name? Carrie or Bernice. What kind of tombstone did you have in mind for your daddy?

HORACE: Just a small one.

SOLL: What the hell do you want a small one for? Did you see the one I put on my daddy's grave? It's the biggest goddamned tombstone ever made. It's got angels all over it and two women crying. Come here. (*He points toward the convicts' graveyard.*) See that? There are eight tombstones in that graveyard. Which do you like best?

HORACE: I don't see any tombstones there, Sir.

SOLL: You don't see any tombstones?

HORACE: No sir. There's none there.

SOLL: Who the hell took them away? Who the hell stole them? It's them damn convicts. They steal everything—even the tombstone off my daddy's grave.

HORACE: No sir. That's not your graveyard, Sir. That's where the convicts are buried.

SOLL: Where the hell is my graveyard?

HORACE: It's over yonder.

SOLL: Let's go find the goddamn place. (*He starts away, then stops and shoots the gun again.*)

HORACE: What are you shooting at now, Sir?

SOLL: Convicts. I'm gonna kill all them convicts. I'm gonna have me a sure enough convict graveyard out here. (*He shoots again, then pauses. He hands* HORACE *the gun.*) Shoot you a convict. (HORACE *takes the gun. He shoots.*) How many have we killed?

HORACE: I don't know, Sir.

SOLL: A lot?

HORACE: Yes Sir, I guess so.

(SOLL *lies down on the grave*.)

It's cold on that ground, Sir. I wouldn't lie down there if I were you. That ground is cold and damp.

(BEN *comes in*.)

BEN: Who were you all shooting at?

HORACE: First he said he was shooting at a bear, and then convicts. But there aren't any—bear or convicts either. I tried to keep him from lying on the cold, damp ground, but he wouldn't listen.

(BEN *goes to him. He tries to rouse him*.)

BEN: Mr. Soll . . . get up, now . . . you're gonna catch your death. Mr. Soll . . . (*He can't move him*.)

SOLL: Damn convicts take all my tombstones off the graves—now they've come to kill me.

(BEN *shakes him*.)

BEN: Mr. Soll . . . Mr. Soll . . . Watch him now while I go for Jackson.

(*He leaves*. SOLL *raises his head up*.)

SOLL: Are you a convict?

HORACE: No sir.

SOLL: You haven't come to kill me?

HORACE: No Sir.

SOLL: One of those damn convicts tried to kill me. He slipped away while they were working in the brush. The damn overseer was half drunk and he didn't notice he was gone until it was dark. We took the dogs and ran the bottom half the night but couldn't find him, and it got to raining and we came back here and I got into bed and had closed my eyes and something told me to keep my gun in the bed with me and I went and got it, and just then I heard a noise in the closet and I told whatever it was to come out of the closet, and the sonofabitch wouldn't answer me and so I said, "I give you fair warning— whoever is in there better come out or I'm gonna kill you." And he wouldn't answer, so I took my goddamn gun and I shot eight or nine times into the goddamn closet. And I said, "Now will you believe me and come out?" And there was no answer from the goddamn closet, and the over- seer . . . (*Pause.*) Who was overseer then? Was Will the overseer then or was it Philip?

HORACE: I don't know, Sir.

SOLL: Anyway, one of them come up to my room and said, "Are you all right?" And I said, "Yes, I'm all right, but there is a sonofabitch in there that won't come out of the closet." And Will or Philip or whoever the hell his name was opened the goddamn closet door and the goddamn convict bastard fell out of the closet riddled with bullets. I think every shot I fired in there hit the bastard, and he was still holding the goddamn knife he used for cutting brush and cane in his hand, and the overseer said . . . I don't remember his goddamn name. Did I tell you his god- damn name?

HORACE: No Sir.

SOLL: Well, anyway, he said, "That sonofabitch was wait- ing in the closet to kill you." There was blood splattered all over the closet; his blood was running all across the floor of my room, so I said, "Get Ben and get the sonofabitch out of here and get the blood cleaned up." And he went for

Ben and he and the overseer came back and Ben said, "You want me to bury him?" And I said, "I don't care what the hell you do with him." And the overseer said, "We're not going to bury him yet. We're going to hang him to a tree for a few days out where the convicts are working so they can see what will happen to them when they get out of line." And it was daylight then and they took the sonofabitch out and hung him from the tree, and he hung there until he began to stink and I said to the damn overseer, "Get rid of him. I can't stand the smell." So they buried him . . . out here someplace, where they bury all the goddamn convicts that die or kill each other.

HORACE: What was his name?

SOLL: Whose name?

HORACE: The convict you shot.

SOLL: I shot four of them. I shot one as he was trying to run. I seen him start and I hollered to him to stop and he wouldn't, but kept on running and I shot him. Killed him with the first shot. I shot two brothers that ran away together and I found hiding in a shack down near the river. I told them to come out or I was gonna set fire to the shack and they came out, but as they did, they ran for the brush and I killed one and wounded the other, but he died before morning. They are all buried out here some-place. The more you kill, the more they are.

(JACKSON *and* BEN *come up.*)

Ben, what was the name of the overseer that was here when I shot that convict that was hiding in my closet?

BEN: Philips.

SOLL: Was that his first name or his last one?

BEN: His last one.

SOLL: Was he white or colored?

BEN: White.

SOLL: White makes the best overseers. One I got now is the meanest one of the bunch. That's the first question I ask when I hire them: "How mean are you?" I think the one we got now is the meanest white man alive.

BEN: I think the sheriff over in Harrison is meaner than he is.

SOLL: Maybe so.

JACKSON: They're working white convicts on the Forgason place across the river. Bud Jenkins is cooking for them. He said the overseer over there has a mean, long whip. He says he whips at least one of them white men every day.

SOLL: Weren't you a convict, Jackson?

JACKSON: Yes Sir. You know I was.

SOLL: How come you ain't down there with the rest of them?

JACKSON: I'm a trustee. I work for you.

SOLL: Who the hell made you a trustee?

JACKSON: You did, Sir.

SOLL: Well, watch yourself, or I'll have you back in chains.

JACKSON: Yes Sir.

(BEN *and* JACKSON *lift* SOLL *up off the ground.*)

SOLL: Where are you taking me to?

BEN: Back to the house.

SOLL: I want to go hunting.

BEN: How you gonna hunt, drunk as you are? (SOLL *pulls away from them.*) You're gonna get put to bed.

SOLL: Not me. I'll be goddamned if I'm going to be. (*He takes his gun.*) You come near me an' I'll kill you. Keep away from me. You hear me? Now get out of here.

(*They start away.* HORACE *goes with them.*)

I want the white boy to stay. (HORACE *pauses.*) He's the only one around here I trust. (*He lies down again holding the gun.*)

BEN: Don't cross him when he's drunk. You stay here with him.

HORACE: I'm scared of him.

BEN: He's not gonna hurt you. He's too drunk to pull the trigger of the damn gun.

(JACKSON *and* BEN *leave.* HORACE *goes over to* SOLL.)

SOLL: Help me up. (HORACE *does so.*) What's your name again?

HORACE: Horace Robedaux. (*He cries.*)

SOLL: What are you crying for?

HORACE: I'm scared.

SOLL: What are you scared of?

HORACE: I don't know, Sir.

SOLL: Are you scared the convicts are gonna get loose one night and kill you?

HORACE: No Sir.

SOLL: What are you scared of, then?

HORACE: I don't know, Sir. I'm scared about a lot of things.

SOLL: Tyre's wife is a jackass. "I want my girls to be educated," she said. "I want a school out here. Everybody should be educated, no matter what color their skin is." "What for?" I said. "I ain't educated, your husband ain't. We knew enough to come here and get hold of eight thousand acres of the richest land in the whole goddamn world. We can grow three crops a year here . . . we . . ." (*Pause. He looks up at the boy.*) Albert says you came out here to work so you could buy a tombstone for your daddy's grave.

HORACE: Yes Sir.

SOLL: Well, I'm going to buy it for you. I'm gonna buy the biggest goddamned tombstone in Texas. I'm gonna have angels on it and two Confederate veterans. Was your daddy a Confederate veteran?

HORACE: No Sir. He wasn't born till after the war, but he remembered people talking about it.

SOLL: I was a veteran. I fought in every goddamned battle they'd let me. What were we talking about?

HORACE: A tombstone for my daddy.

SOLL: Oh, yes. I'll put "Rest in Peace" on it, and three verses from the Bible. Have you seen the tombstones I've had put up out here?

HORACE: No Sir.

SOLL: I'll take you over to my family graveyard tomorrow first thing. You pick out the tombstone you like and I'll have it copied and put on your daddy's grave. (*He grabs the boy.*) Did you hear something?

HORACE: No Sir.

SOLL: I do. It's one of them convicts. See him hiding back over there?

HORACE: No Sir.

SOLL: Yonder. See him yonder? Right through the trees there . . . (*He calls out.*) Come out, you sonofabitch. (*He takes the gun. He can barely lift it. He finally does and finds the strength to pull the trigger.*) Did I get him?

HORACE: No Sir.

SOLL: Has he gone?

HORACE: I guess so, Sir.

SOLL: You know my brother Tyre?

HORACE: I've seen him, Sir.

SOLL: He accused me of cheating him. "Why would I cheat you?" I said. "I got all the land and money I want." "Give me half and you take half," he said. "My wife is against working convicts." "Well, then," I said, "you'll never get the work done." Took him two years to find out. Next thing I heard he had his own convicts.

(*A man is heard singing "Rock Island Line."*)

Who is that over there crossing the back field?

HORACE: It's the convicts.

(ASA *appears.*)

ASA: Uncle, you want any supper?

SOLL: No.

ASA: It is Christmas Eve.

SOLL: I don't give a goddamn what day it is. If I wanted supper, I'd tell you. (*He gets up.*)

ASA: Where are you going?

SOLL: We're going hunting.

ASA: What are you going hunting for, this time of day?

SOLL: We're going to look for the convicts. There are three of them that have escaped.

ASA: There's no damn convict loose.

SOLL: And you're a goddamn liar.

ASA: You're crazy. You've drunk so much whiskey it's finally made you crazy.

SOLL: And you're a whore. My goddamn brother said to me, "You sonofabitch, you're childless. I have two daughters." "Two whores," I said. "Two no-good, sluttish whores. They'll get nothing of mine."

(*He stumbles and falls to the ground.* HORACE *goes to him.*)

ASA: Leave him alone. I hope he broke his goddamn neck. (*She goes over and kicks him.*) Did you hear me? I hope you break your goddamn neck.

SOLL: You'll get nothing of mine. Ben and Martha are to have it all.

(BEN *and* MARTHA *and* JACKSON *have come in. They stand at the background.*)

Are there witnesses here? Ben and Martha are to have it all.

ASA: Who wants any of your goddamn land? I have all the goddamn land I want.

SOLL: Ben and Martha, faithful and trustworthy . . . and the convicts . . . they're all around. Hand me my gun, please . . . allow me to defend myself. Don't leave me here alone, defenseless, to have my throat cut. I sleep with my gun beside me. My cane knife is always near. Where's the boy? Where's the white boy? (HORACE *steps toward him.*) I want him near me. I don't want you to leave me. (HORACE *is beside him now.* SOLL *closes his eyes.*) And tomorrow, first thing, we'll go look at my family's graveyard and you'll tell me the tombstone you like and I'll have it copied. What's your name, boy?

HORACE: Horace.

SOLL: Oh, yes. You're to sleep in my room tonight. I'll have my gun and you'll have yours, and no damn convicts will ever get near us.

(*He reaches out as if to grab the boy and pull him to him, but his arm never quite makes it; he falls back to his side as he rolls over on the ground.* HORACE *and the others watch him as the lights fade.*)

Act Two

The lights are brought up in a room of the GAUTIER *plantation.
The room is empty except for three chairs: two straight, and one
armchair.* SOLL *is in the armchair, dozing, his gun across his
lap.* HORACE *comes in.* JACKSON *goes up to him.*

JACKSON: He's asleep now. But every time he wakes up, he
asks for you. He's about driven me crazy asking for you to
come up here. He says he wants a white person with him
when he dies.

HORACE: Where is Miss Asa and Mr. Billy?

JACKSON: They went over to her daddy's place.

HORACE: Is he dying?

JACKSON: That's what he says he's doin'. But I don't believe
him—I've heard it all before.

HORACE: Don't leave me alone with him, Jackson, if he's
gonna die. I don't want to be here alone when he dies.

JACKSON: He's not going to die. He just talks a lot. He's too
mean to die.

HORACE: I don't want to die. Do you?

JACKSON: No.

HORACE: I was thinking coming over here of that convict,
Leroy, dying this morning. He said it meant nothing to
him. And I thought if I die, I might go to heaven and see

138

my daddy, but much as I'd like to see him, I wouldn't want to die to do it.

SOLL: (*opening his eyes*): Jackson . . .

(JACKSON *goes over to him.*)

JACKSON: That white boy is here.

SOLL: Tell him to come here where I can see him. (HORACE *goes over to him.*) Did they tell you I was dying?

HORACE: Yes Sir.

SOLL: Has anyone sent for a doctor to come see me?

JACKSON: Miss Asa said she was going to send one out here when she got back to town.

SOLL: She's a damn liar. She won't send nobody out here. She wants to see me dead so she can claim all this for herself and her no-good father. (*Pause.*) There was three of us Gautier boys, you know—Tyre, Melvin, and me. Tyre poisoned Melvin, you know. At least, he had him poisoned. Paid a man to mix some jimsonweed in his food, and he poisoned him. He denied it, of course, up and down, but I know he did. I have it carved right on Melvin's tombstone: "Poisoned by his brother Tyre, whose motive was greed." Tyre wants it all. (*To* HORACE.) Come closer, boy. (HORACE *goes to him.*) I'm going to die. Did they tell you that?

HORACE: Yes Sir.

SOLL: Did you ever watch an old man die?

HORACE: No Sir.

SOLL: Promise you won't leave me alone after I die until they get me in my coffin. There are wild varmints out here. I knew a man that died out here and they went off and left his body alone while they went for the coffin or the preacher or something, and when they came back to the body the varmints had come and tore it all apart.

HORACE: What kind of varmints?

SOLL: Wildcats . . . wolves . . . God knows what all. Don't let that happen to me.

HORACE: No Sir.

SOLL: And if I fall asleep, don't leave me.

HORACE: No Sir.

SOLL: Jackson . . .

JACKSON: Yes Sir?

SOLL: Convicts all quiet?

JACKSON: Yes Sir. Been quiet.

SOLL: As soon as it's daybreak, I want you to go down there and tell the overseer I want the convicts to make a coffin for me, if I'm dead or not.

JACKSON: Yes Sir.

SOLL: When you reach my time of life, you'd better have your coffin handy. When it's made, I want it put right under my bed.

JACKSON: Yes Sir.

SOLL: And if you can't get it under my bed, I want it beside it.

JACKSON: Yes Sir.

SOLL: You were a convict, weren't you?

JACKSON: Yes Sir. You know that.

SOLL: What did they send you to the pen for?

JACKSON: I killed a man.

SOLL: Wasn't a white man, I hope?

JACKSON: No Sir.

SOLL: Was it a colored man?

JACKSON: Yes Sir.

SOLL: What did you kill him for?

JACKSON: Because he killed my only brother. He took a club and clubbed him to death and then he took his body into his house and burned it up.

SOLL: The house too?

JACKSON: Yes Sir.

SOLL: Whose house was it? His house or your brother's house?

JACKSON: My brother's house.

SOLL: How long did they give you for killing him?

JACKSON: Life.

SOLL: How old were you at the time?

JACKSON: Nineteen.

SOLL: How old are you now?

JACKSON: Fifty-five.

SOLL: You know how old I am?

JACKSON: No Sir.

SOLL: Be seventy-eight my next birthday. How old were you when you come to work on this place?

JACKSON: Thirty-two.

SOLL: How long you been a trustee?

JACKSON: Eight years. Ever since you killed the convict in the closet over here. You said you wanted someone you could trust to guard you here while you slept.

SOLL: And can I trust you?

JACKSON: Yes Sir, I hope so. I believe so.

SOLL: I believe so too. I'm going to leave everything I got to you.

JACKSON: Thank you.

SOLL: I don't want to wait until dawn. I want you to go out there now and get the convicts to make my coffin.

JACKSON: Yes Sir.

(*He starts away.*)

SOLL: Jackson . . . Jackson . . . Is that your first name or your last name?

JACKSON: My first name.

SOLL: What's your last name?

JACKSON: Hall.

SOLL: Were you born around here?

JACKSON: Matagorda County.

SOLL: On the coast.

JACKSON: Right on the coast.

SOLL: I thought of settling down there once when things got so bad with my brother, but the hurricanes are too fierce down there.

JACKSON: They are fierce here too.

SOLL: Oh, yes, they are. Why did the man kill your brother?

JACKSON: I don't know.

SOLL: How did you kill him?

JACKSON: I shot him.

SOLL: From ambush, or did you walk right up to him and kill him?

JACKSON: I walked right up to him.

SOLL: Did you give him any warning?

JACKSON: Yes Sir. I hollered to him to start running—I was going to kill him.

SOLL: Did he run?

JACKSON: No Sir. He tried to take the gun from me.

SOLL: And you shot him then?

JACKSON: Yes Sir.

SOLL: Did he have a gun on him?

JACKSON: No Sir, just a knife.

SOLL: Did you ever regret killing him?

JACKSON: No Sir.

SOLL: And you would kill him again if you had it all to do over again?

JACKSON: Yes Sir.

SOLL: You were fond of your brother?

JACKSON: Yes Sir.

SOLL: Were you here with me when I shot the convict in the closet?

JACKSON: I was here on the place, but I wasn't working directly for you then.

SOLL: Did you know the convict I shot?

JACKSON: Which one?

SOLL: The one in the closet.

JACKSON: Yes Sir.

SOLL: What was his name?

JACKSON: Tucker, I think, but I'm not sure about that. But I remember what he look like. He was crippled because he had run away once before and he got caught in a bear trap, and it broke his leg and never healed right so he limped around here from then on.

SOLL: What do you think he was doing in that closet? Do you think he was waiting there to kill me?

JACKSON: I don't know, Sir.

SOLL: What is your opinion?

JACKSON: Yes Sir.

SOLL: Yes Sir what?

JACKSON: I think he was waiting there to kill you.

SOLL: I think he was too. (*Pause.*) Do you hear something in that closet over there?

JACKSON: No Sir.

SOLL: I did. (*He calls out.*) Come out of there. You hear me, you sonofabitch? (*There is no answer.*) I'll give you one more chance to come out of there. (*He takes his gun and shoots into the closet*.) I warned you. (*He shoots again and again*.) Go see if I killed anything in there.

(JACKSON *goes*. SOLL *looks up at* HORACE.)

Where you from?

HORACE: Harrison.

SOLL: What are you doing out here?

HORACE: I work for you, Sir, at the store.

SOLL: You're white, aren't you?

HORACE: Yes Sir.

SOLL: We're the only two white people between here and Harrison except for the overseer and the two guards. The rest are convicts.

HORACE: Ben and Martha aren't convicts.

SOLL: No. Where are they?

HORACE: Over at the store.

SOLL: Are you the one I promised the tombstone?

HORACE: Yes Sir.

SOLL: I haven't forgotten.

HORACE: Yes Sir.

SOLL: And I owe you money?

HORACE: Yes Sir.

SOLL: As soon as Jackson comes back, I'm going to have him get your money. How much do I owe you?

HORACE: Eleven dollars and fifty cents.

SOLL: Eleven dollars and fifty cents. I'm gonna give you a

hundred dollars. Maybe even a thousand. I'm gonna reward you for your kindness to an old man. Do you know how much my daddy's tombstone cost?

HORACE: No Sir.

SOLL: Five thousand dollars. Brought it by boat from New Orleans. There used to be a woman out here named Sarah. Have you seen her lately?

HORACE: No Sir. I believe she's dead.

SOLL: How do you know that?

HORACE: I heard Ben say that.

SOLL: Ben Johnson?

HORACE: Yes Sir.

SOLL: He was born on this place.

(JACKSON *comes in.*)

JACKSON: Wasn't anything in the closet.

SOLL: No? I swore I heard something.

JACKSON: Yes Sir.

SOLL: You go tell them to get my coffin ready now.

JACKSON: Yes Sir.

(*He leaves.*)

SOLL: Boy?

HORACE: Yes Sir.

SOLL: You're still here.

HORACE: Yes Sir.

SOLL: Come closer so I can see you. (HORACE *does so.*) Did you hear anything in that closet?

HORACE: No Sir.

SOLL: I had a dream one night last week . . . I had a dream that all the convicts got loose, and they came over here and they caught me here in this very chair, and they shot Jackson and they bound me . . . (*Pause.*) I don't really remember if they shot Jackson or not; part of the time it seemed like Jackson was one of them. (*Pause.*) Did you hear something in that closet over there?

HORACE: No Sir.

SOLL: I did. Come out of there, you sonofabitch. I hear you. (*Pause.*) I give you one last warning. (*He shoots again and again.*) That got whoever was in there. Go see who it was.

HORACE: No Sir.

SOLL: You scared to go?

HORACE: Yes Sir.

SOLL: I'll go. Help me up.

(HORACE *does so.* SOLL *goes out of the area and after a beat, he comes slowly back.*)

I knew there was somebody in there. I killed the sonofabitch—blood everyplace. He's a cripple. (*He sits down.*) What was I telling you before? Oh, yes, about my dream. Well, I was sitting here and Jackson come in with all them convicts. Oh, I never saw so many and they grabbed me, and Jackson had a club and he began to club me, and I said, "Jackson, you're killing me." And then the convicts grabbed clubs and began to beat me, and Jackson set fire to the house. I said, "Why did you do that?" And he said, "We're going to burn you and all you got to the ground."

(JACKSON *comes in.*)

Where have you been?

JACKSON: I went to tell them about your coffin.

SOLL: Have they started?

JACKSON: Yes Sir.

SOLL: Are they making it out of cypress wood?

JACKSON: I don't know, Sir.

SOLL: Will they bring it up here when they finish?

JACKSON: Yes Sir.

SOLL: How long will that be?

JACKSON: They'll have it done in an hour.

SOLL: I killed a man hiding in the closet out there. It's full of blood. You go clean it up and get Ben to help you bury the body.

JACKSON: Yes Sir.

SOLL: It was a convict, so you bury him in the convicts' graveyard.

JACKSON: Yes Sir.

SOLL: He was crippled . . .

JACKSON: Yes Sir.

(*He goes.*)

SOLL: How many convicts do we have out here?

HORACE: I don't know, Sir.

SOLL: If I live, tomorrow I'm going to go out there and count them.

(JACKSON *comes in.*)

JACKSON: Nobody in that closet, Sir.

SOLL: No?

JACKSON: No Sir.

SOLL: Did you see any blood?

JACKSON: No Sir.

SOLL: I saw a crippled convict lying in there, blood over the walls, on the floor . . . (*Pause.*) What was my mama's name? Any of you all remember? (*Pause.*) I think it was Erna. She died when I was born. My daddy raised me and my two brothers. It was my daddy's idea to get convicts. We tried after slavery to have tenants out here. We had 300 at one time living on the place, but we had a series of bad crop years and we all nearly starved. So Papa said, "Get rid of the tenants and hire yourself convicts," and I did. (*Pause.*) Tyre is in New Orleans. If I die, don't send for him. I don't want him at my funeral—not him, not his daughters. (*Pause.*) Asa and Velma—two whores. I don't want any whores at my funeral. (*Pause.*) Where is mama buried? Is she buried out here?

JACKSON: I don't know, Sir.

SOLL: I don't think she is. I think one of them convicts got loose and took a club and clubbed her to death and burned her body up in the house. You remember that house we used to live in? It burned to the ground. That's why we never had a picture of my mama. All her pictures and letters were burned in the fire. (*Pause.*) Do you smell smoke? Is there a fire?

JACKSON: I don't smell nothing.

SOLL: Are you sure?

JACKSON: I'm sure.

SOLL: Boy? Do you smell anything?

HORACE: No Sir.

SOLL: Don't lie to me. Don't let me burn up like my mama did. I have a dread of fire. Anybody know where my mama is buried?

JACKSON: I don't.

SOLL: You, boy?

HORACE: No Sir.

SOLL: I think it's at Salurie. Buried someplace down by the lighthouse. I went there once, looking for it to put up a tombstone, but I couldn't find it. Albert Thornton brought a boy out here, his nephew. He said he wanted to work here to get enough money to put a tombstone on his daddy's grave. He said his daddy is buried next to my mama in Salurie Island. "You'll never find his grave, then," I told him, "because the tidal wave after the last storm swept over the whole island washing all the graves away—my mama's, your daddy's. . . ." They found some bones on the beach later, but they didn't know whose graves they belonged to. (*Pause.*) Jackson . . .

JACKSON: Yes Sir.

SOLL: Are you a convict?

JACKSON: Yes Sir.

SOLL: Have you come to kill me?

JACKSON: No Sir.

SOLL: What's the boy's name?

JACKSON: Horace, Sir.

SOLL: Horace, come near to me. (HORACE *does so*.) When I was your age, this was all dense forest. So thick, a man or a boy couldn't get through it without a cane knife to cut his way, and beside the forest, there was something I've seen no other place—miles of cane. Cane that grew ten and twelve feet high, so thick you couldn't make your way through without a knife . . . and then a cold spell would come and kill the cane, and it would lie rotting on the ground until the spring and a new crop would start up. That's why they call this "cane land." Did you know that?

HORACE: No Sir.

SOLL: Did you know that, Jackson?

JACKSON: Yes Sir.

SOLL: Do you know any songs, Jackson?

JACKSON: Yes Sir. I know some.

SOLL: Do you know "Golden Slippers"?

JACKSON: Let me see now . . .

SOLL: Sing it.

JACKSON (*singing*): "Oh, dem golden slippers. Oh, dem golden slippers." (*Pause*.) That's all I remember of it. I know some hymns. . . .

SOLL: Don't sing them around me. I can't bear them.

JACKSON: Yes Sir.

SOLL: And another thing—when I die I don't want any preacher near me.

JACKSON: Yes Sir. But who's gonna pray over you if you don't have a preacher?

SOLL: I don't want anybody praying over me. And I don't want my brother here or any of his children.

JACKSON: Who you want then?

SOLL: Just you and Martha and Ben and this boy and Sarah.

JACKSON: Sarah? Sarah can't be there.

SOLL: Why?

JACKSON: She's dead too.

SOLL: Oh . . .

JACKSON: Don't you want any white people there except Horace?

SOLL: Is the overseer white?

JACKSON: Yes.

SOLL: And the two guards?

JACKSON: Yes.

SOLL: Then they can come.

JACKSON: It's not going to be much of a funeral if you won't have a preacher to pray for you and you don't like hymns. What kind of a funeral is that going to be?

SOLL: It's the kind I want. Go see how they're getting along with my coffin.

JACKSON: Yes Sir.

(*He goes.*)

SOLL: Did you know that boy Mr. Albert Thornton brought out here?

HORACE: Yes Sir. It was me.

SOLL: Was it? You're the one whose daddy died?

HORACE: Yes Sir.

SOLL: My daddy is dead too, you know. He had a stroke. He got so mad at them convicts, he had a stroke and fell over dead. You think them bastards would call out and tell us? No. They just went on working and left him lying dead there in the cotton fields. My daddy was eighty-four when he died. How old was your daddy?

HORACE: Thirty-two.

SOLL: Well, we all have to go sometime. Is it daylight yet?

HORACE: No Sir.

SOLL: I wonder what time it is?

HORACE: I don't know, Sir.

SOLL: I got a watch. Look and see.(*He takes it out of his pocket and hands it to him.*)

HORACE: It says eleven o'clock, but I think it's later than that. (*He holds the watch to his ear.*) It has stopped.

SOLL: Did you hear something in the closet?

HORACE: No Sir.

SOLL: I did. (*He calls out.*) Come out, you sonofabitch. (*There is no answer.*) Did you hear me? (*There is no answer.*) I'll give you one more chance. (*Again, there is no answer and he raises his gun to shoot, but it is empty. He tosses the gun.*) Do you have a gun?

HORACE: No Sir.

SOLL: What will protect us now? I need bullets for my gun. (*Pause. He sniffs.*) I smell fire. Do you smell fire?

HORACE: No Sir.

(JACKSON *and* BEN *come in with the coffin.*)

JACKSON: Here's your coffin. Where do you want it?

SOLL: Put it down there. (*They put it down.*) I'll try it out and if it fits, you can put it under my bed.

JACKSON: It's bound to fit.

SOLL: Let me be the judge of that. Help me into the coffin, Jackson.

(JACKSON *helps him out of the chair and over and into the coffin.*)

BEN: Horace, you got a chew of tobacco?

HORACE: Sure.

(*He hands him his plug.* BEN *cuts off a piece, puts it in his mouth, and hands it back to* HORACE.)

BEN: Another convict died last night—the one that said he was too sick to work. I guess he was telling the truth.

HORACE: Sherman Edwards?

BEN: That's his name.

(JACKSON *comes up to them.*)

JACKSON: He's gone to sleep in that coffin.

BEN: Maybe he's dead.

JACKSON: No, he's just asleep. He had a whole lot to drink, you know.

BEN: I'm gonna go. I have to bury that convict that died tonight.

(*He goes.*)

HORACE: Did you know him?

JACKSON: Sure. I know them all. Are you sleepy?

HORACE: Yes, I am.

(JACKSON *goes back to the coffin.*)

JACKSON: Mr. Soll, can the boy go on to sleep now? Mr. Soll
. . . (*Pause. He puts his head in the coffin, then takes it out. He
calls out.*) Ben . . . you better get up here. Mr. Soll is dead
in his coffin. (*He comes over to* HORACE.)

HORACE: He was all alone in his coffin when he died.

JACKSON: Yes, he was. He better start gettin' used to bein'
alone in there. He's going to be alone in there for a long
time.

(BEN *enters.*)

JACKSON: He's gone. The old devil is gone.

BEN: Is he? (*He looks into the coffin.*) He sure is. He's gone.
I'm going to have to get word to Miss Asa.

JACKSON: He don't want her here for the funeral. Nor his
brother. And he don't want a preacher.

BEN: Are you going to be the one to tell her that?

(*Pause.*)

JACKSON: I wonder what will happen to me?

BEN: What do you mean?

JACKSON: I was paroled to him. They can take me back to
the pen now.

BEN: Why don't you take off?

JACKSON: Where am I gonna go to? I'm too old to run away. He was right and I was wrong. He said he was going to die and he did.

BEN: What time do you think we should bury him?

JACKSON: I guess as soon as it's daylight.

BEN: We can't have much of a funeral. He don't want no hymns and no preacher.

HORACE: We can say the Lord's Prayer. He didn't say we couldn't do that.

BEN: No.

HORACE: And you could testify. He didn't say you couldn't do that.

BEN: No. (*Pause.*) I can say he always worked hard; I can say that.

JACKSON: And I could say he let me be a trustee; I could say that. And he drank a lot of whiskey.

(*They hear a knock in the coffin.*)

BEN: Did you hear something?

JACKSON: It's a rat, I think. This old house is full of rats.

(*Again there is a noise.*)

BEN: I hear something in that coffin. (*He goes over to the coffin.*) My God! He's risen from the dead! (*He reaches in and helps* SOLL *out.*) We thought you were dead.

SOLL: Well, I wasn't. (BEN *leads him back to his chair.*) Now hand me my gun.

(BEN *does so*.)

JACKSON: Sherman Edwards is dead.

SOLL: Who the hell is Sherman Edwards?

JACKSON. Brother of that convict that had his throat cut.

SOLL: Somebody kill him?

JACKSON: No Sir. He just died. He told you he was too sick to work, but you didn't believe him.

SOLL: Who's burying him?

BEN: I am. I bury them all.

SOLL: Did you think you was going to bury me?

BEN: Yes Sir, I did.

SOLL: Did you think I was dead?

HORACE: Well Sir . . .

SOLL: What did you think happened?

HORACE: I don't know, Sir.

SOLL: I wasn't dead.

HORACE: No Sir.

SOLL: I ain't never gonna die.

HORACE: Yes Sir.

SOLL: Tell them to take that damn coffin out of here. I changed my mind about dying.

HORACE: Yes Sir.

SOLL: Take it out.

BEN: Yes Sir.

(*He and* JACKSON *go out with the coffin.*)

SOLL: I'm gonna outlive them all—Asa and my devilish brother and Ben and Jackson and the other goddamn convicts. How old are you?

HORACE: Thirteen.

SOLL: Maybe I ain't gonna outlive you. I never married. I never had no children I know about anyways. You got a daddy?

HORACE: No Sir.

SOLL: What happened to your daddy?

HORACE: He died.

SOLL: You an orphan?

HORACE: No Sir. I have a mother.

SOLL: Where the hell is she?

HORACE: Houston.

SOLL: I'm going to tell you something, boy. One minute I think I'm gonna live and the next minute I think I'm gonna die. Right now I think I'm gonna die. Come close to me. (HORACE *does so.*) I got money hidden in here. Back in that closet in a suitcase. Go bring me the suitcase so I can pay you what I owe you and reward you handsomely, besides, for all your kindness to an old man.

(HORACE *goes. He comes back with a suitcase.*)

Now, hand it to me. (HORACE *does so.*) You know how much money I have in here?

HORACE: No Sir.

SOLL: More than ten thousand dollars, last I counted, and

you're to get half. Open up the suitcase. (HORACE *does so*.) Now reach in there and hand me the money.

HORACE (*reaching in*): There's no money in here.

SOLL: Don't lie to me, boy. Don't try to fool me.

HORACE: I'm not lying to you.

SOLL: Hand me that goddamn suitcase. (HORACE *does*. SOLL *reaches in*.) My God! I've been robbed! Call Ben! Call Jackson! Call the goddamn overseer. I want all them goddamn convicts searched. Someone has robbed me of my money. (HORACE *starts away*.) Boy, don't leave me. Don't ever leave me. Come here to me. I don't care about the goddamn money. Don't leave me. (HORACE *goes to him*.) Anyway, the money wasn't in that goddamn suitcase. I just remembered I buried that money out there in one of them convict's graves. Help me up. (HORACE *does so*.) Which grave did I put it in? Call Ben.

HORACE (*calling*): Ben. . . .

(BEN *comes in*.)

SOLL (*turning to* BEN): Ben, do you remember which convict's grave I hid the money in? I want to pay this boy what I owe him.

BEN: No Sir.

(BEN *goes out*.)

SOLL: Can you read?

HORACE: Yes Sir.

SOLL: Get that paper over there. (HORACE *gets it*.) Read me the news.

HORACE (*looking at it*): This is an old paper. This paper is dated 1865. It says Texas can't come back into the Union yet.

SOLL: Why?

HORACE: Because she was in the Confederacy.

SOLL: Oh, yes. Read it to me. (HORACE *begins to read*.) Come close to me. (HORACE *does so*.) Don't let them bury me with my own family, because my brother and his daughters are going to be buried there and I don't want to be buried by them or near them. I'd rather have convicts near me than that stinkin'—

(SOLL *dies*.)

HORACE (*calling*): Ben . . .

(BEN *comes in. He looks down at* SOLL.)

BEN: He's dead now. He's dead for sure. There'll be no more hollering and cussing from him now.

HORACE: Is that all there is to dying? Your breath just stops?

BEN: Yes . . . when you die that way. When you get shot or stabbed, or you're in pain, it's different. I've known men to beg to die, they were in such pain.

HORACE: That's all that happened to my daddy, my grandmother said. One minute he was breathing and the next minute he stopped. That's not so bad. Do you think Mr. Soll minded dying?

BEN: I don't know.

HORACE: Do you think my daddy minded dying?

BEN: I don't know.

HORACE: Ben, I can't get loose from him. He won't let me go.

(BEN *takes* SOLL'*s hand away from the boy*.)

BEN: I think he minded dying. I think he minded it the worst way.

HORACE: I think he did too. And I think my daddy did. That's what worries me.

BEN: Go get Jackson.

HORACE: No, you better go. I promised him I would sit by his side with a gun after he died, until he was buried.

BEN: Don't let that bother you. Look at all he promised you. Didn't keep none of them.

HORACE: I'd feel better if I kept mine.

BEN: How much did that old devil owe you?

HORACE: Eleven dollars and fifty cents. He said one time he was going to give me a hundred dollars, and another time a thousand, and then a tombstone for my daddy.

BEN: He said a lot of things. He was always making promises. And Miss Asa is going to wind up with it all. You'll see.

(BEN *leaves*. HORACE *gets his gun and sits by* SOLL. *In the distance "Rock Island Line" is heard*. JACKSON *and* BEN *come in with the coffin*.)

BEN: He's not playing possum this time. Let's put him in.

(*They put* SOLL'*s body inside the coffin and carry it out*. HORACE *follows after them as the lights fade*.)

(The lights are brought up near the convicts' graveyard. BEN *and* JACKSON *bring in the coffin.* MARTHA *and* HORACE *follow. They put the coffin down and crowd around it self-consciously.)*

JACKSON: Well, he has a pretty day for his funeral. Anybody else coming, you think?

BEN: No. I guess this is all there is gonna be. Miss Asa say she won't come. She don't care what we do with him. Bury him here, throw him in the creek—she don't care. Mr. Billy is still drunk, the overseer don't want to come, so it's just us'ns. An' he don't want no hymns an' no prayers an' no preacher. An' he won't have no tombstone unless Miss Asa puts it up. You know she won't do it.

HORACE: I went over to his family's graveyard this morning. He said his daddy's tombstone had angels all over it and it came from New Orleans, but I couldn't find it.

BEN: He was lying. Didn't have nothing on it—just a slab of marble sticking up with his name on it. If the convicts didn't keep it weeded over there, you wouldn't be able to find it for the brush in a week.

(In the distance we hear a convict singing "Ain't No More Cane On the Brazos.")

I told Miss Asa you were still here and you stayed with him all last night until he died, and that he still owed you money, and she said that was your hard luck because she would pay none of his debts, and I asked how you were to get back into town and she said you could walk. An' we'll all be walkin', I guess, because she's gonna close the store and take the convicts over to her daddy's place. Says she's gonna let the weeds and trees and the cane get this land. Six months from now you won't know where anybody's buried out here. Not my people, not the convicts, not Mr.

Soll. The trees and the weeds, and the cane, will take everything. "Cane land" they called it once, cane land it will be again. The house will go, the store will go, the graves will go, those with tombstones and those without.

JACKSON: I could sing "Golden Slippers." He liked that. He asked me once to sing it and I couldn't remember it, but now I can.

BEN: Sing it then.

JACKSON (*singing*): "Oh, dem golden slippers. Oh, dem golden slippers . . ."

BEN: Yes Sir. The house will go, the store will go, the graves will go, those with tombstones and those without.

(JACKSON *continues singing as the lights fade.*)

Lily Dale

Characters

HORACE ROBEDAUX
MRS. COONS
LILY DALE ROBEDAUX
CORELLA DAVENPORT
PETE DAVENPORT
WILL KIDDER
ALBERT THORNTON

Act One

Place: A railroad car on the way to Houston, Texas; and Houston.
Time: 1910

As the lights are brought up down left, we see a section of a train. HORACE ROBEDAUX, *twenty, is seated and looking out of the train window. A woman in her late forties comes in. She is* MRS. COONS.

MRS. COONS: Mind if I sit beside you, son?

HORACE: No Ma'am.

MRS. COONS: I can't stand a train trip without a little company. I wouldn't care to ask to sit beside those older gentlemen. They might think I was forward. They're all drummers, you know. I can tell by looking at them. (*She looks at* HORACE.) How old are you, young man?

HORACE: Twenty.

MRS. COONS: When's your birthday?

HORACE: In April.

MRS. COONS: In April! I have a boy just your age. He'll be twenty in June. Almost your age, that is—two months younger. Where are you going?

HORACE: Houston.

MRS. COONS: Another coincidence; so am I. Houston your home?

HORACE: No Ma'am. I'm going on a visit.

MRS. COONS: Who are you visiting? Your grandma?

HORACE: No, my mother.

MRS. COONS: Your mother? Not your mother and your daddy?

HORACE: No Ma'am. My daddy is dead; she's married again.

MRS. COONS: Did you used to live with them in Houston?

HORACE: No Ma'am. My stepfather doesn't have a whole lot and it's all he can do to take care of my sister and mother.

MRS. COONS: Oh, well, times are hard all over. I think they'll get better though, don't you?

HORACE: I certainly hope so.

MRS. COONS: So do we all. I have a rich uncle, thank God . . . from New Orleans. When things get too tight, I just write dear Uncle Julius and I say, "Here I am begging again." He's real sweet about it too, just sends me whatever I need. Hardest part for me is my mama. Now, I've known nothing but lean times all my life, so naturally I don't know anything different. But Mama, she was born with a golden spoon in her mouth, to hear her tell it. And being poor has been a real cross to her. You got on the train in Harrison. Do you live there?

HORACE: No Ma'am. I used to. I live in Glen Flora now. I've been working there at the general store.

MRS. COONS: Well, I live in Harrison now. Been there two months . . . like it real well. I used to live in Houston, but my husband lost his job there and he got a position at the gin in Harrison. He's a bookkeeper. I hope he'll keep that. (*Pause.*) We have a problem—my husband, that is. He drinks. He does fine on a job and then he gets to drinking after two or three months and they let him go. He's taken the Keeley Cure more times than I can count, but so far nothing seems to help. He swears this time he's learned his lesson. I hope to goodness he has. I'm going in now to see about shipping our furniture out to Harrison. We just sold our home in Houston. We won't buy a house in Harrison until we see if we are going to be permanent.

HORACE: Whose house are you renting in Harrison?

MRS. COONS: They call it the old Robedaux place. They say it's a sad house. The man was a brilliant lawyer and drank himself right into the grave. Mr. Coons said—

HORACE: That was my house. At least it was my father's. I lived there until I was eight. Until my mama and daddy separated.

MRS. COONS: Separated? Oh, mercy! What a terrible thing. I hope it didn't end in divorce?

HORACE: No Ma'am.

MRS. COONS: Did your mama and daddy reconcile before he died?

HORACE: No Ma'am.

MRS. COONS: Have you been inside that house lately?

HORACE: No Ma'am.

MRS. COONS: Well, it is awful run-down. We're paying twelve dollars a month rent, but I swear it's not worth it. It leaks like a sieve. I don't know when it's been painted. The yard is full of weeds. (*Pause.*) Is it your daddy died a drunkard?

HORACE: Yes Ma'am.

MRS. COONS: I feel sorry for you, son. Deeply sorry. I know what that can mean. I get on my knees every night praying Mr. Coons will lose his taste for it. I hope your stepdaddy don't drink.

HORACE: No Ma'am. Not that I know of.

MRS. COONS: Thank God for that. Pansy Greenwood is my best friend. She's been married three times now. Every one has turned out to be a drunkard except for the last, and he's a morphine addict. That's the worst of all. I tell Billy Joe—that's my boy—"Thank God Daddy ain't a morphine addict." (*Pause. She sighs dolefully and then looks up at* HORACE.) Are you a Christian, son?

HORACE: Yes'm. I guess so.

MRS. COONS: What do you mean you guess so, son? There's no guessing about being a Christian. You're either saved or not. Are you baptized?

HORACE: I don't know, Ma'am.

MRS. COONS: You don't know?

HORACE: No'm.

MRS. COONS: Why don't you know?

HORACE: Well, I hadn't thought about it one way or the other. If I was baptized, I was too young to remember it.

MRS. COONS: Mercy! You ask your mama the first thing you see her. You ask her if you're baptized. Your soul is in terrible danger if you're not, son. An' don't you put that question off. That's all Satan would have you do is postpone that question. Do you attend church?

HORACE: No Ma'am.

MRS. COONS: You don't?

HORACE: No Ma'am. The church my people go to doesn't have a congregation in Glen Flora.

MRS. COONS: What church is that?

HORACE: The Episcopal.

MRS. COONS: I guess they don't. They only have a small one in Harrison. (*Proudly.*) I'm a Baptist.

HORACE: Yes Ma'am.

MRS. COONS: My mama was a Baptist and her mama before her. We have churches everyplace. Black and white. We're flourishing. If we'd baptized you, you would have known it.

HORACE: Yes Ma'am.

MRS. COONS: I was baptized in the river. Made clean in the river. Gave all my sins to Jesus in the river. Washed in the blood of the Lamb in the river. I'm ready to meet my Maker, son. I am ready. I am ready. (*Pause.*) Did you go to school in Harrison?

HORACE: As far as the sixth grade . . . then I quit.

MRS. COONS: Billy Joe wants to quit, but I beg him not to. Didn't your mama try to get you to stay in school?

HORACE: No Ma'am. She didn't have any education to speak of. She only went to the fourth grade. And my stepfather only got as far as the second grade. (*Pause.*) My father was an educated man . . . all his family were. They were Greek scholars and Latin scholars. You know the *Harrison Spectator*?

MRS. COONS: Read it every week.

HORACE: My uncles started that. One of them never worked at all, they say. He just sat around and read books in Greek all the time. My mother says she'd rather see me dead than that way. She said he lived a useless life. (*Pause.*) I like to read, though. I can't help it. I don't tell my mother because it would worry her. But I read all the time . . . newspapers and magazines and books about famous men. I don't care for novels.

MRS. COONS: And the Bible, son. Do you read the Bible?

HORACE: No Ma'am.

MRS. COONS: Oh, poor child. Why not?

HORACE: I don't have a Bible.

MRS. COONS: You don't have a Bible?

HORACE: No Ma'am.

MRS. COONS: Son, what are you going to say to your Maker when he asks you that question, "Did you read your Bible?" an' you say, "No, Sir," an' he says, "Why not?" an' you say, "Because I had no Bible," an' he says, "Why not?" What will you say?

HORACE: I don't know.

MRS. COONS: You better think up a good answer, son. Because that question is coming to you one of these days. An' my heart trembles for you when I think of the wrath of my God. Get yourself a Bible, son. Promise me that. Promise me you'll get yourself a Bible and ask your mama about your baptism, and if you're not baptized, see that you have it done right away. Do you say your prayers every night?

HORACE: No Ma'am.

MRS. COONS: Then you start praying every day. On your knees . . . morning and night. You can hear me praying all over town. Mr. Coons says, "Mrs. Coons, you're praying too loud, you're keeping people awake with your prayers." "It's good for them," I say. "Let them hear the prayers of a true Christian." An' I just pray that much louder. Why, sometimes I even shout. Shouting down the devil, I say. An' you have to shout loud to shout down the devil. Would you join me in a little prayer now, son?

HORACE: No Ma'am. That's all right. I don't believe so.

MRS. COONS: Don't be embarrassed, son. Never be ashamed to let people know you're a Christian. (*She prays.*) Father, take this boy here . . . (*She turns to* HORACE.) What's your name, son?

HORACE: Horace.

MRS. COONS: Horace. Cleanse Horace of his worldly ways, Father. Open his eyes to the need of baptism.

(*She continues praying as the lights fade, and the train section is taken off stage.*)

(*As the lights come up, we see the* DAVENPORT *living room. The room is simply furnished.* LILY DALE ROBEDAUX, *eighteen,* HORACE's *sister, is practicing at an upright piano. There is a knock at the front door. She doesn't hear it at first and continues playing. There is another knock. She hears this and stops playing.*)

LILY DALE (*calling*): Mama . . . Mama . . .

(CORELLA, *her mother, thirty-eight, enters up right.*)

CORELLA: What is it, Lily Dale?

LILY DALE: Someone is at the door, Mama.

CORELLA: Can't you open the door, honey?

LILY DALE: I'm scared to, Mama.

CORELLA: Lily Dale . . . heavens!

LILY DALE: Doris Violet tells me the city is alive with beggars and gypsies and white slavers. She says her mother forbid her ever to open her door.

CORELLA: I think that's a good idea when you're alone, honey, but I don't think you have to worry when I'm in the house. (*Again a knock.*) Just a minute.

(*She opens the door.* HORACE *is there.*)

Horace. . . . (*She embraces him.*) Lily Dale, it's Horace.

LILY DALE (*going over to him*): Hello, Brother. (*She hugs him.*) We thought you were the gypsies. Mr. Davenport is in Atlanta seeing his kin and Mama and I are here alone in the city. And my girlfriend, Doris Violet, says it is dangerous for ladies and young girls to be alone in this wicked city, as it is filled with gypsies and beggars and white slavers. You heard about Charlie Parker?

HORACE: No, I don't believe I did.

LILY DALE: Well . . . he didn't live in Houston but in Philadelphia . . . and one day he went out to play and the gypsies came by and grabbed him and took him off and he has never been seen or heard of by his family until this very day . . . An' Mama was on the porch last week and this beggar man came by all bandaged up and he stopped and asked her if she would fix his bandages as they were coming loose. So she invited him up on the porch and she began to retie them for him and he reached out an' tried to grab her.

CORELLA: Yes, he did, Son. Like to have scared me to death . . . I screamed and ran into the house as fast as I could and locked every door in the house.

LILY DALE: The city is filled with danger, Brother. The white slavers put a pill in your tea or coffee that knocks you out and then they carry you off to China and force you to become a prostitute.

HORACE: Is that right?

CORELLA: Yes, a girl has to be careful in the city, Son.

HORACE: Yes Ma'am. I guess so.

CORELLA: Did you take the streetcar here from the station?

HORACE: Yes Ma'am.

LILY DALE: How do you like my piano?

HORACE: That's nice, Lily Dale.

LILY DALE: When Mama and Mr. Davenport first got married, he said he had always wanted a daughter and though he weren't a rich man, he was going to spoil me in all ways and make up for the daddy I never had. And my heaven, he has. He got me a secondhand piano straight off, and then after I learned to play some, he said he wouldn't have me using a secondhand piano and he went out and bought this one for me.

HORACE: Well, that is sure a nice piano.

LILY DALE: Oh, he's so sweet to me. He is the best thing that ever lived. My own daddy, if he had lived, couldn't have been sweeter to me . . . could he, Mama?

CORELLA: No, precious.

LILY DALE: He bought this dress for me from Munn's just before he left for Georgia; and, Brother, he has to work so hard.

HORACE: Is that so?

LILY DALE: Oh, yes. He is up at four every morning and then he takes the streetcar to the railroad yards and he works there until four in the afternoon and he comes home and then he works out back until way dark in his garden.

HORACE: My goodness.

LILY DALE: And then he comes in and he's so tired he can't eat and he sits here; and while Mama is getting his supper, I take off his shoes and get him a pillow to rest his head on and then I go to the piano and I play him an étude of Chopin.

HORACE: Do you?

LILY DALE: Yes. Chopin is his favorite, he says. Brother, you haven't heard me play the piano, have you?

HORACE: No.

LILY DALE: Want me to play for you now?

CORELLA: Honey, your brother just got here. He's tired. Let him rest for a while first. What time were you up this morning?

HORACE: Four. Randall, the colored man that works with me in the store, brought me into Harrison in Mr. Galbraith's wagon. I caught the seven o'clock train.

CORELLA: Did you have breakfast?

HORACE: Yes Ma'am. Randall's wife fixed me a big breakfast.

LILY DALE: We know all about getting up early in the morning. Mr. Davenport is up every morning at four. Even on Sundays. Isn't he, Mama?

CORELLA: Yes, he is. Horace, you've grown. Stand up. Let me take a good look at you. (*He stands.*) You've turned into a fine-looking young man.

HORACE: Thank you.

CORELLA: Do you realize it's a year since we've seen each other?

LILY DALE: How long are you planning to stay, Brother?

HORACE: Oh, I don't know exactly; you mentioned a week in your letter and—

CORELLA (*interrupting nervously*): Are you hungry, Son?

HORACE: Well . . .

CORELLA: If I fixed you a sandwich could you eat it?

HORACE: Sure.

CORELLA: And I have a cake I made this morning. Would you like a piece of that too?

HORACE: Yes Ma'am. (CORELLA *exits*. HORACE *looks around*.) Is this a two-story house?

LILY DALE: Yes, it is. We rent the upstairs to a quiet couple that works all day. They get up at four too. They are in bed by eight. Do you think I've changed?

HORACE: Yes, you have.

LILY DALE: Would you have recognized me if you'd passed me on the street?

HORACE: I think so.

LILY DALE: I keep having this terrible dream that I'm kidnapped and they won't let me go until I'm an old woman, and I come home and no one recognizes me . . . an' I keep saying, "I'm Lily Dale. Lily Dale Robedaux," but no one will believe me. Did you ever have a dream like that?

HORACE: No.

LILY DALE: Do you ever have dreams?

HORACE: Sometimes.

LILY DALE: What about?

HORACE: Oh, I don't know. Once I dreamed . . . (*Pause.*) I forget.

LILY DALE: We didn't think you were coming when you didn't answer Mother's letter.

HORACE: I didn't get the letter right away, and when I did get it, I just decided to come on.

LILY DALE: How much did it cost you to get here?

HORACE: Two dollars.

LILY DALE: Where did you get two dollars?

HORACE: Mama sent it to me.

LILY DALE: She did? Did you ask her for it?

HORACE: No, she just sent it to me.

LILY DALE: How are you gonna get back?

HORACE: Mama said she would give me the two dollars to get back after I got here.

LILY DALE: You have a job, don't you?

HORACE: Yes.

LILY DALE: How much do you get paid a week?

HORACE: Three dollars.

LILY DALE: Some of my friends have jobs, but Mr. Davenport said he won't hear of me working.

HORACE: Is that right?

LILY DALE: He spoils me in every way. See my shoes? He bought them just before he left.

HORACE: They're very pretty, Lily Dale.

LILY DALE: They were very expensive. I miss him. I'll be glad when he comes home.

HORACE: How much longer will he be gone?

LILY DALE: He was to be gone three weeks, but we got a letter yesterday and he said things had changed so in Atlanta, it didn't seem like home any longer and he longed to get back to us. So he's cutting his trip short.

HORACE: Oh, I see.

LILY DALE: He didn't say how much, though. When Mama got the letter, she said it was a blessing you hadn't come because she would be a nervous wreck having you here and expecting Mr. Davenport to walk in any minute, unexpected. You see, she sent for you behind his back.

HORACE: Did she?

LILY DALE: She kind of hinted around for his permission to ask you here while he was gone, but he said he didn't think it would be a good idea to encourage you to take off from work, and so she didn't press it any further.

HORACE: Oh.

LILY DALE: But then she decided to write to you anyway . . . which I thought at the time was a mistake. I always think deceit is a mistake. Don't you?

(CORELLA *enters with a glass of milk and a sandwich. She hands it to* HORACE.)

I told Brother about Mr. Davenport coming home. Why didn't you tell me you sent him two dollars for a ticket?

CORELLA: It was my own secret, honey. I have to have a few secrets.

LILY DALE: Does Mr. Davenport know you gave him that money?

CORELLA: No, and I don't want you to tell him. You hear me?

LILY DALE: Can I play the étude for you now, Brother?

HORACE: Sure.

LILY DALE: Mr. Davenport says he'd take his last cent to pay for my music lessons. Do you have musical ability, Brother?

HORACE: I don't know.

(LILY DALE *goes to the piano and plays a Chopin étude. She does not play well, but with enormous confidence.*)

Mama, I was hoping that I—

CORELLA (*again nervously interrupting him*): Have you been to Harrison lately?

HORACE: I try to get in every week. I get up early Sunday morning and I walk into Harrison along the railroad tracks and have Sunday dinner with Aunt Virgie or Aunt Inez or sometimes Aunt Gladys. Then I get up early Monday morning and walk back to Glen Flora in time to get the store open.

CORELLA: How long does it take you to walk it?

HORACE: Three hours. Aunt Virgie has taught me to dance.

CORELLA: She would. You can't be around Virgie for five minutes without some kind of dancing going on.

LILY DALE (*stopping her playing and turning to them*): I'm not going to play anymore if you all are going to talk.

CORELLA: I'm sorry, Sister.

(LILY DALE *begins again.* HORACE *listens for a moment.*)

HORACE (*speaking while* LILY DALE *is playing*): Mama . . .

(LILY DALE *stops.*)

CORELLA: Shh . . . shh. (*Whispering.*) We'll talk when Lily Dale finishes. She's very sensitive.

(*Again there is a silence as* LILY DALE *continues to play.* HORACE *, after a few moments, begins to nod and then falls fast asleep. Soon he begins to snore.* LILY DALE *hears this and stops playing.*)

LILY DALE: Mama . . . he's asleep. I think that's very rude of him.

CORELLA: He doesn't mean to be rude, Lily Dale. I just don't think he's used to hearing music like that and he's probably very tired from the train ride.

LILY DALE: How long is he planning to stay?

CORELLA: I don't know. When I invited him, I asked him to stay a week, but that was before I knew about Mr. Davenport cutting his trip short. I'm going to tell him he can't stay more than a day.

LILY DALE: What would you do if Mr. Davenport walked in right now?

CORELLA: I'd die, Lily Dale.

LILY DALE: What do you think Mr. Davenport would say?

CORELLA: I don't know. I just pray he doesn't come until Horace leaves. (*Pause.*) I don't think Mr. Davenport will come home before the day after tomorrow. We got his letter yesterday and it takes two days from Atlanta. (HORACE *wakes up*.) You've been asleep. You had a good nap.

HORACE: Oh, I didn't know where I was for a minute.

LILY DALE: How long do you plan on staying, Brother?

HORACE: I had planned on staying a week, and I thought while I was here I might look for a job.

LILY DALE: Where?

HORACE: In Houston.

LILY DALE: Why?

HORACE: Well, I just thought it might be nice to live near you and Mama for a change.

LILY DALE: Oh, you couldn't live here, Brother. There is no room here at all.

HORACE: I didn't mean here. I meant somewhere in Houston, but near you.

LILY DALE: What could you do in Houston, Brother?

HORACE: Maybe I could get a job working in a store.

LILY DALE: Doing what?

HORACE: Waiting on customers like I've always done.

LILY DALE: Have you ever been in a store in Houston?

HORACE: No.

LILY DALE: Well, you'd change your tune if you ever did. They have beautifully dressed men and women working in those stores. Cultured men and women. Not country people.

HORACE: Well, then I thought Mr. Davenport might help me find work at the railroad.

LILY DALE: Doing what?

HORACE: I don't know.

LILY DALE: Do you know, Brother, they are laying off people down at the rail yards all the time? And if Mr. Davenport wasn't such an exceptional worker, he would be in mortal danger of losing his job. Goodness, Brother, be practical.

CORELLA: Albert writes he is opening a dry goods store in Harrison. Maybe he will give you a job. Let's all go to the Palace this afternoon and see a play. I'll get an early supper for us when we get back. Would you like that, Horace?

HORACE: Sure!

LILY DALE: Have you ever seen a play?

HORACE: Sure. A lot of times at the Opera House in Harrison. I heard Chauncey Olcott sing there too, last spring. When he sang "Hello, Central, Give Me Heaven," there wasn't a dry eye in the house. And then he sang "My Wild Irish Rose," and the audience went wild! They just tore the house down.

CORELLA: I'll get dressed. I don't know how to tell you this, Son, but you won't be able to stay a week after all. You see, Mr. Davenport—

LILY DALE (*interrupting*): I told him about Mr. Davenport. An' I told him he didn't want you to have him in the first place. Are you gonna give Brother money for a ticket home?

CORELLA: Yes, I am.

LILY DALE: Where are you getting all this money from, Mama? Buying tickets to plays and train tickets for Brother?

CORELLA: It's none of your business, Lily Dale. I have a little of my own, you know, from the sewing I take in now and then. What I'm trying to say, Son, is that I think we can only have you stay just today and tomorrow, at this time.

HORACE: Yes Ma'am.

CORELLA: I'm awfully sorry.

HORACE: Don't worry about it.

(CORELLA *exits.* LILY DALE *peeks out the door to make sure* CORELLA *has gone.*)

LILY DALE (*crossing to* HORACE): Do you have a sweetheart, Brother?

HORACE: No.

LILY DALE: I have one. Don't tell Mama I told you that, though. She'd have a fit. He's a lovely boy. (*She leans in toward him.*) Mr. Davenport can't stand him. He won't let him come to the house. He says he is dissolute. I have to slip out to see him. Mr. Davenport found out just before he left that I had slipped out to see him and he was in a fury. He didn't speak to me until the morning he left for Atlanta. He can be very moody, Brother. He is usually very sweet to me, but sometimes he comes home from work and he looks so unhappy. Why do you think our stepdaddy is so unhappy?

HORACE: I don't know, Sister. I've seen very little of him anytime—unhappy or otherwise.

LILY DALE: Mama says it is because of the terrible childhood he had. He doesn't tell us much, but she knows he was supporting his mother and five brothers and sisters when he was twelve. She says all he's ever known is hard work. (*She pulls out a chain that she has hung around her neck.*

*It has a "going steady" ring on it that is hidden under her dress.
She shows this to* HORACE.) This is the ring my boyfriend
gave me. He wants to marry me. He thinks I'm beautiful.
He thinks I'm pretty enough to be an actress. He's very
handsome too. He does drink, though. And smokes cigarettes. I told him he would have to stop both before I
married him. I told him I had a father who was a drunkard and a cigarette fiend and that those habits had killed
him. (*Pause.*) Do you remember Papa?

HORACE: Sure.

LILY DALE: I don't have a picture of him. Do you?

HORACE: No.

LILY DALE: I wonder if anyone has a picture of him? I tell
you, I can hardly remember anymore what he looks like.
Sometimes I remember him looking one way . . . sometimes another. (*Pause.*) Well . . . it can't be helped. I can
hear his voice, though. I can remember the way he always
called me Sister and you Brother.

HORACE: He never called you Sister or me Brother.

LILY DALE: Yes, he did.

HORACE: No, he didn't.

LILY DALE: Yes, he did!

HORACE: No, he didn't! He always called me Horace Junior
and you Lily Dale.

LILY DALE: Who called me Sister and you Brother?

HORACE: I called you Sister and you called me Brother. But
Papa . . . (*He takes a handkerchief out of his jacket pocket. A
pocket watch is wrapped lovingly inside. He shows it to* LILY
DALE.)

LILY DALE: What's that?

HORACE: Papa's watch. It doesn't run. I'll have it fixed someday. It has his initials engraved, see?

LILY DALE: Where did you get it?

HORACE: I found it stuffed in a drawer at the house when I came back after you all had gone that time. And look here. . . . (*He takes a wedding ring out of his pocket.*) This is Mama's wedding ring.

LILY DALE: How do you know?

HORACE: Look inside. It says "To C.T. from H.R."

LILY DALE: Yes, it does.

HORACE: I used to have some of Papa's books.

LILY DALE: Where are they now?

HORACE: I don't know. They just disappeared after I went out to work at the Gautier plantation. I used to read all the time when Mr. John Howard was alive. I read newspapers now, mostly.

LILY DALE: I can't stand reading. Mama doesn't like to read either.

HORACE: I know.

LILY DALE: Mr. Davenport says he's never read a book in his life and doesn't intend to. When Mama told him once how Papa used to like to read, he said, "No wonder he drank."

(*She takes another peek out the door after* CORELLA, *then runs to the piano bench, lifts up the seat cover, and takes out a picture. She crosses back to* HORACE.)

LILY DALE: This is my sweetheart. Isn't he good-looking? He plays baseball on the city team. He's first baseman. He's a wonderful athlete. He's twenty-two. Mr. Davenport says he's old enough to be my father, but I think a boy should be quite a bit older than a girl. Don't you?

HORACE: I hadn't thought about it one way or the other.

(CORELLA *enters dressed for the theater. She has her gloves on and carries a purse and hat. As she enters,* LILY DALE *hides her picture inside her dress.*)

CORELLA: Are you ready? (*She crosses up into the hallway by the coatrack and looks into the mirror as she puts on her hat.*)

LILY DALE: What are we going to see?

CORELLA: I don't know, but I'm sure it will be good. It usually is.

LILY DALE: I like music best. We went to hear Galli-Curci when she sang here, and Paderewski, and John McCormack.

HORACE: I would like to have heard him. I love Irish tenors. I heard Chauncey Olcott.

LILY DALE: I know. You told us.

HORACE: Did John McCormack sing "Mother Machree"?

CORELLA: Yes, he did.

HORACE: So did Chauncey Olcott. As an encore.

CORELLA: We have a record of John McCormack singing. Play it for him, Sister. We have time.

(LILY DALE *crosses to a Victrola and puts the record on as the lights fade.*)

(*A few hours later. The lights are brought up.* CORELLA *comes in followed by* LILY DALE *and* HORACE.)

LILY DALE: I don't believe you cared for the play, Brother.

HORACE: Yes, I did . . . what I could understand.

CORELLA: He's never seen Shakespeare before, Sister. He can be hard to understand at first.

LILY DALE (*laughing*): You went to sleep twice. Once you were snoring so loud I had to poke you. Mama, what did Papa call me? Did he call me Sister or did he call me Lily Dale?

CORELLA: I don't remember.

LILY DALE: I think he called me Sister, but Brother says he called me Lily Dale.

CORELLA: Yes, he did call you Lily Dale. I remember now.

LILY DALE: All the time?

CORELLA: I think so. He thought we should all be called by our given names.

LILY DALE: How old were you when you married our father?

CORELLA: Eighteen. I had Horace when I was nineteen.

LILY DALE: How old was our father?

CORELLA: Twenty-two. We were all moving around every-place after the war. We had lived for a while in Goliad and then gone to Salurie Island, where my papa was in charge of a lighthouse; but then there was a terrible storm and the water came up to the second story of our house and Papa couldn't get to us and we almost drowned. Anyway, when the storm was over, my papa took us off the island and we went back to Goliad, and then we moved back to Harrison because he was trying to save some of the land from his papa's plantation he'd been cheated out of. And I think your father was already there then. I believe they had moved there by that time from Tyler. He was very handsome, I remember. Very distinguished, even as a young man. His brothers had started a newspaper. He had a law office.

(PETE DAVENPORT *slams the bedroom door and enters the room. Both* LILY DALE *and* CORELLA *scream.*)

PETE: Don't be frightened.

CORELLA: Oh, you gave me such a start.

LILY DALE: Oh, me too. I couldn't imagine who you were or what you wanted.

CORELLA: Oh. . . . (*She laughs with relief.*) I don't know when I've been so frightened. My heart is beating so. I didn't know who it was. When did you get here?

PETE: I've been here two hours. I took a nap.

LILY DALE: We got your letter. But we didn't expect you until tomorrow. I am so glad you're home. I have missed you so much. I learned two new pieces while you were gone. I just love my new piano.

CORELLA: Pete, this is my boy. This is Horace. He surprised us this morning by walking in here. He said he decided to take the day off and pay us a visit.

HORACE: Hello, Sir.

PETE (*very coldly*): Hello.

CORELLA (*nervously*): Did you have a good time, Mr. Davenport?

PETE: Yes, I guess so. (*He starts out of the room.*)

CORELLA: How were your people?

PETE: All right.

(*He exits.*)

LILY DALE: Oh, he's mad. He can be the sweetest thing in the world, but when he's crossed he can be a terror. I only saw him mad once and I hope to never see it again.

CORELLA: Horace, there's no room here for you now. You see, Sister was going to sleep with me in my bed and I was going to give you her bed, but now. . . . You can get a train back to Harrison tonight. You go right to Virgie and explain just what happened and she'll put you up. I know Albert will give you a job in his store.

HORACE: I don't have any money for my ticket home.

CORELLA: Oh, yes, I forgot. You wait here. I have my money in my sewing closet. I'll be right back.

(*She hurries out.*)

LILY DALE: How are all our old friends in Harrison?

HORACE: All right. Willie Roseberry left.

(PETE *comes back in.*)

LILY DALE: Mama has gone to get him money to get back home on. She sent him two dollars to get here and she . . .

(CORELLA *comes back in.*)

PETE: Are you giving him money?

CORELLA: Well . . . you see, Mr. Davenport . . .

PETE: You're a grown man. Aren't you ashamed to take money from your mama? When I was your age, I had been supporting my mother and my brothers and sisters for eight years. Nobody ever gave me anything and I never asked for anything. What kind of man are you gonna make, taking money from a woman at your age?

(*He exits.*)

CORELLA: He doesn't mean that. He's not as bad as he sounds. Take the money.

(*She gives it to him. They hug, and he leaves. She watches him through the front door.*)

LILY DALE (*at the piano, calling*): Mr. Davenport . . . he's gone. Come listen to my new pieces. (*She starts to play.*)

CORELLA: Be quiet, Lily Dale. I have a splitting headache. Just be quiet for once.

(*She exits.* LILY DALE *continues playing, but in a subdued manner.* PETE *enters and sits.*)

PETE: Play the étude I like.

LILY DALE: All right. (PETE *starts to read the newspaper he has carried in with him.*) I won't play if you're going to read the paper.

PETE (*putting the paper down*): I'm not going to read the paper.

(LILY DALE *begins to play the Chopin étude. There is a knock on the door.* PETE *goes to it and opens it.* HORACE *is there.* LILY DALE *stops playing.*)

PETE: What do you want?

HORACE: I forgot my suitcase. (CORELLA *enters.*) I forgot my suitcase.

CORELLA: Oh . . . (*She gets it, gives it to him, and he puts it down.*)

HORACE: I brought some presents for you all. (*He opens the suitcase and takes out three gifts, all wrapped in brown wrapping paper. Two have ribbon around them. The third, which is* PETE's, *has string around it. He gives* CORELLA *her gift.*)

CORELLA: Thank you, Son. (*She opens it. It is a painted cup and saucer.*) That's certainly pretty. I do appreciate it.

HORACE: And this is for you, Lily Dale.

(*He hands her gift to her, and then hands* MR. DAVENPORT *his.*)

LILY DALE (*unwrapping her gift, which is a memory book*): I got one of these already. Anyway, I haven't been to school in four years. Mrs. Davenport said I could just stay home and practice the piano and compose music.

CORELLA: She wrote a rag. She called it the Davenport Rag for her stepdaddy. What did Horace bring you, Mr. Davenport?) (*He holds up an unwrapped cigar box.*) That's nice.

PETE: It would be, if I smoked. (*He puts them down and continues to read the paper.*)

CORELLA: You can give them to somebody at the train yard.

PETE: I expect I can.

(*Pause.*)

CORELLA (*to Horace*): You tell Virgie and the rest of them hello if you see them.

HORACE: I will. (*He starts out.*)

CORELLA: Goodbye again, Son.

HORACE: Goodbye.

(*He leaves.*)

CORELLA (*calling after him*): And don't forget to tell Albert you are looking for a new job.

LILY DALE: Mama, why did you do that?

CORELLA: Do what?

LILY DALE: Tell Mr. Davenport about the rag I composed. I wanted to surprise him.

CORELLA: I'm sorry.

LILY DALE: It was to be his Christmas present. I was going to play it for him on Christmas Morning.

(*She crosses the stage to a trunk. Inside is the music she has written. She takes it out and crumples it up as she goes back to the piano.*)

PETE: You can write me another one for Christmas. You can call that one the Christmas Rag. You play this one for me now.

LILY DALE: All right.

(*She opens and smooths out the crumpled music and hands it to* PETE. *She starts to play the Davenport Rag.* CORELLA *goes to the window and looks out.*)

What are you looking out the window for?

(CORELLA *doesn't hear her. She stops playing.*)

What are you looking out the window for?

CORELLA: What?

LILY DALE: I said, why are you looking out the window?

CORELLA: I just wanted to see if your brother got on the streetcar all right. You go on playing.

LILY DALE: No. I don't want to play unless everybody is going to listen.

CORELLA: I'm listening, Lily Dale.

LILY DALE: You're not listening if you're looking out the window.

CORELLA: All right. (*She sits on the couch.*) Now I'm listening. Go ahead and play.

(LILY DALE *continues with her rag as the lights fade.*)

(*Two hours later. As the lights are brought up, we see* PETE *asleep in his chair.* CORELLA *is darning some socks on the couch.* LILY DALE *is sitting on the floor.*)

LILY DALE: Mama?

CORELLA: Yes?

LILY DALE: Can I see Will again?

CORELLA: No.

LILY DALE: Why not, Mama?

CORELLA: You know why not. Mr. Davenport doesn't approve of him.

LILY DALE: I like him, Mama.

CORELLA: You're too young to know whether you like him or not.

LILY DALE: If he promised to stop drinking, could I see him?

CORELLA: No, because he wouldn't do it.

LILY DALE: Yes, he would. I know he would.

(*We hear a trio of young men out in the yard. They start to sing "Juanita."*)

That's Will. He's come to serenade me. (*She looks out the window.*)

PETE (*waking up*): What's that?

CORELLA (*looking out the front door window*): It's Will Kidder. He's come to serenade Lily Dale again.

PETE: I think he's crazy. Doesn't he know there are working people that live here? Mr. and Mrs. Westheimer go to bed at eight o'clock. They work hard all day long and they are tired. Send him away, Lily Dale. I forbid you to have anything to do with him. I've told you and told you that.

LILY DALE: And I've told him, Mr. Davenport, I have. I've told him and told him, but he says he will just die if I never see him again. He says he is going to reform and never drink again as long as he lives.

PETE: I don't believe it. He'd tell you anything to see you. Tell him to clear out of here or I'm going to. (PETE *crosses toward his room.*) I think he's crazy, coming around people's houses this time of night acting that way. (LILY DALE *begins to cry.*) What's the matter with you, Lily Dale?

LILY DALE: You're just breaking my heart. That's what's the matter with me. You're breaking my heart. I love him and he loves me.

PETE: Come on now. Don't cry. Just don't cry now.

LILY DALE: I can't help it. My heart is breaking. I'm so unhappy and so miserable.

CORELLA: Come on now, Lily Dale. You can't hear the singing if you're gonna cry like this.

PETE: Don't cry, Lily Dale. Please stop crying. You won't have to send him away. Just don't cry!

LILY DALE: Will you talk to him?

PETE: What about?

LILY DALE: About . . . about how he's reforming. About how he intends to behave himself from now on.

PETE: All right, I guess so.

LILY DALE (*going to the front door*): Will . . . Will, come on inside. Mr. Davenport will speak to you now.

(*The singing stops.* WILL KIDDER *comes in. He is a tall, well-built young man. He seems very sure of himself.*

WILL: Evening, folks.

CORELLA: Good evening, Will.

WILL: I hope you didn't mind the serenade.

CORELLA: It was very pretty. "Juanita" is one of my favorite songs.

WILL: Lily Dale says you object to our seeing each other because of my habits. (*He gets no answer.*) Did Lily Dale tell you I'm changing my habits? I've stopped drinking.

CORELLA: We're glad to hear that, Will. You won't ever regret that, I'll tell you.

WILL: No, Ma'am, I know that. I never drank a whole lot anyway.

PETE: What do you call a whole lot? I saw you drunk three times.

WILL: Those were the only three times in my whole life I was ever drunk. I said to Lily Dale, I said, "Wouldn't you know the only times in my whole life I got drunk I had to meet your stepdaddy?"

PETE: She's too young for you. She's only eighteen. An eighteen-year-old girl has no business—

LILY DALE: I'm almost nineteen, Mr. Davenport. I'll be nineteen next month.

PETE: Well, if you want to come call on her here, all right. But you'll have to sit right here. She can't leave the house with you until she is nineteen. And if I ever so much as smell one drop of liquor on your breath . . . you'll not be allowed back in here ever again.

WILL: Yes Sir.

LILY DALE: Oh, thank you, Mr. Davenport. Thank you.

PETE: Now, go on so we can get to bed around here.

(LILY DALE *runs over to* WILL *and takes his hand for a moment. She lets go, he leaves, and she runs back to hug* PETE. *The singing begins again. We hear "Let me call you sweetheart, I'm in love with you" as* WILL *and his friends go down the street.*)

LILY DALE: Oh, Mr. Davenport. You are the sweetest man in the whole world. You have made me so happy and you have made Will so happy.

(PETE *goes back to sleep in his chair.* CORELLA *continues darning socks.* LILY DALE *sings along with the trio under her breath. There is a knock on the door.* LILY DALE *heads towards it.*)

CORELLA: Do you think that's Will?

LILY DALE: No, I saw Will walking away, singing with the others.

CORELLA: Don't open the door then. It's awful late. You'd better let Mr. Davenport answer it. (*There is another knock.*) Mr. Davenport . . . someone's at the door . . . Mr. Davenport . . .

PETE (*calling out*): Who is it?

HORACE (*from outside*): It's Horace.

PETE: Who?

HORACE (*outside the door*): Horace. . . .

CORELLA (*nervously*): I think it's Horace. (*She goes to the door.*) You say you're Horace?

HORACE: Yes Ma'am.

CORELLA (*opening the door*): What happened, Horace?

HORACE: I took the wrong streetcar, and by the time I got to the railroad station the train had gone. There is no train to Harrison until the morning.

CORELLA: Oh, I'm sorry. Did you hear that, Mr. Davenport?

PETE: Don't you have enough sense to get on the right streetcar?

HORACE: I didn't know there were different streetcars.

CORELLA: Of course you didn't. How were you to know that?

HORACE: I thought all the streetcars took you to the railroad station. But they don't. The one I took ended up in the heights someplace.

(PETE *walks out of the room.*)

LILY DALE: Brother, guess what happened? You know the young man I was telling you about? Will Kidder? Tonight after you left, he came around to serenade me with some friends. He thought Mr. Davenport was still in Atlanta, I guess, but he wasn't. (HORACE *has begun to tremble.*) What are you trembling about, Brother? Are you sick? You look pale.

CORELLA: Are you all right, Son?

HORACE: I don't feel well, Mama.

CORELLA: You're feverish. Your head is on fire with fever. I think you've got malaria. Have you been taking your quinine and calomel regular?

HORACE: Yes, Ma'am. I don't know what's wrong with me. (*He faints and falls to the floor.* LILY DALE *screams.*)

CORELLA (*calling out*): Mr. Davenport . . . Mr. Davenport . . . Mr. Davenport . . .

(PETE *comes into the room.*)

CORELLA: Help me lift him up on the sofa . . . please.

LILY DALE: Oh, he's gonna die. I know he's gonna die. That's another one of my terrible dreams. I'm always seeing Brother dead in his coffin. Sometimes he is drowned in the river, sometimes he has been in a terrible train wreck, sometimes—

CORELLA: Shh, Lily Dale, shh. (*She covers* HORACE *with a quilt.*)

PETE: He's not going to die. He's just got a fever, Lily Dale.

CORELLA: Feel his forehead. I think he has a very high fever.

PETE (*feeling his forehead*): Yes, he does.

CORELLA: Do you think it's malaria? It's just rife down home.

PETE: I don't know anything about malaria. I don't come from the swamps and the bottoms, remember? I come from Atlanta—the best climate in the world.

CORELLA: Do you mind if he stays here tonight?

PETE: What else can he do? I hope he doesn't lose his job tramping around the country this way.

LILY DALE: He was about to quit his job. He was hoping to find one here in Houston working in a department store. I told him that was the craziest idea I ever heard of. He could never get a job in a Houston department store. He's not qualified. And then he said maybe you could get him a job in the railroad yards and I said, "Brother, that is even wilder yet. Do you know they're laying off people in the railroad yards and it's only because of the great respect they have for Mr. Davenport's abilities down there that he has a job at all?"

CORELLA: Shh, Lily Dale. Now, shh!

PETE: He'd better not ask me for a job. Let him get his own job. Nobody ever helped me get a job. I've never asked anybody for anything. Not one solitary thing. I'd have too much pride to ask help of anyone.

(*He leaves.* CORELLA *feels* HORACE'S *head again as the lights fade.*)

Act Two

Two weeks later. As the lights are brought up., we see HORACE
*asleep on the couch. It has been made into a sickbed with a sheet,
pillow, and quilt.* LILY DALE *tiptoes in and goes to her piano. She
very quietly plays a few notes. She turns to look at* HORACE,
who has been awakened by this.

LILY DALE: Brother?

HORACE: Yes?

LILY DALE: How do you feel?

HORACE: Better.

LILY DALE: Well, I'm glad. Welcome back to the land of the
living.

HORACE: Thank you.

LILY DALE: This is the first time in a week you have
responded to us at all. We were so afraid for you, Brother.
We thought we were going to lose you.

HORACE: Was I sick?

LILY DALE: Sick? I guess you were sick. At the point of
death for almost two weeks.

HORACE: I was?

LILY DALE: Out of your head nearly the whole time . . .
talking the wildest kind of nonsense.

HORACE: I was?

LILY DALE: I tell you, it was awful. Night before last, Mama, Will, and I had to hold you in bed by sheer force. You thought Mr. Davenport had a butcher knife and was trying to kill you. You kept screaming, "He's trying to slit my throat. Don't let him slit my throat." Mrs. Westheimer heard you all the way upstairs and thought we were being murdered and made Mr. Westheimer go for the police.

HORACE: My goodness.

LILY DALE: There was a great deal of excitement then, let me tell you. There's good come from it, though. You know what happened? Will came to call the next night, like Mr. Davenport said he could, and made himself so helpful, Mama and Mr. Davenport fell in love with him and he's been invited over every night for supper.

HORACE: He has?

LILY DALE: Yes. And when Mr. Davenport heard day before yesterday he had lost his job, he took him right down to the railroad yard and got him a job working there. Now they ride the streetcar together every day to and from work and Mr. Davenport says I can marry Will as soon as he saves a little money. Isn't that thrilling?

HORACE: Where am I?

LILY DALE: What, Brother?

HORACE: Where am I?

LILY DALE: Where are you? Oh, heavens, Brother, don't scare me that way. You're in Houston. Don't you know where you are?

HORACE: How did I get here?

LILY DALE: How did you get here? On the train.

HORACE: How long have I been here?

LILY DALE: Two weeks. You've been sick the whole time. Don't you remember? I had to go over to my girlfriend's to practice my music.

HORACE: Have I been baptized?

LILY DALE: What, Brother?

HORACE: Have I been baptized?

LILY DALE: Oh, Lord, Brother! I don't know.

HORACE: Have you been baptized?

LILY DALE: I don't know that either. What makes you ask a question like that at a time like this?

HORACE: Is Mama here?

LILY DALE: No, she went to the store to get me some material. She's going to make me a ball gown. Will is taking me to a dance. Mr. Davenport says we can go unchaperoned. Isn't that sweet of him? Would you like a little music to cheer you up? I've just gone crazy over rags. I wrote the "Davenport Rag" (*she plays part of it*) for Mr. Davenport, and then I wrote the "Willie Rag" (*she plays again*) for Will. And now I'm working on the "Lily Rag," which I'm dedicating to myself. (*She plays this now. They all sound pretty much the same.*)

(CORELLA *comes in the front door with a paper bag.* LILY DALE *stops playing.*)

Well, he's much better. He doesn't remember a thing that's happened to him, but he talks sense now.

CORELLA: You feel better, Son? (HORACE *nods that he does.*) Did you give him any nourishment, Lily Dale?

LILY DALE: No.

CORELLA: Would you like a little broth, Son? I bet you would. I'm going to get some for you. You have to keep up your strength, you know.

HORACE: Have I been baptized, Mama?

CORELLA: No, you haven't, honey. What makes you ask a thing like that?

HORACE: I met this lady on the train coming down here and she asked me and I said I didn't know. She said I was in mortal danger if I wasn't baptized. (*Pause.*) I thought for sure I was going to die . . . I was going to die without being baptized.

CORELLA: Well, you didn't die.

LILY DALE: Was I baptized, Mama?

CORELLA: No. I told you that.

LILY DALE: How come we weren't baptized, Mama?

CORELLA: Because every time I started to baptize you when you were babies, something came up to prevent it. Either you got sick or I got sick or your father, and then all our troubles started and I just never got around to it. Did you tell him about Mr. Tom Galbraith's store, Lily Dale?

LILY DALE: No.

CORELLA: A terrible thing happened—Virgie wrote me yesterday his store burned to the ground. Two weeks ago. It must have been right after you left. They say the fire started around three in the morning and by the time they discovered it, it was almost all destroyed. Virgie says the worst part is that since Mr. Galbraith was in debt, people are implying he did it for the insurance, but she says she just heard he had very little insurance.

(WILL *and* PETE *come in. They wear overalls and carry lunch pails.*)

LILY DALE: Well, look who's home.

WILL: How does the young man feel?

CORELLA: I think he's going to live now.

WILL: He's strong as an ox. Did you tell him how I had to wrestle with him to keep him in that bed? He thought Pete here was trying to kill him.

CORELLA: How was work?

WILL: Fine. I like it better every day. I think they like me. Don't you, Pete?

PETE: Yes, they do. They told me today. They said you're as good a worker as they've ever seen.

LILY DALE: Mama, show them the material and the pattern for my dress.

(CORELLA *takes them out of the bag and hands them to* WILL.)

WILL: That's mighty good-looking. I'm going to have the prettiest and best-dressed girl at the ball.

LILY DALE: See it, Mr. Davenport? (*She shows it to him.*) Isn't it pretty?

PETE: It sure is.

WILL (*to* HORACE): Young man, you'd better get well and come go with us.

HORACE: Thank you.

LILY DALE: Can you dance, Brother?

HORACE: Yes.

CORELLA: Virgie taught him. She's the dancer in the family. She loves music and dancing.

PETE (*to* HORACE): When are you going back home?

CORELLA: He'll be going back before long. He'll have his strength back now in no time, now the fever has broken.

HORACE: I'm going back tomorrow.

CORELLA: No, Son.

HORACE: Oh, I'm going to. But first I'm going to get dressed and get baptized. I'm going to find me a preacher. (*He tries to get up.*)

CORELLA: Oh, Lord! He's delirious again.

HORACE: I'm dirty and I want to be washed clean.

WILL (*going to him*): Come on, fellow. Take it easy.

HORACE: Don't come near me. You're trying to kill me before I can get baptized. (*He is struggling to get up.* WILL *can hardly manage him.*)

WILL: Help me, Mr. Davenport. I can't hold him by myself.

(PETE *goes to help* WILL. *They hold* HORACE *until his struggling subsides.*)

PETE: I just think he's putting on an act to get us to keep him here so he can get free room and board.

CORELLA: Why would anybody want to do that? He's sick and you know he's sick. You should be ashamed of yourself, Pete!

(HORACE *is exhausted. He closes his eyes.*)

PETE: Does he know he lost his job in Glen Flora?

CORELLA: He didn't lose his job. He just got laid off temporarily.

PETE: That's a polite way of putting it.

(*He exits.*)

HORACE (*opening his eyes*): What about my job?

CORELLA: Shh, shh . . . now don't get excited, honey. Everything will turn out all right. You'll see. We'll talk about all that at another time.

HORACE: What about my job, Mama? Don't I have a job in Glen Flora?

LILY DALE: Brother, there has been a terrible fire in Glen Flora. Mr. Galbraith's store burned down. We told you about it.

HORACE: Oh, my God!

CORELLA: But Mr. Galbraith sent word he is building it again. A lovely brick building this time, and you can have your job back then.

(HORACE *closes his eyes as the lights fade.*)

(*A few days later. As the lights are brought up we see* HORACE *on the couch reading a newspaper. There are two more on the floor beside the couch.* CORELLA *comes in.*)

CORELLA: Well, I don't need to ask you today how you feel. I know you are feeling better. One look at you tells me that.

HORACE: I am. Thank you. Who brought me the papers?

CORELLA: Will did. I asked him to. I hope you like them.

HORACE: Oh, yes, I do.

CORELLA: He asked what you liked and I said, "Oh, anything from out of town." I remembered someone telling me once how you asked everyone you knew going to Houston to bring you back a paper from some other city. What did he get you?

HORACE: The *New Orleans Picayune*, the *St. Louis Star*, and the *Galveston News*.

CORELLA: The *Galveston News*—that's not very far away.

HORACE: I know, but I like it. It's my favorite paper.

CORELLA: Is that so? Of course, I can't tell one from another. I never read the papers. It's my eyes, I guess. You see, I sew so much that my eyes are tired at the end of the day. (*Pause.*) Do you remember Mrs. Clint Harris?

HORACE: No Ma'am.

CORELLA: She is kin to the Vaughn's some way—or Mrs. Vaughn, I guess, who was a Miss Speed. you know, before she married Henry Vaughn. We were friends before I was married. She came to Harrison to work in the courthouse and she lived in a boardinghouse around the corner from our house and we used to have her over a lot and—

HORACE (*interrupting*): What about Mrs. Harris?

CORELLA: Oh, yes, excuse me. I ramble so lately. I'll start on one thing and before I know it I'm off on ten different other subjects. Well, anyway, Myrtle Harris lives across the street in that big house with the stone lions in front. It cost all kinds of money, they say. She called on me when I first came here, but I never returned that call because I'm always working. Virgie wrote me that she had been in Harrison recently and Virgie met her at a bridge club. She told Virgie that I had hurt her feelings because I hadn't returned her call. Virgie said I hadn't, she was sure, because I was always working. "What does she do?" Virgie said she asked her. "Takes in sewing," Virgie told her. "Oh, heavens!" Virgie said Myrtle said. "Oh, heavens what?" Virgie asked her. "You know, she's as poor as you were when you lived here. She didn't happen to marry a rich husband." Virgie said that shut her up. (*Pause.*) Why do you like the *Galveston News* so much?

HORACE: I don't know. I've always loved Galveston, you know.

CORELLA: No. I didn't know that.

HORACE: Oh, yes. I went down there the last three summers when they ran the overnight excursion from Harrison. I loved it. Papa used to talk about it once in a while, you know, when he was growing up there as a boy.

CORELLA: He didn't grow up there. They left there after his father died when he was two years old and his mother had to start the boardinghouse over in Tyler, so he couldn't remember much about Galveston except what he heard from his mother and brother and sisters.

HORACE: How did they get from Tyler to Harrison?

CORELLA: I don't know. I never heard. I remember your father once talking about his mother and saying that she had never even buttoned or tied her own shoes before the war. She had never lifted her hand to do a single thing. But after it, when they lost their shipping fleet, she had to learn to work and feed a family. And she did.

HORACE: Mama, Will Kidder tells me that for fifty dollars you can go to a business school here in Houston and get a business course. I think I'm going to do it.

CORELLA: Where will you stay?

HORACE: Well . . .

CORELLA: I'd like to ask you to stay here with us, Horace,

but I can't. You understand that. We've no room. We made do while you were sick . . .

HORACE: No. I know. I didn't expect to stay here.

CORELLA: Where would you stay?

HORACE: Will says I can find a boardinghouse that's cheap.

CORELLA: How cheap?

HORACE: He didn't say. He just said cheap.

CORELLA: Where will you get the money to do all this, Horace?

HORACE: I'm going to try to borrow it.

CORELLA: I can't help you, Son—you understand that?

HORACE: I wasn't going to ask you, Mama.

CORELLA: Where will you get it?

HORACE: I'll ask Aunt Virgie—Uncle Doc's practice is pretty good now. Or I'll try the bank. They might loan me the money.

CORELLA: What if you can't borrow the money?

HORACE: Then I can't go.

CORELLA: Why do you want to study, Son?

HORACE: I don't know . . . I just don't want to clerk in a dry goods store all my life. There's no future in that unless you own the store . . . which I don't see how in this world I can ever do. I thought if I had a business course, I would have a few more opportunities to get work.

CORELLA: I see. (*Pause.*) I could do this much. I could see that you get a good breakfast every morning. Mr. Davenport leaves for work by five or five-thirty, and if you come over here between six and six-thirty, I could fix you a good hot breakfast. I would ask you here to have all your meals, but Mr. Davenport is tired when he comes home and he likes it quiet; and I just don't like to impose on him too much, you know. He's peculiar in many ways, I know, but he has been good to me and your sister. He's no bad habits. Doesn't even smoke, as you know. He worships your sister and he's crazy about Will now. I'm thankful for that, although I tell him not to encourage them too much. Will, you know, wants her to marry him. And, oh, I worry so about it. She seems so young to me to be marrying. Of course, she throws up to me that I was married by this time too, and I know I was. I wasn't ready for the responsibility of it all. And neither was your father, for that matter. And we had you children so soon. (*Pause.*) Do you have a girl, Son?

HORACE: I go with several.

CORELLA: No particular one?

HORACE: I've been seeing quite a bit of Dolly Parker when I come in from Glen Flora. You know, she lives with the Garretts now and her two brothers live there too. So there are four young people living there, and Mr. and Mrs. Garrett are grand hosts. They have a piano; there are always a lot of young people over there and Rosa Garrett has a lovely voice. And someone is always there that can play the piano, and Rosa has the sheet music of every song you've ever heard of.

CORELLA: Is Dolly pretty, Son?

HORACE: Yes Ma'am. She is pretty.

CORELLA: And Rosa?

HORACE: She has a very nice disposition and so she has a lot of friends, and like I say, her mother and father are always very kind and hospitable to young people.

CORELLA: Are they still poor as church mice?

HORACE: Yes Ma'am, I guess they are, but they always seem to have a lot to eat. There is always a ham or a chicken or a turkey on the table, and sometimes they ask as many as twelve or fourteen of us to stay for dinner. Where's Sister?

CORELLA: She's getting dressed for the dance in her room.

HORACE: Where's Mr. Davenport?

CORELLA: He's out in the backyard fixing the chickens' fence so they can't get into his garden. He has quite a garden this year. (*Pause.*) I suppose you'll be thinking about getting married one day.

HORACE: I suppose so.

CORELLA: Have you thought about it?

HORACE: Oh, I've thought about it, but I can't think of marrying now, Mama. I don't even have a job. I want to have a job and at least a few hundred dollars saved before I even think about marrying.

CORELLA: And I think that's very sensible. I wish I had been as sensible as that before I married. I hope your sister will be.

LILY DALE (*entering, wearing her evening dress and evening slippers.*): How do I look?

CORELLA: Beautiful. Like a picture.

LILY DALE: How do I look, Brother?

HORACE: Very pretty, Sister.

LILY DALE: Thank you. I feel pretty. I thought just now, as I looked at my dress in the mirror, not a girl at that ball, I don't care how rich they are, will have a dress as pretty as mine. Thanks to my sweet Mama who sews so beautifully. And works so hard so that I can have all these pretty things. (*She kisses* CORELLA.)

CORELLA: Thank you.

LILY DALE: Where is Mr. Davenport? I want him to see me.

CORELLA: He's out in the backyard working. I'll call him.

(*She exits.*)

HORACE: I was thinking, lying on the couch here this afternoon, Lily Dale, Papa used to sing a song to the two of us called "Lily Dale." Do you remember how it went?

LILY DALE: No, and I don't want to. Brother, you always want to talk about the past. I have no interest in it, really, at all.

HORACE: No?

LILY DALE: No! I want to think of now. This minute. Why do you always want to talk about the past, what Papa did or didn't do? I don't care what he sang and I don't care what he called me. All I know is that he smoked cigarettes like a fiend and was a drunkard and broke my mother's heart, and he died and left her penniless to go out into the world to work and support two children.

HORACE: She didn't support me.

LILY DALE: Well, she supported me. And she's the only one I want to talk about except for Mr. Davenport, who has been more to me than a real father ever could have been. (HORACE *pulls the quilt over his head and turns away from her.*) What's the matter with you? Why have you turned your face away? You are jealous of me. That's why. And you should be ashamed of yourself for allowing yourself to be jealous. Mama said that's the Robedaux disposition: jealousy, spitefulness, and vindictiveness. I don't have an ounce of it, thank God, and if I thought I did, I'd jump off the highest building in Houston and kill myself. Because

that kind of disposition makes you miserable, Mama said.
And she doesn't have to tell me that. I see it every time I
meet Minnie Robedaux, who teaches school here now in
Houston. No matter where she sees me or who I'm with,
she stops me and begins a perfect tirade about what she
says is her family's side of the story. "I don't want to hear
your family's side of anything," I say. "They're your family, too," she says. "Not mine," I told her. "My mother and
Mr. Davenport are my family and I want none other. My
mother is a living, unselfish angel and I won't have you
say a word against her. You and your family mooched off
her and my father and drove him to drink. So don't come
around here anymore and ask me anything about my
father. I only know one thing about him: he died and left
us all alone in this world." (*Pause.*) Of course, I hope you're
happy now. I was feeling so happy and joyful and you
had to spoil all my wonderful feelings by asking me questions about things I don't want ever again to think about.
That's why I love Will. He only talks about the future—
what he's going to do with his life, how much he's going to
accomplish. He doesn't sit around and talk and wonder
why this happened or that happened, or what happened
when we were five years old or seven years old. I have not
heard him mention his mother or father or childhood
once, and he had just as difficult a time as we had. (*Pause.
Lily Dale sings, half to herself, "Let me call you sweetheart, I'm
in love with you." She peeks out the front door curtain, looking
for Will.*) Are you going to lie on that couch forever,
Brother? You'll never get your strength back lying around
on that couch, Mr. Davenport says, and I agree with him.
Never. You should make yourself get dressed now every
day and start walking around the block at least. (*Pause.*)
Why are you so sad, Brother? Why are you always so sad?
It's not fair. Turn around and look at me! I can't help it if I
have a happy disposition and you don't. Mama said you
were never happy even as a child, and I was born with a

sweet, loving, happy disposition. Oh, Brother! Brother
. . . let's be close. I want to be close to my brother, and I
feel we aren't. I have to tell you this: we are not close as
brother and sister should be. Why, I should be able to
come to you with my troubles and I can't. I want to be
close, Brother. Please, let's be close.

HORACE: Sister, I feel close to you.

LILY DALE: Do you?

HORACE: Yes.

LILY DALE: And you're not jealous of me?

HORACE: I don't know what you're talking about. I've
never been jealous of you in my life.

LILY DALE: Oh, I'm relieved to hear that. I thought you
were jealous of me because Mr. Davenport spoils me and
prefers me to you. But that's natural, Brother, that he
would. You're a stranger to him, really, and I was raised
up here in the house with him.

HORACE: I know.

LILY DALE: He's always been so sweet and considerate to
me, Brother. You must love him for that. Say you do? Why,
I remember when Mama decided to marry him and she
came to tell me of her decision. And Mama asked Mr.
Davenport to come and talk to me after she had told me
they would be married. And he came into the living room
of the house we rented then and took me in his arms and
he said he was going to be a daddy to me. He was going to
see that nothing bad ever happened to me ever again, and
that he was going to make up for all the unhappiness I
had known in my young life, and make up to me for the
loss of a father. And he has. He certainly has. And I do
love you, dear Brother, but we have lived apart because of
circumstances and . . . Brother, try to be a little more

friendly with Pete. He doesn't mean to be so abrupt. Reach out to him, Brother.

HORACE: I can't stand him.

LILY DALE: Brother, don't say that. I can't bear to hear this.

HORACE: You think I'm faking, lying here on this couch? Do you think if I had the strength right now to walk across this room I wouldn't do so? Do you think I don't choke on every piece of food of his I eat? How can I get well lying here eating the food of a man I despise?

LILY DALE: Brother! Brother! Brother!

HORACE: I despise him. I despise him. I would never have come here if I had known he would come here and that I would have gotten sick and been at his mercy.

LILY DALE: Stop it! Dear Brother, please . . . please!

HORACE: I despise him! I despise him! I despise him! And if I had the strength, I would put on my clothes right now and leave. I would leave here right now. (*He falls weakly back on the couch.*)

LILY DALE: Now you've spoiled it for me. I hope you're satisfied, Brother. I do hope you are. You have ruined an evening for me that I had been looking forward to for a very long time!!

(*She runs out, crying.* HORACE *tries to get up off the couch but can't. He tries again, stands, takes a step or two, and then falls to the floor.* CORELLA *comes in. She sees him on the floor, screams, and runs to him.*)

CORELLA: Lily Dale . . . Lily Dale . . . run for Mr. Daven-port in the backyard. Your brother has fallen. He's fainted from weakness. I need help . . . hurry, Lily Dale . . . Lily Dale . . . can you hear me?

LILY DALE (*offstage, calling back weakly*): I can hear you.

CORELLA: Oh, my God, what's the matter with you?

LILY DALE (*offstage*): Nothing.

CORELLA: You sound so funny. Don't tell me your period has started?

LILY DALE (*offstage*): No Ma'am.

CORELLA: Then why on earth do you sound so funny?

LILY DALE (*offstage*): No reason. No reason at all.

CORELLA: Then hurry and go for Mr. Davenport. Your brother may be dying for all we know. His father was dead at thirty-two. And bring some smelling salts out of my room. Hurry! Hurry! For God's sake, hurry! (*She gets one of* HORACE's *newspapers and begins to fan him with it.*) Oh, Son! Son! Please! Wake up! Please!!

(*She is crying.* PETE *comes in.*)

Mr. Davenport . . . look here!

PETE: How did he get there?

CORELLA: I don't know. I guess he was trying to go to the bathroom. I went out to call you to see Lily Dale's dress, and I stayed and held the lantern for you so you could see to finish nailing the fence, and I came in here to tell Lily Dale you would be here in another five minutes at the most.

(LILY DALE *comes running in with the smelling salts.*)

And I found him here, half dead, on the floor. Half dead. . . .

(*She is sobbing now.* PETE *takes the smelling salts from* LILY

DALE *and holds them under* HORACE'S *nose.* CORELLA *controls her sobbing and looks at* HORACE *as* PETE *administers the smelling salts.*)

HORACE (*opening his eyes and seeing* PETE): I despise him. I despise him!

CORELLA: Oh, he's delirious again! Poor boy! He has such a sweet, uncomplaining nature.

HORACE: I despise him! I despise him!

CORELLA: Who are you talking about, boy?

LILY DALE: Pete. Mr. Davenport. (*She is sobbing now.*) He says he hates and despises him.

CORELLA: Shh, honey . . . shh . . . shh . . . he didn't mean that. Never! Never! It's the fever coming back. Don't repeat what he said when he's sick and out of his head.

LILY DALE: He was not out of his head and he has ruined this precious night for me by his hate. (*She runs out of the room crying.* PETE *goes after her.*)

CORELLA (*holding* HORACE *in her arms*): You were out of your mind weren't you, Son? Tell your sister you were. Don't spoil her evening. Please, Son. She's had so little happiness in her life. So very little. Oh, my God! I want us all so to get along now.

(*There is a knock on the door.* CORELLA *turns to call to* PETE *to answer it, but the knock is repeated and she goes herself.* WILL *is there, dressed for the dance, with a corsage for* LILY DALE.)

WILL: Hello there, young lady. How do you feel?

CORELLA: Come in, Will. Help me get Horace up on the couch. He fainted.

WILL (*going to* HORACE, *picking him up, and placing him back on the couch*): Come on, boy. What did you think you were doing? Up we go.

CORELLA: Are you feeling better?

HORACE: Yes Ma'am.

CORELLA: You gave us quite a scare.

HORACE: Yes Ma'am.

CORELLA: You were delirious.

HORACE: Yes Ma'am.

CORELLA: You kept looking at Mr. Davenport and saying you despised him. Of course, he knew you were delirious and didn't mean a word of it.

WILL: Where's my girl? I thought she'd be all dressed and waiting.

CORELLA: She was, but when her brother fell, she got very nervous and upset and ran out of the room. I'll get her.

(*She exits.*)

WILL: Did Lily Dale tell you about my new job?

HORACE: No.

WILL: I'm leaving the railroad. I'm going into the produce business—a great new company that's just started up. They have the rights to handle some great new products here in this area. Admiration Coffee—you know, that's the one they advertise as "the cup of Southern hospitality." (*Pause.*) Say, you need a job. Speak to Pete about getting my job for you out at the yards. Anyone can do it.

PETE (*entering*): Corella says to tell you Lily Dale will be here in a minute.

WILL: Plenty of time, Pete, plenty of time. Say, I've just had a great idea. What about Horace for my job in the railroads?

PETE: It's already been taken. It was filled this afternoon.

WILL: That's too bad. We just weren't on the ball, Pete, were we? Why didn't we think about it sooner?

(LILY DALE *and* CORELLA *enter.*)

WILL: Say, look here. This sight was worth waiting for. Man . . . you are beautiful.

LILY DALE: Thank you, Will! Mama made the dress.

WILL: And it's something! Yes, it is! Doesn't she look gorgeous, Pete?

PETE: Yes, she does.

WILL: Shoot . . . she'll be the prettiest girl there, I'll tell you that. What do you think of your sister, Horace? Put a waltz on the Victrola, Pete. Lily Dale and I will show you the Texas Castles: Irene and Vernon.

(PETE *goes to put it on.*)

LILY DALE: I don't feel like it, Will. I have a headache.

WILL: A headache! Well, get over it. No headaches are allowed on this night. We're going to dance all night.

(*He takes hold of her and as "The Blue Danube" waltz is heard, they dance a few steps, then stop.*)

WILL: How is that?

CORELLA: You are both lovely dancers. You make a very handsome couple. What time are you coming home?

(PETE *takes the needle off the Victrola and the music stops.*)

WILL: Don't wait up for us.

CORELLA: Oh, I always do. I never close my eyes until she's home.

WILL: Don't you trust me, lady? Don't you trust me to take care of your daughter?

CORELLA: I trust you, Will. You know that.

WILL: Then you go to sleep.

CORELLA: No. I can't do that. I don't close my eyes until she's in the house.

WILL: What are you going to do when she's married and not living here?

CORELLA: Then I can't help it. She's somebody else's responsibility.

WILL: What if we're out until dawn?

CORELLA: Then I won't get to sleep until dawn, but surely you're teasing me about dawn. You'll surely be home at twelve.

WILL: Or one.

CORELLA: Twelve!

WILL: All right—twelve. (*To* LILY DALE:) Let's go, princess.

LILY DALE: All right. Good night, Mama. (*She kisses her.*)

CORELLA: Good night, darling. Have a wonderful time . . .. both of you.

LILY DALE: Thank you. Good night, Mr. Davenport. (*She hugs him.*)

PETE: Good night, honey.

WILL: Good night, Pete. Don't take any wooden nickels.

PETE: I'll try not to. Take care of her now.

WILL: I will.

LILY DALE: Good night, Brother.

HORACE: Good night, Lily Dale.

WILL: Good night, young man; now you take care of yourself.

(*They leave.*)

CORELLA: She did look pretty, didn't she?

PETE: Yes.

(*He exits.*)

CORELLA (*to* HORACE): I told him that whatever you said to him just now, you were delirious.

HORACE: I wasn't delirious, Mama. I knew what I was saying.

CORELLA: Then what possessed you to say it, honey? (*Pause.*) Surely you didn't mean it? (*Pause.* HORACE *doesn't respond.*) I don't think you understand him is all. He's been good to me and to your sister. He's gruff, I know, and doesn't talk a lot—

HORACE: I'm leaving tomorrow, Mama.

CORELLA: How are you leaving, honey, when you're so weak you can't even make it across the floor?

HORACE: I'm going if I have to crawl out of here. (*Pause.*) I'm going to ask Will to come and help me out of here and ride to Harrison with me on the train . . . or put me on the train and I'll make it by myself. And I can make it by myself—once I get on the train.

CORELLA: I don't want you to do that now. I don't know what's gotten into you and why you are so sensitive, but I tell you—

HORACE: I'm going, Mama. You are wasting your breath. Nothing will keep me here. Nothing!

CORELLA: What will Virgie and the others say to me, my allowing you to go back that way? Where will you go? You've no job. What will you do?

HORACE: I'll go to Aunt Virgie's. She'll nurse me.

CORELLA: I want to nurse you. I want to do something for you. Please let me. (*Pause.*) Anyway, I hope if you come back and study at the business school, I want you to remember what I said to you about having breakfast here every morning. (HORACE *closes his eyes.*) You're tired. You want to rest. I'll go now . . . (*She starts to exit.*)

HORACE: Mama?

CORELLA (*stopping*): Yes, Son?

HORACE: Do you remember that song "Lily Dale," the one Papa always sang to Sister?

CORELLA: Let's see. I remember his singing it . . . but I forget how it goes.

HORACE: Try to remember it, Mama.

CORELLA: Why, honey? (*He doesn't answer.*) Why, honey?

HORACE: Because I want to remember it.

CORELLA: All right. I'll try. I'll certainly try. (*Pause.*) Right now?

HORACE: Yes.

(*Pause.*)

CORELLA: I just can't. But I'll keep trying.

(CORELLA *exits.* HORACE *closes his eyes as the lights fade.*)

(*Later that night. The lights are brought up as* CORELLA *waits for* WILL *and* LILY DALE *to return.* HORACE *is asleep on the couch.* CORELLA *hears them and goes to open the door.*)

WILL: Didn't I tell you I'd get her home by twelve-thirty?

CORELLA: Shh . . . shh . . .

(*She points to* HORACE. WILL *and* LILY DALE *come into the room.*)

CORELLA: Did you have a good time?

LILY DALE: Oh, a wonderful time!

WILL: We danced every dance. Tell your mother what the reporter from the paper said to you.

LILY DALE: He said I was the most graceful dancer he had ever seen. He thought I should consider dancing professionally.

CORELLA: How was the orchestra?

WILL: Perfection! Show her your present.

(LILY DALE *holds her hand up for her mother to see.*)

CORELLA: My goodness!

WILL: How do you like that?

CORELLA: It's beautiful, Will.

WILL: What do you think it cost me?

CORELLA: Oh, I have no idea.

WILL: Plenty. But I thought nothing is too much for my sweetheart.

CORELLA: What does it mean, Will?

WILL: It means we're engaged. I've asked her to marry me.

CORELLA (*crying*): You're too young to be married, darling. Will, believe me. She's too young. I have nothing, absolutely nothing against you, nothing in this world.

WILL: What's the matter with you? We're not getting married tomorrow. I have some sense, you know. I am making my plans. I'm going to work hard for a year and save my money, and when I have a few thousand in the bank, we'll marry. Do you have any objections to that plan?

CORELLA: No, I guess not. But promise me you'll wait at least a year. Will you both promise me that?

WILL: I'm not making any promises. I might want to get married tomorrow.

CORELLA: Now, Will, be serious.

WILL: I'm serious. We'll wait as long as you want us to. Won't we, honey?

(LILY DALE *nods her head, begins to cry, and runs out.*)

CORELLA: Lily Dale . . .

WILL: She'll be all right. She's been a little upset all evening. (*He points to* HORACE, *then whispers.*) I think his being here gets her upset. He talked mean to her tonight, she said.

CORELLA: I don't know what all went on. He's upset too. He says he wants you to take him to the station tomorrow—that he's going home. I don't think he's strong enough to make it by himself, but he says he's determined to go.

WILL: Well, we all have troubles. My brother is about to drive me crazy. He can't keep a job.

CORELLA: Is he older or younger than you?

WILL: Younger.

CORELLA: Your father is dead, isn't he?

WILL: Yes.

CORELLA: Lily Dale says you've been the head of your family for a long time.

WILL: Since my father died.

CORELLA: How old were you then?

WILL: Going on thirteen. I can tell you about hard work. It was up to me to put the food on the table . . . if there was any food.

LILY DALE (*entering*): I'm sorry, Will. I bet you think I'm crazy.

WILL: No, I don't. I just think you're sweet and pretty. (*Pause. To* CORELLA:) Can I kiss her good night? We're engaged.

CORELLA: All right.

(*He kisses* LILY DALE.)

WILL: Good night.

LILY DALE: Good night, Will.

WILL (*heading out the front door*): Good night, Miss Corella.

CORELLA: Good night, Will.

(WILL *exits.*)

CORELLA: Well, he's a fine boy. I'm very pleased for you. We better get to bed. (*She starts out.*)

LILY DALE: Mama? (*Pause.*) What do they do to you when you're married to make you have children?

CORELLA: Don't ask me questions like that this time of night, Lily Dale. Heavens!

LILY DALE: Myra Kate says your husband does terrible things to you. Does he?

CORELLA: No. It's not so terrible.

LILY DALE: What is it?

CORELLA: It's just what you have to do with your husband when you get married, that's all.

LILY DALE: What?

CORELLA: You'll find out.

LILY DALE: When?

CORELLA: When you get married.

LILY DALE: Does it hurt?

CORELLA: I've heard some say it does. It didn't hurt me.

LILY DALE: Does it hurt to have children?

CORELLA: Yes, and I pray to God you never have to go through that.

LILY DALE: Will wants children.

CORELLA: He's a fool, and don't you ever let him talk you into it.

LILY DALE: Women die in childbirth, don't they?

CORELLA: All the time. Every minute of the hour. While I was having you and your brother, I prayed I would die.

LILY DALE: Why?

CORELLA: Because it hurt so much.

LILY DALE: Which hurt the most? Me or Brother?

CORELLA: I don't know. I was in terror the whole time I had you both.

HORACE (*waking up*): Is the dance over?

CORELLA: Oh, we've awakened you. I'm sorry. Go on back to sleep.

HORACE: How was the dance, Lily Dale?

LILY DALE: Very nice.

CORELLA: Lily Dale is engaged to be married. Show him your ring.

LILY DALE (*crossing to him and showing him her finger*): It cost a hundred twenty-five dollars.

HORACE: How do you know?

LILY DALE: Will told me. He paid cash for it.

HORACE: You know Papa did sing "Lily Dale" to you when you were a girl, and you got your name from that song. Mama told me.

LILY DALE: I don't care whether you're right or not. It doesn't mean a thing to me one way or the other.

HORACE: And Mama . . . I remember how the song goes.

(*He sings:*)
　'Twas a calm still night
　And the moon's pale light
　Shone soft o'er hill and vale.
　When friends, mute with grief,
　Stood around the deathbed
　Of my poor, lost Lily Dale.

CORELLA (*having joined in with him on the last line*): Oh, yes, that's it.

HORACE: You'll have to learn it and teach it to your children, Lily Dale.

LILY DALE: I'm not going to have children.

HORACE: You're not?

LILY DALE: No.

HORACE: Why?

LILY DALE: Because it hurts too much to have children. Mama says she prayed to die while she was having us. Anyway, if I had children I wouldn't sing them that song.

HORACE: Why?

LILY DALE: Because I want to forget everything that happened back then. Everything. I want my children to know about happy times, pleasant things. I don't want to tell them about drunkards and dying and not having enough to eat. And I want you to quit talking to me about it. Every time I feel the least bit good you begin on all that. What did Papa call us? What did Papa sing? Did Papa do this? Did Papa do that? I don't care about him. How many times do I have to tell you that? I don't care if I ever hear his name again. Mr. Davenport is my father. I want no other. You have no father, but that's not my fault. I have one—the only one I want. (*She runs out.*)

CORELLA: She didn't mean that, you know. She's excited because, well, you know, the dance and getting engaged and—

HORACE: I don't care, Mama, if that's how she feels.

CORELLA: It might be better if you didn't talk about your papa so much, Horace. You know, Mr. Davenport is very sensitive and I don't think he likes it.

HORACE: I don't talk to him about my father. I wouldn't, thank you.

LILY DALE (*coming back in and still in a fury*): I'm going to tell you something else! Mama didn't love our papa. She loves Mr. Davenport because he doesn't drink and neglect her; he's been good to her and to me. So don't you ever let me hear you say a word against him again. Because if you do, I'll tell him exactly what you said and he'll throw you out and never let you in this house again to upset me and Mama. Never! Never! Never! Never! Never!

HORACE: He's not going to throw me out. (*He starts out of bed.*) He'll never get the chance to throw me out. (*He's out of bed.*) I'm getting my clothes on and I'm getting out of here.

CORELLA: Horace, Horace . . . it's two in the morning. You can't leave now.

HORACE: Oh, yes, I can. And I will leave. I can leave if I can crawl on my hands and my knees.

(*He takes a step or two, then falls.* LILY DALE *sees him falling and tries to catch him.* CORELLA *screams.*)

LILY DALE: Oh, Brother. Brother! I'm sorry! Oh, dear Brother! I'm so sorry! I didn't mean a word of those terrible things I said. Not a one. I don't know what gets into me. I have a terrible disposition, Brother, a terrible disposition. It's the Robedaux coming out in me. Forgive me, please, please forgive me. (*She and* HORACE *are crying.*) I loved Papa. Believe me, I did. Just as much as you did. I loved him, but it hurts me so to talk about him, Brother. And it scares me, too. You don't know how it scares me. I wake sometimes in the night and I think I hear Papa coughing and struggling to breathe like he used to. And I didn't mean that about your leaving, Brother. I'm glad you're here and I want you to stay until you're all well and strong again. Because you're the only brother I have, and sometimes at night I see you dead and in your coffin, and I cry in my dreams like my heart will break. I am really crying because my crying wakes me up and I say to myself, "Brother is alive and not dead at all; that's just a dream." But still I feel so miserable, I just lie there sobbing, like my heart will break. And sometimes Mama hears me and comes in and says, "Why are you crying, Lily Dale?" And I say, "Because I dreamt again that Brother was dead and had gone to heaven and left us." (*She holds him.*) You're all the family I have, Brother, you and Mama. And we must never leave each other. Promise me you'll never leave me and promise me you'll forgive me. Promise me, promise me. . . .

CORELLA: I know he does forgive you, Lily Dale. He's just too weak to talk much now. (*She goes to* HORACE.) Do you think we can help you back to bed ? Or should I call Mr. Davenport?

(*She and* LILY DALE *try to lift* HORACE *to his feet. They can't manage.*)

I'd better call Mr. Davenport.

HORACE: Don't you call him. I don't want him to help me. I don't want him near me. I don't want him to touch me. I'll get back on the couch by myself.

*(He tries to get up. He can't. He tries again and fails. He slowly
begins to pull himself towards the couch. As* HORACE *just gets
himself up onto it,* PETE *comes in with his robe on.)*

PETE: What the hell is going on out here?

CORELLA: It's all right, Mr. Davenport. Horace fell again,
but he's all right.

PETE: What time is it?

LILY DALE: It's two or after.

PETE: Let's get to bed. My God, I have to be up at five, you
know. I have to work for a living!

*(*PETE *goes to the bedroom door.* LILY DALE *slowly follows him.
As she gets to the door, she looks at* HORACE *before she turns and
exits to her room.)*

HORACE: I despise him!

CORELLA: Go to sleep. Get your rest.

HORACE: Mama . . .

CORELLA: Shh!

HORACE: Mama, Mama . . .

CORELLA: Shh. . . . *(She sings:)*
　Go tell Aunt Rhodie,
　Go tell Aunt Rhodie,
　Go tell Aunt Rhodie
　The old grey goose is dead.

(As she sings the last line, the lights fade.)

(One week later. The lights are brought up as LILY DALE *is
playing the piano.* WILL *is seated. He listens for a moment, then
slides onto the piano bench with* LILY DALE*.)*

LILY DALE: Will, behave yourself. Mama and Brother may come in at any moment, not to mention Mr. Davenport. You know he's very old-fashioned. He would be furious if he knew Mama had left us alone in the house unchaperoned. Now you go over there and sit down and behave yourself. (*He doesn't move.* LILY DALE *stands up.*) Will. . . .

WILL: I'm not leaving your side until you promise to marry me.

LILY DALE: I promised to marry you a year from now.

(WILL *stands and comes towards her.* LILY DALE *backs up.*)

WILL: I don't want to wait a year.

LILY DALE: You told Mama you would. That was our agreement when we became engaged. (*Pause.*) Why are you going back on your word? Why are you doing that to me? And stop looking at me that way. You are making me very nervous. Now, go sit down in that chair over there (*she points to a chair*) or I'm leaving here and I'm going to find Brother and Mother and tell them I won't stay here alone with you because you have not behaved like a gentleman.

(WILL *takes another step towards her. She stops him by pointing at the chair.* WILL *stops, shrugs, laughs, and goes to the chair and sits.*)

WILL: Is this how a gentleman behaves?

LILY DALE: Yes. Thank you. (*She goes back to the piano and begins to play.*)

WILL: Lily Dale?

LILY DALE (*stopping her playing*): What?

WILL: Something is wrong with you.

LILY DALE: Nothing is wrong with me. Now, be quiet and let me practice. (*She plays again.*)

WILL: Lily Dale?

LILY DALE: What?!

WILL: Something is troubling you.

LILY DALE: Oh, I don't know, Will. I'm very nervous. I think it's Brother's being here. He's been so sensitive and touchy. And it's not easy, four of us living on this one floor. Mr. Davenport has been so silent and morose, too, not his usual jolly self, and poor Mama, she's just torn into little pieces trying to make peace between us all.

WILL: It will soon be over. He's leaving tomorrow.

LILY DALE: I must say it will be a relief to have the house back to ourselves. Brother just doesn't fit in. We all try. I do, Mama does, Mr. Davenport, and Brother too, but he just doesn't fit in. Now, you fit in. Isn't that funny? You're here five minutes and you cheer everybody up and Mr. Davenport begins to talk like a normal human being, but once you leave we're silent and gloomy and unhappy. (*Pause.*) I had this dream about Brother again last night. I dreamt he was dead, and this time I didn't cry. I said a terrible thing. I said, "It's about time." And Mama said, "We'll bury him in our family plot here in Houston." And I said, "No, we won't. I'll not have him buried with you and Mr. Davenport and me. I want him buried with his father where he belongs." Wasn't that terrible for a sister to have a dream like that about her brother?

WILL: You probably ate something that didn't agree with you for supper.

LILY DALE: No, I didn't. I'm always having terrible dreams. I dreamt once last week that I was a very old woman and I was a famous concert pianist and I had come to Houston to give a concert, and before the concert I looked out through the curtain into the audience and I called out and I said, "Is Will Kidder there?" "No," they said, "he is dead." "What did he die of?" I asked. "A broken heart," they said.

WILL: Shoot . . . don't ever worry about that dream. I'm not ever going to die of a broken heart.

LILY DALE: Will . . .

WILL: What?

LILY DALE: Look the other way. I want to tell you something.

WILL: Where shall I look?

LILY DALE: Anywhere away from me. (*He does so.*) I don't want to get married.

(*Will looks at her; she turns away.*)

WILL: Why?

LILY DALE : Don't look at me, please.

WILL (*turning away again*): Why?

LILY DALE: Because you're going to hurt me if we do.

WILL: How am I going to hurt you?

LILY DALE: You know.

WILL: Oh. (*Pause.*) Why do you think I will hurt you? Who told you I would?

LILY DALE: Sissy Douglas.

WILL: She's a fool.

LILY DALE: I asked Mama about it too.

WILL: What did she say?

LILY DALE: She didn't want to talk about it. (*Pause.*) She said Papa didn't hurt her, but some women told her they were hurt by their husbands.

WILL: I'm not going to hurt you.

LILY DALE: How do you know?

WILL: I just do. (*She cries. He holds her.*) Lily, what's the matter?

LILY DALE: I'm scared. I want to marry you, but I'm scared.

WILL: Now, I told you—

LILY DALE: I'm scared that I'll have a baby. I know that hurts when you do, and I'll die while I'm having the baby. Mama says it's the worst pain in the world. She said she prayed to die the whole time she was having her children.

WILL: Don't you want to have children?

LILY DALE: I do, but I'm scared to, Will. I'm scared of the terrible pain and I might die and . . .

WILL: We won't have them, then.

LILY DALE: You mean you can get married and not have children? (*She pulls away and looks at him.*)

WILL: Yes.

LILY DALE: How?

WILL: There are ways. Pete and your Mama are married and they have no children.

LILY DALE: Pete and Mama! Oh, my God, Will! What are you saying? Are you saying that Pete and Mama . . .!?

WILL: Honey, they're married.

LILY DALE: But they're too old, Will.

WILL: No, they're not. Your mama is only thirty-eight. She could still have a child if she wanted to.

LILY DALE: My God Almighty, Will! I wish you wouldn't tell me things like that. God knows what kind of terrible dreams I'll start having now.

WILL: Honey, I only told you so you could understand that married people don't always have to have children if they don't want to. (*He sits with her.*)

LILY DALE: I don't want to. I mean, I want to, but I'm scared to.

WILL: Then we'll never have them.

LILY DALE: Do you promise?

WILL: I promise. Does that make you happy?

LILY DALE: Yes, it does. It certainly does. (*She hugs him.*) You are so sweet. You are the sweetest person in this whole world.

WILL (*returning her hug*): You're mighty sweet yourself.

(PETE *comes in the front door. They don't hear him. He slams the door.* LILY DALE *screams.*)

PETE: What's going on here?

LILY DALE (*standing*): Mr. Davenport, I'm nervous enough without your coming in here and scaring me this way.

PETE: I'm sorry, little girl, I didn't mean to scare you. (*He crosses in front of* WILL *and looks at him.* WILL *doesn't look at him.*) Where is your mama?

LILY DALE: She's gone for a walk with Brother to help him get his strength back.

WILL: We're going to lose the old boy tomorrow.

LILY DALE: Uncle Albert's coming for him on the seven o'clock train from Harrison and they'll go back together on the three o'clock.

PETE: Will if Albert doesn't get into a gambling game. I think they're a fool to send Albert. Every professional gambler in Houston knows him.

LILY DALE: He has to go back. He has a store now, you know.

PETE: That never stopped Albert. Nothing has ever stopped him from gambling. Not a job, not his wife, not his children. I'm surprised he hasn't gambled his store away long before this.

LILY DALE: He only opened his store two weeks ago.

PETE: I'm surprised he didn't gamble it away the day after it opened. I'll give him six months. It will be gone and he'll be clerking for someone else again.

(CORELLA *and* HORACE *come in the front door.*)

WILL: Did you have a nice walk?

HORACE: Slow. I had to stop and rest every now and again. (HORACE *sits in a chair.*)

CORELLA: Now, you mustn't be discouraged. Naturally, you are weak after that long stay in bed. In another week you won't know yourself.

WILL: I hear you have a job?

HORACE: Yes . . . clerking for my uncle in Harrison.

CORELLA: He's going to live for the time being with my sister Virgie. At least until he gets his strength back. She's a wonderful cook and she loves him.

WILL: Does she have any children of her own?

CORELLA: One. A little girl. Her husband said after he saw what she went through having that one, they could drag him around the courthouse square but he'd never put her through that again. You hungry, Pete?

WILL: Pete's always hungry. I never knew the time he wasn't hungry.

CORELLA: You do pretty well yourself, Will. Are you going to eat with us?

WILL: No. I'm afraid if I eat another meal over here, you'll send me a board bill. (*He gets up and heads for the front door.*)

PETE: Now, come on. Stay for supper.

WILL: All right, you don't have to twist my arm. I'll stay . . . on one condition—that Lily Dale will play for us the rag she wrote for you for Christmas time.

LILY DALE: I want to play you my classical piece, Will.

WILL: No. I don't want any classical pieces. I want something lively. I want one of your rags and I don't want to wait for Christmas time.

LILY DALE: All right. If I play one of my rags, then can I play one of my serious pieces?

WILL: No. Then you can play another rag.

LILY DALE: Will . . .

WILL: Nothing serious tonight. This is Horace's last night with us and we want him to leave feeling happy.

LILY DALE: Oh, Will.

(*She starts to play.* HORACE *begins to cry and runs out the front door.* LILY DALE *stops.*)

What's the matter with him, Mama?

CORELLA: I think it's weakness. He cried twice on our walk, but then it passed and he apologized. I said, "What was there to apologize for?"

(*Pause.* HORACE *comes back in.*)

HORACE: I apologize. Forgive me.

CORELLA: Don't apologize.

LILY DALE: Shall I continue?

HORACE: Would you play "Lily Dale" for me?

LILY DALE: I don't know "Lily Dale." How can I play it for you?

HORACE: I'll sing it for you—maybe you can play it then.

LILY DALE: All right. I'll try.

(HORACE *hums the first verse.*)

CORELLA: You have a sweet voice, Son.

HORACE: No, I don't.

CORELLA: Yes, you do. Sing the words to the song, Son.

HORACE (*singing as he crosses towards* LILY DALE):
　'Twas a calm still night
　And the moon's pale light
　Shone o'er hill and vale.
　When friends, mute with grief,
　Stood around the deathbed
　Of my poor, lost Lily Dale.
　Oh, Lily, sweet Lily,
　Dear Lily Dale.
　Now the wild rose blossoms

O'er her little green grave
'Neath the trees in the
Flowery vale.

CORELLA: Can you play it now, Sister?

LILY DALE (*making an attempt, then stopping*): I can't play that.

CORELLA: Sing it again, Horace.

HORACE: No, that's all right. Maybe I can find the sheet music in Houston someplace and Sister can learn it from that.

LILY DALE: Can I play my classical piece now?

CORELLA: Why don't you play something Horace can sing, Lily Dale? He has such a sweet voice. Do you know "Drink To Me Only," Son? Lily Dale, play that.

HORACE: No.

CORELLA: What do you know?

HORACE: I know "Love's Old Sweet Song."

CORELLA: Oh, that's lovely. Play that, Sister.

LILY DALE: I don't want to, Mama. I want to play my classical piece.

CORELLA: All right, then, honey, play your classical piece.

LILY DALE: Well, I won't play it if you all don't want me to play it, Mama.

CORELLA: I want you to play it, sweetheart. Why do you think I don't want to hear it?

LILY DALE: No, I don't want to play my piece now.

CORELLA: But we want you to, don't we, Pete?

PETE: Yes, we do. I always like to hear her play her classical pieces. Does it have a lot of runs in it?

LILY DALE: Yes, it does.

PETE: I always love it when you have a lot of runs. Play it for us.

LILY DALE: No. Will doesn't want to hear me play it. He wants me to play rags.

WILL: No, I want to hear your classical piece.

LILY DALE: What about you, Brother?

HORACE: Sure, I want to hear it.

LILY DALE: You're sure, now?

HORACE: Yes, I'm sure.

CORELLA: He's leaving tomorrow. It's the last chance he'll get to hear it.

LILY DALE: Well, all right.

(*She begins to play as the lights fade.*)

(*The next day. The lights are brought up and we see* LILY DALE *and* CORELLA *at the piano. We also see, in a low light,* HORACE *and* UNCLE ALBERT *sitting on the train.*)

LILY DALE: I guess Brother and Uncle Albert are halfway to Harrison by now.

CORELLA: I guess so.

LILY DALE: I hope dear Brother will be happier now that he will work for dear Uncle Albert in Harrison and live with Aunt Virgie.

CORELLA: I hope so.

LILY DALE: Brother has never seemed very happy to me in his whole life. Was he ever happy?

CORELLA: I think so. I hope so.

LILY DALE: Maybe you are born with a happy, contented disposition.

CORELLA: Maybe so.

LILY DALE: I'm happy and contented. I wish Brother could be.

CORELLA: I wish so.

LILY DALE: He's determined—that's for sure. He took Will aside before he left last night and asked him to stop by Goggan's and find this sheet music for me to play for him. (*She takes the "Lily Dale" sheet music off the top of the piano.*)

CORELLA: I'm glad you got to play it for him once, at least, before he left.

LILY DALE: Do you think it is a pretty piece?

CORELLA: I think it is very sweet.

LILY DALE: Do you think the girl on the cover looks like me?

CORELLA: Yes, I guess so.

LILY DALE: I'm prettier, though, don't you think so?

CORELLA: Yes, I do. I think you are much prettier.

LILY DALE: Do you think I'm beautiful?

CORELLA: Yes, I do.

LILY DALE: Will says I'm so beautiful I should be in motion pictures. I hope he is sincere when he says it.

CORELLA: I'm sure he is. He always seems very sincere to me. Will is a very sincere, nice person.

LILY DALE: Mama, Will says that you and Mr. Davenport could, if you wanted to . . . I mean, that Mr. Davenport and you . . .

CORELLA: We what?

LILY DALE: Nothing. I forgot what I was going to ask. (*She goes back to playing the piece very softly.*)

(*The lights on the train section are brought up.*)

ALBERT: How do you feel, Horace?

HORACE: I'm all right.

ALBERT: Would you like a sandwich from the butcher boy?

HORACE: No Sir.

ALBERT: An orange?

HORACE: No Sir. Thank you. I'm not hungry.

ALBERT: I'm going back in the smoking car for a cigar.

HORACE: Yes Sir.

ALBERT: Do you want to come back with me? I have an extra cigar.

HORACE: No, thank you. I don't feel like smoking.

ALBERT: I have some chewing tobacco on me, too.

HORACE: No Sir, thank you.

ALBERT: I may be awhile . . . there is a poker game going on back there, the conductor told me, and I think I'll get into it. I feel very lucky today.

HORACE: Yes Sir.

ALBERT: But I know you won't tell my wife or Virgie about this.

HORACE: No Sir.

(ALBERT *exits.* HORACE *closes his eyes and leans back. The lights fade a bit.*)

LILY DALE (*stopping her playing*): Mama, did you love Papa when you married him?

CORELLA: Yes, I did. I thought I did.

LILY DALE: Who did you love most—Papa or Mr. Davenport?

CORELLA: Mr. Davenport is a good man. He's been very good to me. (*Pause.*) He doesn't seem to like your brother. I wish that would change.

LILY DALE: Brother doesn't like him either. Who do you love the most—Brother or me?

CORELLA: I love you both, honey.

LILY DALE: But you love me the most, don't you?

CORELLA: I love you both.

LILY DALE: I think you love me the most.

CORELLA: You're a girl. You have needed me more, perhaps.

LILY DALE: I'm never going to leave you, and you are never going to leave me.

CORELLA: When you marry, you will have to leave me, sweetheart, and live with your husband.

LILY DALE: Why can't Will move in here with us?

CORELLA: That wouldn't be practical, darling.

LILY DALE: That's what Will says too. Anyway, we'll get a house next door and if we can't do that, as close as we can.

(*She starts to play quietly again as the lights are brought up on the train section.*)

(MRS. COONS *enters and comes up to* HORACE. *His eyes are*

still closed and he is not aware of her. She looks at him a moment before speaking.)

MRS. COONS: Excuse me. (HORACE *opens his eyes.*) Aren't you the young man I met on the way to Houston three weeks ago?

HORACE: Oh, yes Ma'am.

MRS. COONS: I thought so. Was that Mr. Albert Thornton from Harrison sitting with you?

HORACE: Yes Ma'am.

MRS. COONS: I thought so.

HORACE: He's my uncle.

MRS. COONS: Of course. You look terrible, son. Have a spell of malaria?

HORACE: I had a spell of something. I've been pretty sick.

MRS. COONS: You still look sick to me. May I sit and visit for a while?

HORACE: Yes Ma'am.

MRS. COONS (*sitting beside him*): I don't know why I'm not down myself, as much as I have to bear. Mama said yesterday, "Arabella, where do you get your strength from?" "I don't know, Mama," I said. But I do know— it's my faith that gives it to me. My Christian faith. Mr. Coons got sick again, you know.

HORACE: No.

MRS. COONS: Oh, yes. Lost his job, of course. So we have to move again. I've just taken him into Houston to start another Keeley Cure. He swears this is the last time this will happen. "What's to become of us, Mr. Coons?" I said. "I'm not educated, I can't work, and you get sick and can't keep a job." (*Pause.*) Of course you understand what kind of sickness I'm talking about. Whiskey. That's the kind of sickness I'm talking about. He just can't seem to leave it alone. (*Pause.*) How did you find your mama?

HORACE: She's well.

MRS. COONS: And your sister?

HORACE: Just fine.

MRS. COONS: I bet they were glad to see you and sorry to see you go. Did you ask your mother about your baptism?

HORACE: Yes Ma'am. I wasn't.

MRS. COONS: Mercy! Sick as you look, I wouldn't put it off any longer. It would be terrible if you died without being baptized. How would you explain that to your Maker?

HORACE: Pray for me, Mrs. Coons.

MRS. COONS: What do you want me to pray about? That you live until you're baptized?

HORACE: No Ma'am. Just pray for me and my sister and my mother. . . .

MRS. COONS: All right, I will. I don't know your sister and your mother, but I'll be glad to include them in my prayers.

HORACE: Now, Mrs. Coons. Pray for us now. This very moment.

MRS. COONS: Why certainly, son. (*She takes his hand and closes her eyes.*) Father . . . I am turning to you here on this train . . . this train filled with miserable sinners . . . Father, I turn to you and I ask your forgiveness of our sins and your blessings—

HORACE: My mother and my sister and me. Pray for us, Mrs. Coons, pray for us.

MRS. COONS: Give me time, son. I'm getting to all of you. Father . . .

(LILY DALE *begins to sing "Lily Dale" as she plays it.*)

What's your mother's name, son?

HORACE: Corella.

MRS. COONS: And your sister?

HORACE: Lily Dale.

MRS. COONS: Father, I've been asked to remember in my prayers this young man, Horace, and his dear mother, Corella, and his dear sister, Lily Dale. Father of mercy, Father of goodness, Father of forgiveness . . .

(*The lights fade out on the train section.* LILY DALE *continues singing and the lights on the living room slowly fade to black.*)

The Widow Claire

Characters

HORACE ROBEDAUX
ARCHIE GORDON
FELIX BARCLAY
SPENCE HOWARD
ED CORDRAY
CLAIRE RATLIFF
BUDDY RATLIFF
MOLLY RATLIFF
VAL STANTON
ROGER CULPEPPER

Place: Harrison, Texas
Time: 1912

The lights are brought up on the downstage right area. We see a section of a furnished room with a cot far right. Four young men, ARCHIE, FELIX, SPENCE, *and* ED, *are at a table playing poker. They are in their shirtsleeves.* HORACE ROBEDAUX, *twenty-two, tying his tie, watches the poker game.*

SPENCE: When I get some money ahead, I'm going into Houston and get into some big games. (*Pause.*) They have some big games in Houston. (*Pause.*) They have a game going day and night at the Milby Hotel. They say you don't need to know nobody. You just go into the lobby of the Milby and ask the desk clerk the room where the game is being held and he tells you, and you go up to the room—

ED (*interrupting*): Shut up and play cards.

(*There is silence.* HORACE *finishes tying his tie. He whistles "Waltz Me Around Again, Willie."*)

ED: Shut up, Horace.

(HORACE *stops whistling and puts his coat on.*)

FELIX: Archie is the ladies' man to beat all ladies' men. When a girl calls up and he answers the phone, they ask him what he's doing and he says, "Thinking of you."

ED: Will you shut up, Felix? Get out of the game if you're going to talk.

(HORACE *gets a clothes brush and brushes his coat.* ED *throws his cards down.* ARCHIE *begins to take money from the pot.* ED *walks away from the table.*)

ED: I'm through. I'm cleaned out.

SPENCE: Don't you have any more money?

ED: No.

ARCHIE: Come on and play, Horace.

HORACE: I can't. I have a date.

ED: Loan me a little money until Saturday, Horace.

HORACE: I can't, Ed.

ED: Come on, be a friend.

HORACE: I can't. I leave for business school tomorrow. I need all my money for that.

SPENCE: I'll loan you some money until Friday, Ed. (*He gives him five dollars.*)

ARCHIE: You better get in the game, Horace—you could double your money.

HORACE: No, thank you. I tried that before.

FELIX: Horace has worse luck at poker than his Uncle Albert.

ARCHIE: Let's shoot some craps. Maybe you'll have some luck with that.

HORACE: Not me. (HORACE *looks again at his watch and then at himself in the mirror.*)

ARCHIE: Who is your date with?

HORACE: Claire.

ARCHIE: The Widow Claire?

HORACE: Yes.

FELIX: I had a date with her a month ago, but her kids wouldn't leave us alone.

HORACE: No?

FELIX: No.

(HORACE *glances at himself again in the mirror; he whistles "Waltz Me Around Again, Willie."*)

FELIX: How do you get away from them kids? My God, how can you ever feel romantic with kids everyplace?

ED: I'd keep away from her. Who wants those kids around your neck? Whoever gets her is gonna get it.

ARCHIE: Do you think she's good-looking?

ED: Kind of. . . .

FELIX: She used to be. I think she's losing her looks. She used to be a beauty.

(HORACE *looks at his watch.*)

FELIX: Are we keeping you, boy? Don't let your old pals keep you from your date.

HORACE: No, it's still early. I want to give her time to put the kids to bed.

ED: How many dates have you had with her, Horace?

HORACE: Two.

SPENCE: Were those kids always there?

HORACE: In the house. Sometimes they are in bed.

FELIX: They weren't in bed the night I was there. They were crawling all over me the whole time, asking me every five minutes if I'd brought them a present. Finally I had to give them both a nickel to shut them up.

ED: I never went out with a widow.

ARCHIE: Hell, you never go out with anybody.

ED: I've had a date.

FELIX: Who with—Cowpen Annie?

ED: You're kind of funny, aren't you?

SPENCE: They tell me widows can be dangerous. You be careful over there, Horace.

HORACE: I can take care of myself.

SPENCE: Famous last words.

HORACE (*looking again at his watch*): I've got to go.

FELIX: Give me five dollars and I'll come over and entertain the children while you're courting the mama.

ED: I'll do it for three. I'll even take them for a nice long walk, and I'll whistle loud to let you know when I'm bringing them home.

HORACE: Thank you. I may take you up on it one of these nights.

FELIX: She's seeing a lot of other fellows too, you know.

ED: She's seeing Val and she's seeing—

HORACE (*interrupting*): I know who all she's seeing. She makes no secret about it.

(HORACE *leaves.* SPENCE *gets up and walks around to the door.*)

SPENCE: Maybe old Horace is turning into a ladies' man like Archie. What does Archie say when those gals call up, Felix?

FELIX: Thinking of you. (*He tries to whistle a tune.*) What was the name of that last song Horace was whistling?

SPENCE: "Waltz Me Around Again, Willie."

FELIX: That's right. I can't get the damn thing out of my head. What are the words?

SPENCE: Search me.

FELIX: Do you know the words, Archie?

ARCHIE: Maybe. (*Pause. He tries to think of them.*) "Waltz me around again, Willie . . . Da-da-da-da . . ." That's all I know.

FELIX: Claire has that song on her Victrola. That's where I heard it last.

(ED *starts out.*)

Where are you going?

ED: Just going to wander downtown. See what's up.

(*He goes.*)

FELIX: How does that song go again?

ARCHIE: "Waltz me around again, Willie. Da-da-da-da . . ."

FELIX: That's right. (*He attempts to sing it.*)

(*We hear "Waltz Me Around Again, Willie" being played on a phonograph as the lights fade. The men gather up their money and cards. One man exits with two of the chairs, and another takes the remaining two chairs to the center of the stage.*)

(The lights are brought up center and upper left on the living room section of CLAIRE's *house, while the yard section of the house down left remains in darkness. The room is simply furnished: a small sofa right center, the Victrola up right, and the two chairs.)*

*(*CLAIRE, *twenty-eight, comes into the area. She lights a cigarette and begins to dance around the room. She is obviously not an experienced smoker.)*

*(*HORACE *enters far down left. He knocks and stands waiting.* CLAIRE *quickly puts the cigarette out, waving away the smoke.)*

CLAIRE *(calling out)*: Who is it?

HORACE: It's me. It's Horace.

CLAIRE: Oh, Horace . . . come in.

(He comes into the living room area and hands her a small box of candy.)

HORACE: This is for you.

CLAIRE: Oh, thank you. Sit down. *(He goes to a chair and sits.)* I just finished putting the children to bed. I pulled down the shades so I could smoke a cigarette. The neighbors watch everything I do over here.

HORACE: Do they?

CLAIRE: They sure do. And I'm sick and tired of it. I'm going to sell my house and move.

*(*HORACE *gets out of the chair and goes toward her.)*

HORACE: Where will you move to?

CLAIRE: Someplace where I can have some privacy and not be spied on all the time.

(HORACE *draws her to him. They embrace, then kiss. They hear a noise and separate as* MOLLY, *nine, comes into the room.*)

Molly, what are you doing out of bed?

MOLLY: Buddy won't let me sleep. He's made a tent out of his bed and he's playing soldier.

CLAIRE: Go tell him I said to stop it and get to sleep.

MOLLY: I did, but he won't listen to me. He says he's the major and nobody can give orders but him.

CLAIRE: Well, you go on back to bed and I'll be in in a minute and tell him he has to go to sleep right away.

MOLLY: I want you to tell me a story first.

CLAIRE: I told you two stories.

MOLLY: I want another one.

CLAIRE: Not now, Molly. (MOLLY *cries.*) My God, Molly, won't you ever give me any peace?

HORACE: I'll tell her a story. Come here to me, Molly.

(MOLLY *goes to him.*)

CLAIRE: I'll go straighten Buddy out.

(*She leaves.*)

HORACE: What story do you want me to tell you?

MOLLY: What story do you tell your little girl?

HORACE: I don't have a little girl.

MOLLY: Do you have a little boy?

HORACE: No.

MOLLY: What stories did your mama and daddy tell you when you were a little boy?

HORACE: They didn't tell me any.

MOLLY: Didn't you have a mama and a daddy?

HORACE: Yes, but they didn't tell me any stories.

MOLLY: How did they get you to go to sleep?

HORACE: My daddy used to sing to me when I was real little. He would rock me and sing.

MOLLY: Do you know the story about Goldilocks?

HORACE: Yes, I do.

MOLLY: Tell me that one.

HORACE: All right. Once upon a time there was a little girl with long golden curls. They called her Goldilocks—

MOLLY (*interrupting*): Don't tell me that one. Tell me about Red Ridinghood.

HORACE: All right. Red Ridinghood was going to see her grandmother one day and—

MOLLY (*interrupting again*): What was the song your daddy used to sing to you?

HORACE: He sang a lot.

MOLLY: Do you live with your mama and daddy?

HORACE: No, my daddy is dead.

MOLLY: Is your mama dead too?

HORACE: No, she lives in Houston.

MOLLY: Did your daddy have a pretty voice?

HORACE: Yes, he did.

MOLLY: Sing me one of the songs.

HORACE (*singing part of "Lily Dale"*):
'Twas a calm still night
And the moon's pale light
Shone soft o'er hill and vale—

MOLLY (*interrupting*): I like you.

HORACE: Thank you. I like you.

MOLLY: I like you better than the other men that come to see my mama. Do you know old Val?

HORACE: Yes, I do.

MOLLY: Do you like him?

HORACE: Well . . . I . . .

(CLAIRE *comes in.* MOLLY *doesn't see her.*)

MOLLY: I don't like Val at all.

CLAIRE: Why don't you like Val?

MOLLY: Because Buddy said he hit you and made you cry.

CLAIRE: Buddy has a big mouth.

MOLLY: I'm going to tell him you said that.

CLAIRE: I'll tell him myself. Come on, let's go to bed. Buddy promises to behave himself.

MOLLY: I haven't heard my story.

HORACE: Come on, I'll tell it to you in bed.

CLAIRE: Are you sure you don't mind?

HORACE: No.

CLAIRE: And will you promise me to go to sleep then?

MOLLY: Yes Ma'am.

(*He takes her out.* CLAIRE *gets water, whiskey, and glasses.* HORACE *comes back in.*)

HORACE: I don't want Val pushing you around. I'm going to speak to Val.

CLAIRE: He was drunk, Horace. You know how he gets when he's drunk. He was sorry the next day. Would you like a drink?

HORACE: Thanks.

(*She pours him some whiskey.*)

CLAIRE: Are you jealous of Val?

HORACE: No, why should I be?

CLAIRE: Well, don't be. I don't like him at all.

HORACE: What do you see him for then?

CLAIRE: I see lots of fellows. You know that. I see him to pass the time.

(*She pours a drink for herself. They embrace.* BUDDY, *ten, comes in.*)

BUDDY: Mama, Molly's crying.

CLAIRE: Oh, Jesus! You didn't do anything to her to make her cry, did you?

BUDDY: No Ma'am.

CLAIRE: You're sure?

BUDDY: I swear to you, Mama.

CLAIRE: Well, you better not have.

(CLAIRE *puts down the glass of whiskey, and goes out of the room.*)

BUDDY (to HORACE): Hi. . . .

HORACE: Hi, Buddy.

BUDDY: You got a nickel for me?

HORACE: I think so. Here's one for Molly too. (*He gives them to him.*)

BUDDY: Thanks. Molly is crying because she says she misses our daddy. Did you know our daddy?

HORACE: I sure did.

BUDDY: Our daddy is dead.

HORACE: I know.

BUDDY: He had the typhoid. He died in that room in there. Did you ever see the room he died in?

HORACE: No.

BUDDY: You want to see it?

HORACE: No, thank you.

BUDDY: I was scared to go in there for a long time. I was afraid his ghost would be in there. There is nothing in there, though. Mama used to keep his clothes in there, but she gave them all away last month. (*Pause.*) Did she give any to you?

HORACE: No.

BUDDY: I think they would have fit you. There was a winter suit and a summer suit. He's been dead a year. He worked at the wholesale grocery. Another man has his job now. Molly says your daddy is dead.

HORACE: He is.

BUDDY: Did he die with the typhoid?

HORACE: No.

BUDDY: What did he die of?

HORACE: He just died.

BUDDY: How old were you when he died?

HORACE: Twelve.

BUDDY: I was nine when my daddy died.

HORACE: I know.

BUDDY: Were you sad when your daddy died?

HORACE: Yes, I was.

BUDDY: Did you cry?

HORACE: Yes, I did.

BUDDY: I cried too. Do you have a picture of your daddy?

HORACE: Yes, somewhere.

BUDDY: We don't have a picture of my daddy. He died before he even had his picture taken. I remember him, though. Do you remember him?

HORACE: Sure I do.

BUDDY: Tell me what he looked like.

HORACE: Well, he was good-looking and he had a real nice personality and he was certainly well liked by everybody.

BUDDY: Mama says he had a good character. Do you think he did?

HORACE: Oh, yes, I do. And he was smart, Buddy. He was a very smart man and a good businessman. I expect in time he would have been rich.

BUDDY: Are you rich?

HORACE: No, I'm just starting out in life.

BUDDY (*opening his hand, which holds a pocketknife*): Look here.

HORACE: Where did you get that?

BUDDY: Uncle Ned. He's a drummer that comes to see us every time he gets to town. He brought Molly a doll. He got them in New Orleans, he said. I like him better than Uncle Val. He never brings us anything. He just tells us to get out and leave him and Mama alone. Where do you work?

HORACE: I've been working in Mr. Jackson's store. I'm going to school day after tomorrow.

BUDDY: High school?

HORACE: No, business school. Mr. Jackson has been very nice to me.

(CLAIRE *comes back in with* MOLLY, *who carries a doll.*)

CLAIRE: Molly is scared. I told her she could sit with us for a while.

BUDDY: Can I too?

CLAIRE: All right.

BUDDY: He gave us a nickel. Here's yours.

CLAIRE: Did you ask him for that nickel, Buddy?

BUDDY: No.

CLAIRE: Are you sure?

BUDDY: Yes.

CLAIRE: I don't like you asking my friends for things, Buddy.

BUDDY: I know that.

CLAIRE: If you want a nickel you ask me for it. I can afford to give you a nickel.

BUDDY: That's the doll Uncle Ned gave Molly.

MOLLY: I call it Eunice Anne.

BUDDY: Uncle Ned is always giving us presents. Isn't he, Mama?

CLAIRE: Uncle Horace brought us some candy.

BUDDY: Who is Uncle Horace?

CLAIRE (*pointing to* HORACE): He is.

MOLLY (*looking at the box and reading*): Assorted chocolates. What does that mean?

CLAIRE: It means all kinds.

(HORACE *takes the candy and opens it.*)

HORACE: Have a piece.

BUDDY: How many pieces can I have?

CLAIRE: One.

BUDDY: Two?

CLAIRE: All right, two.

MOLLY: Can I have two, too?

CLAIRE: Yes.

BUDDY: If she's going to have two, I should have three.

MOLLY: Why?

BUDDY: Because I'm older than you are.

CLAIRE: Now be quiet or you won't have any at all.

MOLLY: I want the ones with pecans in them. I got vents on them, Buddy. What kind do you want?

BUDDY: I want the ones with pecans too.

MOLLY: Well, you can't have them because I want them.

CLAIRE: Be quiet, both of you. And be polite. Offer Uncle Horace a piece first.

(MOLLY *thrusts the box of candy toward him.*)

HORACE: No, thank you.

MOLLY: Don't you like candy?

HORACE: Not too much.

MOLLY: I love it. Mama, do you like candy?

CLAIRE: Oh, yes, I do.

MOLLY: Uncle Ned brings us candy too.

CLAIRE: Yes, he does. Ned just spoils the children to death.

BUDDY: He brought me a knife and a mouth organ and a BB gun and a slingshot.

MOLLY: He almost killed me with the BB gun.

BUDDY: I did not.

MOLLY: You did too. You pointed it right at me and said, "I think I'll kill you."

BUDDY: I was only joking.

CLAIRE: That's no way to joke, Buddy. If you joke that way again, I'll get Uncle Ned to take the BB gun back to New Orleans.

BUDDY: I know where you live—over behind the courthouse.

HORACE: That's right.

BUDDY: Can I come over and see you sometime?

HORACE: Sure—when I get back from Houston.

BUDDY: When will that be?

HORACE: In about six weeks.

MOLLY: Mama's wearing a new dress tonight.

BUDDY: It cost a lot of money.

CLAIRE: It didn't cost that much, Buddy. I bought the material and picked out the pattern myself, and Sissy made it for me. Do you think it's becoming?

HORACE: Oh, yes, I do. I think it's very becoming.

MOLLY: My mama smokes cigarettes, but don't tell anybody.

CLAIRE: He knows I smoke cigarettes.

BUDDY: Do you smoke cigarettes, Horace?

CLAIRE: Uncle Horace, Buddy.

BUDDY: Do I have to call him Uncle Horace?

HORACE: No, you don't.

BUDDY: Do you smoke cigarettes?

HORACE: Cigars.

BUDDY: Give me one.

HORACE: Wait until you're older, Buddy.

BUDDY: How old were you when you started smoking?

HORACE: About twelve.

BUDDY: Cigars?

HORACE: No. I started on a pipe.

BUDDY: Do you chew tobacco?

HORACE: Sometimes.

BUDDY: Mama says that's a filthy habit.

CLAIRE: Buddy!

MOLLY: Buddy smokes.

BUDDY: I do not.

MOLLY: You do too. You smoke Mama's cigarettes. I seen you.

CLAIRE: Be quiet, Molly.

MOLLY: Can I smoke one of your cigarettes, Mama?

CLAIRE: No.

MOLLY: Can I have some of your whiskey?

CLAIRE: No. And stop being fresh or you'll go right back to bed.

BUDDY: Mama, let me see you and Horace dance.

CLAIRE: Maybe he don't want to dance, Buddy.

BUDDY: Do you want to dance, Horace?

HORACE: Sure.

CLAIRE: Are you sure?

HORACE: Sure, I'd love to.

CLAIRE: All right.

(HORACE *turns on the Victrola. He extends his hand to* CLAIRE *and she takes it. They begin to dance around the room as* BUDDY *and* MOLLY *watch in delight.*)

BUDDY: He's a good dancer, Mama.

CLAIRE: Of course he is. He's kin to Miss Virgie. He has to be.

(HORACE *twirls and dips with* CLAIRE.)

BUDDY: Look there, Mama. He's a fancy dancer.

(*They continue dancing around the room.* MOLLY *and* BUDDY *watch in silence for a while.*)

MOLLY: Val can't dance.

BUDDY: He sure can't.

MOLLY: Val is mean. I don't like Val.

CLAIRE: Shh, Molly. Don't talk that way.

MOLLY: Can Uncle Ned dance, Mama?

CLAIRE: He sure can.

BUDDY: Uncle Ned is an old man. He's too old to dance.

CLAIRE: He is not old, Buddy.

BUDDY: He is too.

CLAIRE: Well, don't you ever tell him that. He would die. (*To* HORACE.) He's a lonely fellow. He travels with the J.C. Taylor Tailoring Company. They have headquarters in Chicago. He has the southern territory.

HORACE: I know him. He sold tailoring to my uncle.

BUDDY: He asked Mama to marry him.

CLAIRE: Buddy!

BUDDY: Didn't he?

CLAIRE: Yes, but you're not supposed to tell the whole world.

MOLLY: Are you going to marry him?

CLAIRE: I don't know. One day I think I will and the next day I decide nothing can ever get me to marry again.

BUDDY: Show Horace the ring he gave you.

CLAIRE: I don't have it on.

BUDDY: Why don't you have it on?

CLAIRE: Because I haven't decided to keep it.

BUDDY: Why won't you keep it?

CLAIRE: Because it's an engagement ring.

MOLLY: It's a diamond ring.

(*The music ends,* HORACE *turns off the Victrola.* BUDDY *goes over to a table and gets some pictures and a stereoscope.*)

BUDDY: Uncle Ned brought us these pictures of the wonders of the world. We got pictures of the Leaning Tower of Pisa and the Eiffel Tower and Niagara Falls. You want to see them?

CLAIRE: Not now, Buddy. Some other time.

MOLLY: Have you ever been out of Texas?

HORACE: No.

MOLLY: Uncle Ned has. He travels all over the South.

(CLAIRE *turns on the Victrola.*)

HORACE: I hope to travel too, when I finish business school.

CLAIRE: Wouldn't I love that!

BUDDY: Uncle Ned has a house in Galveston. We're going to visit him sometime.

MOLLY: I'm going to marry and have twelve children.

CLAIRE: God help you, then!

HORACE: May I?

CLAIRE (*turning to* HORACE): Certainly. (*They begin to dance.*) When do you leave?

HORACE: Tomorrow.

CLAIRE: How long will you be gone?

HORACE: Six weeks.

CLAIRE: I'll miss you.

HORACE: I'll miss you too.

CLAIRE: I bet there are a lot of pretty girls in Houston.

HORACE: I expect so. I won't have time for girls. I'll have to study a lot to keep up with the courses.

CLAIRE: I bet you will. I know it will be hard. I'd be scared to go to school in Houston.

HORACE: My cousin Minnie is going to help me.

CLAIRE: I remember her. Where has she been all this time?

HORACE: Living in Houston. She's a schoolteacher now.

CLAIRE: Oh, everything has changed so much around here. Why, half the people lived on this street when I was growing up have moved away. (*Pause.*) There's to be a dance at the courthouse next week. You better postpone your trip until after then.

HORACE: I wish I could, but the term starts day after tomorrow.

BUDDY: How old are you, Horace?

CLAIRE: He's twenty-two.

BUDDY: You're twenty-eight. You're six years older than he is.

CLAIRE: Buddy . . .

HORACE: That don't make any difference, Buddy. My Aunt Virgie is six years older than my Uncle Doc.

CLAIRE: What are your plans when you finish business school?

HORACE: I don't have any, except to find a job.

CLAIRE: Will you go back to work for Mr. Jackson?

HORACE: No. I want to do better than that, if I can. That's why I'm going to business school—to help me get a better job. Do you remember Barsoty? He used to live here and—

CLAIRE: Why, yes, I do.

HORACE: He's a traveling man now, too. He wrote me a letter and he said to get in touch with him when I finished business school and he would see if he could help me get a traveling line.

CLAIRE: Would you like that?

HORACE: Yes, I would. As long as it's in the South someplace. I wouldn't care to travel up north because of the cold.

CLAIRE: It can be plenty cold here, let me tell you.

(*The music ends.* HORACE *turns off the Victrola.*)

HORACE: It sure can. If it gets so cold here, imagine what it will be like in the North.

MOLLY: Uncle Ned is a traveling man. He travels in the South.

CLAIRE: He knows that, Molly.

MOLLY: Do you know Uncle Ned, Horace?

HORACE: Yes, I do.

BUDDY: And he knows Val too.

CLAIRE: Laura Lee is going with Mr. Barsoty still?

HORACE: Yes.

CLAIRE: I wonder if they'll ever marry? Have you heard who's taking her to the dance?

HORACE: No.

CLAIRE: Have you heard who's going with who?

HORACE: Archie is taking a girl from out of town who is here visiting the Pridgen girls.

CLAIRE: I heard that. Who are the Pridgen girls going with?

HORACE: I don't know.

CLAIRE: Didn't you used to take out Gladys?

HORACE: I had two or three dates with her.

CLAIRE: Do you think they are attractive?

HORACE: Who?

CLAIRE: The Pridgen girls.

HORACE: Yes. I think they are. In a way. . . .

CLAIRE: Which do you think is the prettiest—Gladys or Lovella?

HORACE: I hadn't thought about it one way or the other.

CLAIRE: I heard they are both very cold. Vernon Dale went with them both and he said they were very cold.

HORACE: He did?

CLAIRE: Yes. Frigid. Do you think they have good personalities?

HORACE: Well . . .

CLAIRE: Vernon said they never would talk when he took them out. He said he had to do all the talking.

BUDDY: What happened to him, Mama?

CLAIRE: Who?

BUDDY: Uncle Vernon. He never comes around anymore.

CLAIRE: No. He likes to own people. Nobody likes to be owned, you know.

HORACE: Ed and Felix don't have dates yet.

CLAIRE: They don't?

HORACE: No.

CLAIRE: Well, they better hurry. All the gals in town will be asked.

HORACE: I know.

CLAIRE: Well, I don't think I've ever known Ed to have a date. Have you?

HORACE: No, I don't think I have. He said tonight he had, but I don't remember it.

CLAIRE: I think he's very shy.

HORACE: I guess.

CLAIRE: Sissy said she would watch the children for me if I wanted to go, but I don't think I will—even if anybody asks me, which they haven't. Sissy said, "You've mourned a year. No one can criticize your going to the dance now." "I'm not worrying about that," I said, "but no one has asked me. I can't go by myself. No one wants to take an old married woman with two half-grown children to a dance." "You were a child when you married," Sissy said, "all of sixteen." "I can't help that," I said. "I'm not a child now."

(HORACE *turns the Victrola on; then he goes to* CLAIRE *and they begin to walk slowly around the room, ending up center.*)

HORACE: I wish I were going to be here. I would take you.

CLAIRE: You're just saying that to be nice.

HORACE: No. I would love to take you.

CLAIRE: You're not just saying that?

HORACE: No.

CLAIRE: I haven't been to a dance in so long I wouldn't know how to act.

HORACE: You know, I don't think I've ever seen you at a dance.

CLAIRE: I guess you haven't. When I went, you were still in knee breeches.

HORACE: Didn't you ever go after you were married?

CLAIRE: No. We went to the first Christmas dance after we were married and then we stopped going. (*Pause.*) Yesterday was the anniversary of my wedding.

HORACE: Was it? I remember the day you got married.

CLAIRE: Do you?

HORACE: Sure.

CLAIRE: Did you go to the wedding?

HORACE: No, but I remember my Aunt Inez coming home and telling about it.

CLAIRE: She was my matron of honor.

HORACE: I remember.

CLAIRE: I had a big church wedding. The church was full. I had a beautiful dress. (*Pause.*) I was a mother at seventeen. "Don't look back" is my motto . . . "look ahead." None of my sisters are married, except Sissy. The others say they are going to learn from my experience and marry them rich husbands. I thought I was so in love with my husband when I married him that I didn't worry if he was rich or not. He didn't leave me destitute, you know. He left me this house. It's got five bedrooms—four upstairs and one downstairs—and two rent houses. Both of my rent houses are rented, thank God—although you don't get rich renting houses here. The children and I can always stay in one room and I could rent out the other four in this house if I had to. Sissy nags me all the time to marry again, find someone who is fond of children. (*Pause.*) But not me. I'm twenty-eight, and I've been married twelve of those twenty-eight years—a mother for ten of them. (*Pause.*) You're a very good dancer. I guess you know that.

HORACE: Thank you. You're very good too. Very light on your feet.

CLAIRE: Thank you. I love to dance.

HORACE: So do I.

CLAIRE: I was nervous when you first asked me to dance. I was afraid I'd forgotten how.

HORACE: I don't think you ever forget something like that.

CLAIRE: I guess not.

HORACE: Do you think dancers are born or can it be taught?

CLAIRE: Oh, I don't know. What do you think?

HORACE: Aunt Virgie says they are born. She says you can't really teach someone to dance who wasn't born with the gift.

(*The record ends. They go to the Victrola.*)

CLAIRE: She should know. I expect she's taught more people to dance than anyone in town.

HORACE: I guess she has.

CLAIRE: What's your favorite song?

HORACE: I have a number of them. I like "Hello, Central, Give Me Heaven." I was at the opera house the night Chauncey Olcott sang that song. When he finished, there wasn't a dry eye in the house.

CLAIRE: Wasn't there?

HORACE: Not a one. But I like "Good Night, Mr. Elephant," "Mighty Lak a Rose," "I Love You Truly," and "Waltz Me Around Again, Willie" . . . I like a lot of them.

CLAIRE: Sometimes I think I'll sell the house and go into Houston with the children. I've never lived in a city.

HORACE: Neither have I.

(*He puts another record on the Victrola and turns it on.*)

CLAIRE: Sissy and her husband leave in the winter for Houston. Your mother still lives there?

HORACE: Yes.

CLAIRE: And your sister?

HORACE: Yes.

CLAIRE: Will you live with them?

HORACE: No. At the boardinghouse where my cousin Minnie stays.

CLAIRE: Oh, yes, you told me. Why don't you live with your mother in Houston?

HORACE: She's no room. She has a very small house.

(*They begin to dance very slowly. They stay down center.*)

HORACE: If I can, I'll try to come down and see you one weekend before my school is finished.

CLAIRE: That would be nice.

HORACE: I'll write you and tell you what weekend.

CLAIRE: I look forward to that.

HORACE: Maybe you can get someone to stay with the children and we could go to a picture show.

CLAIRE: All right.

HORACE (*glancing over at the children, who are both asleep*): Look there—they're sound asleep.

CLAIRE (*glancing over at them*): They're worn out. They go so hard all day. (*He tries to kiss her.*) Be careful. They might wake up and see us. They tell everything they see, you know.

(He persists. She lets him kiss her. They dance a while longer, then he kisses her again.)

CLAIRE: Your Aunt Inez has stopped speaking to me. Do you know why? We used to be best friends, even though she is a lot older than I am. Do you know why she is angry at me?

HORACE: No.

CLAIRE: She was so attentive all the time my husband was sick, and afterwards she used to come to see me almost every day. But then she stopped coming, and she's given a tea and a bridge party since then and didn't invite me to either one. Sissy says it's because I'm receiving company again. She says she doesn't approve of that. "Sissy, what does she want me to do?" I said.

(He kisses her.)

CLAIRE: We better take them back to bed.

(She picks up MOLLY *and he lifts up* BUDDY. *They take them out as the Victrola continues.* VAL *and* ROGER *enter the yard area extreme down left.* VAL *calls "Claire . . . Claire . . ." Claire comes into the living room area. Val calls again: "Claire . . ." She goes to the edge of the living room area.)*

CLAIRE: Oh, I thought I heard someone.

VAL: What are you doing?

CLAIRE: I have a date.

VAL: Who with?

CLAIRE: Horace Robedaux.

VAL: Can we come in and visit for a little?

CLAIRE: I guess so.

(*The two men come into the living room area as* HORACE *enters.*)

Are they still asleep?

HORACE: Yes.

CLAIRE: They didn't move a muscle when we were carrying them in.

HORACE: No.

CLAIRE: Horace and I had to carry the children to their beds. They fell asleep on the couch watching us dance. Horace is a grand dancer. Do you dance, Roger?

ROGER: A little. (*Pause.*) Val can't dance.

VAL: Who the hell wants to dance?

CLAIRE: Some people like to dance, Val.

VAL: Dancing is for sissies.

ROGER: I guess so, if you say so.

VAL: I know so. Mrs. Keith has started a dancing school. For young ladies and gentlemen, she says. My fool sister-in-law enrolled my brother's oldest boy in the dancing school without telling him. When he found out about it, he had a fit. "What are you trying to do—turn him into a sissy?" he said. He yanked him out of that damn dancing school, bought him a twenty-two, and took him deer hunting.

ROGER: Did they get any deer?

VAL: They got all the law allowed. "I'm not gonna have any sissy for a son," my brother said.

HORACE: How do you think a dancing school will do here?

VAL: I think she's gonna starve to death. Would you let a son of yours go to dancing school?

CLAIRE: Sissy wants me to go to the dance next week. "How can I go, Sissy," I said, "unless someone asks me?"

ROGER: Who's Sissy?

CLAIRE: My oldest sister, Bertie Lee. We all call her Sissy.

ROGER: Oh, hasn't anybody asked you to go to the dance?

CLAIRE: No.

HORACE: I want to take you, but I'll be in Houston.

CLAIRE: Horace is going to Houston to business school for six weeks. (*There is an uncomfortable pause.*) Do you boys want a drink?

ROGER: I don't know. Do you, Val?

VAL: It doesn't make any difference to me one way or the other. What have you got to drink?

CLAIRE: Whiskey.

VAL: Is that the whiskey that old traveling salesman brought you?

CLAIRE: Yes, but he's not old.

VAL: He's forty-two.

CLAIRE: I don't consider that old. Do you, Roger?

ROGER: I don't know. I don't have any opinion about it one way or the other.

VAL: Don't you have any opinion about anything?

ROGER: Some things I do.

VAL: You don't call forty-two old?

ROGER: I don't know. I hadn't thought about it.

VAL: What the hell do you call old, Roger?

ROGER: I don't know. What do you call old, Horace?

VAL: What are you bringing Horace into it for?

ROGER: I don't know. I guess I just wanted to hear what he had to say.

VAL: Where is the whiskey?

(CLAIRE *gets it and puts it on the table.*)

CLAIRE: I'll get two more glasses.

VAL: We don't need glasses. (*He takes a swig from the bottle and hands it to* ROGER.)

CLAIRE: Anyway, he is not forty-two. He is thirty-eight.

VAL: Who says?

CLAIRE: He did.

VAL: You'd believe anything. He looks more like fifty-two to me. He dyes his hair.

CLAIRE: He does not dye his hair.

(ROGER *has a drink and hands the bottle back to* VAL.)

VAL: You want a drink, Horace?

HORACE: Thanks. (*He takes the bottle and has a drink.*)

CLAIRE: What makes you think he dyes his hair?

VAL: Because I know he does.

(HORACE *hands the bottle back to* VAL. VAL *offers it to* CLAIRE.)

Claire? . . .

CLAIRE: No, thank you. (*She lights a cigarette.*)

VAL: Give me one of your cigarettes. (*She hands him the package and he takes one.*) Roger, you want a cigarette?

ROGER: Thank you. (*He takes one and he gives the package back to* VAL.)

VAL: You want a cigarette, Horace?

HORACE: No, I smoke cigars.

VAL: What are you trying to do? Act the big man and show off? When did you start smoking cigars?

HORACE: I always have.

(*The Victrola has stopped.* CLAIRE *puts another record on.*)

CLAIRE: Anybody feel like dancing?

(*Pause. No one says anything.*)

Horace? . . .

HORACE: Sure.

(*They dance.* MOLLY *comes in.*)

MOLLY: Mama, I can't sleep with that music.

CLAIRE: All right, honey. (*She turns the Victrola off.*) Go on back to bed now.

MOLLY: I want Horace to take me to bed.

CLAIRE: Oh, Molly!

HORACE: I don't mind.

(*He goes out with her.*)

VAL: Get rid of him.

CLAIRE: You go on and then I will.

VAL: Come on, Roger.

(*He and* ROGER *go.* HORACE *comes back in.*)

CLAIRE: I'm sorry they came by that way. I didn't know what to say.

(HORACE *goes over to her.*)

Horace, I'm going to have to excuse myself. I have a headache.

HORACE: I was going to go anyway.

(*She kisses him.*)

CLAIRE: You're a very nice fellow. I'm going to miss you.

HORACE: Thank you. I'll miss you too.

CLAIRE: You'll write to me?

HORACE: I sure will.

(*She kisses him again.*)

CLAIRE: Good night.

HORACE: Good night.

CLAIRE: You're very sweet. . . .

HORACE: Oh, no, I'm not.

CLAIRE: Yes, you are, and I'll miss you. Write me, now.

HORACE: I will.

(*He goes as the lights fade.*)

(*The lights are brought up down right.* FELIX *and* ARCHIE *bring the chairs back in.* FELIX *has a bottle of whiskey.*)

FELIX: I wonder where Ed got to?

ARCHIE: What time is it?

FELIX: Eleven.

ARCHIE: Then he's probably sitting around down at the drugstore. Let's walk over to Little Bobby's and watch the poker game.

FELIX: No. I don't enjoy watching.

ARCHIE: I think I'll walk over and see how they're doing. Sure you won't go with me?

FELIX: Nope.

(ARCHIE *goes.* FELIX *has a drink of whiskey. He tries again to whistle "Waltz Me Around Again, Willie," then begins a game of solitaire.* HORACE *comes in.*)

FELIX: You're back early.

HORACE: She had a headache. (*Pause.*) Who are you taking to the dance?

FELIX: I don't know yet. Archie is taking an out-of-town girl. She's visiting the Pridgens.

HORACE: I know that.

FELIX: They asked me to take her, but I said I wouldn't unless they showed me a picture first. "She might be homely," I told them. "She's not homely," they said. "Then let me see her picture," I said.

HORACE: Claire doesn't have a date. Her year of mourning is up. I think she would like to go if someone would ask her.

FELIX: Nobody has asked her?

HORACE: No.

FELIX: How do you know?

HORACE: She told me. Why don't you ask her?

FELIX: A date costs a lot of money. It's cheaper going stag. (*Pause.*) Did she tell you to ask me to take her?

HORACE: No.

FELIX: What made you ask me?

HORACE: Because I think she would like to go, and she said her sister Sissy said she should go since her mourning was over, but no one had asked her. I said I would ask her if I were going to be here.

FELIX: Would you ask her?

HORACE: sure.

FELIX: Do you like her?

HORACE: Yes, I do.

FELIX: Does she like you?

HORACE: She likes me. I don't know how much. She sees Val Stanton too. And a traveling man, and some others too, I guess.

(FELIX *has a drink. He passes the bottle to* HORACE, *who has a drink. The courthouse clock strikes twelve.*)

FELIX: I'm going to bed. Are you turning in now?

HORACE: In a little. I can stay up as late as I want tonight. I don't have to get up in the morning and go to work.

FELIX: You sure don't.

HORACE: Felix . . .

FELIX: Yes?

HORACE: Will you take her to the dance?

FELIX: Who?

HORACE: Claire.

FELIX: Let some of these fellows she's seeing take her.

HORACE: They haven't asked her. Will you take her as a favor to me?

FELIX: I can't afford to take a girl I like.

HORACE: I'll give you the money.

FELIX: I thought you had to be so careful with your money.

HORACE: I do, but I'll cut down on something else.

FELIX: All right.

HORACE: Don't tell her I asked you to do this.

FELIX: I won't. (*He takes his shirt off.*)

HORACE: I've changed my mind. I think I'll turn in too.

FELIX: And I've changed my mind. I don't want to take Claire. If she's seeing Val, let him take her.

HORACE: He can't dance.

FELIX: Let him learn. (*He lights a cigarette.*)

(BUDDY *comes to the edge of the area.*)

BUDDY (*calling*): Horace . . .

HORACE: What do you want, Buddy?

BUDDY: Val is beating up my mama.

FELIX: You better stay out of that, boy.

HORACE: I can take care of myself, Felix.

(*He goes out.* BUDDY *follows after him, then pauses. He goes to* FELIX.)

BUDDY: Give me a nickel.

FELIX: I don't have a nickel.

(BUDDY *runs after* HORACE *as* ED *comes in. He is very drunk.*)

FELIX: Where the hell have you been?

ED: I'm drunk.

FELIX: I know you're drunk.

ED: No, I mean I'm real drunk. I'm so drunk it took me an hour to find the damn house. I'm so drunk I got mixed up and walked and I walked and I kept hollering "Where the hell is my boardinghouse?" but nobody heard me and so I kept on walking, and you know where I ended up?

FELIX: No.

ED: Damn right you don't. Guess.

FELIX: No. I don't want to guess. I want to go to bed.

ED: The graveyard. I was in the middle of the damn grave-yard, and I said this sure as hell ain't the boardinghouse and I met old Matt Johnson.

FELIX: In the graveyard?

ED: I weren't in the graveyard then. I don't know where the hell I was, and I said, "Matt, where the hell is the boardinghouse I live in?" And he brought me to the cor-ner and he pointed and he said, "There it is yonder." And so here I am. Where's the bed? I'm so drunk I can't find the bed.

FELIX: There's the bed over there.

ED: Where?

FELIX: Right there. Get your clothes off and get in it.

ED: I'm drunk. (*He falls over the bed.*)

FELIX: I thought you were broke. How did you buy whiskey if you were broke?

ED: I got friends.

(*He collapses over the bed as the lights fade.*)

(*The lights are brought up down left on the yard area.* HORACE *comes running in and stops at the edge of the area as* BUDDY *joins him.*)

HORACE: Did your mama tell you to come for me?

BUDDY: Yes Sir.

HORACE: You're sure?

BUDDY: Yes Sir. Give me another nickel, please.

HORACE: I gave you a nickel earlier.

BUDDY: I lost it on the way to get you.

(HORACE *gives him a nickel.* CLAIRE *comes out from the house area.*)

CLAIRE: Horace, you're going to think we're crazy. Val came over here after you left and Buddy and Molly heard him and asked me to tell him to go and I did and he began to get upset and started talking loud and arguing . . .

BUDDY: He hit you.

CLAIRE: He didn't hit me, Buddy.

BUDDY: He did too.

CLAIRE: He did not, now. He threatened to hit me. He's a bully, but I'm not afraid of him.

BUDDY: He hit you . . .

CLAIRE: Buddy, he didn't hit me.

BUDDY: He did too—I saw him and Molly saw him.

CLAIRE: You thought you saw him hit me.

BUDDY: And he wouldn't leave when you asked him to go.

CLAIRE: Well, he's gone now, so let's all go to bed. You won't be able to keep your eyes open tomorrow in school.

(BUDDY *starts to go.*)

Aren't you going to thank Horace for coming over here?

BUDDY: Thank you, Horace. (*He pauses.*) Can I have another piece of that candy before I go to bed?

CLAIRE: No.

BUDDY: Why?

CLAIRE: Because I don't want you eating candy this time of night.

BUDDY: I just want one piece.

CLAIRE: All right. Just one piece and then get right into bed.

(BUDDY *goes into the house area.*)

HORACE: How is your headache?

CLAIRE: It's a little better. I'm awfully sorry we bothered you.

HORACE: I can sleep in there on the couch the rest of the night if it would make you feel better.

CLAIRE: No. Val won't be back tonight. He wouldn't have come here in the first place if he hadn't been drinking. I made the mistake of offering him another drink, thinking that would get rid of him, but it didn't, of course. It just set him off, and he began to act in a way he shouldn't and I had to ask him to behave, and he began to argue and that woke the children up and they got frightened.

(BUDDY *comes out of the house area.*)

BUDDY: Not but three pieces of candy left out of that whole box. What hog has been into that candy?

CLAIRE: I don't know, Buddy. I only had one piece.

BUDDY: I think the name of the hog is Val.

CLAIRE: Don't be fresh, Buddy, and go on to bed. You probably have been helping yourself to that candy all night behind my back.

BUDDY: I have not.

CLAIRE: Well, don't stand there and argue with me in the middle of the night. Go on to bed, please.

(BUDDY *goes back into the house area.*)

CLAIRE: Look, there's the new moon. Make a wish.

(*She closes her eyes and makes a wish.* HORACE *closes his eyes, and makes a wish. She opens her eyes. He opens his.*)

Did you make a wish?

HORACE: Yes, I did.

CLAIRE: Don't tell me what it was, though, because then it won't come true. (*Pause.*) Did any of the wishes you ever made on a new moon come true?

HORACE: I don't think so.

CLAIRE: One of mine almost did. I wished last summer we could take the children to Colorado during the hottest part of the summer, but we ended up in Galveston instead because it was cheaper to go there. Anyway, we got out of the heat here. I think if I hadn't gotten away someplace after my husband died, I'd a gone crazy. (*Pause.*) This was the hottest summer of all, I think. I wished many a day this summer I was back in Galveston. My friend Ned has a house in Galveston and he keeps asking us there, but I don't like to be obligated. His sister keeps house for him. He says she would love to have us, too. She's never married. How did you feel when your mother married again?

HORACE: Well . . .

CLAIRE: Did you want her to marry again?

HORACE: Yes and no. Sometimes I did and sometimes I didn't.

CLAIRE: How long did she wait before she married again?

HORACE: Not too long.

CLAIRE: Did your father leave her some money?

HORACE: No.

CLAIRE: How did she support you and your sister?

HORACE: Well, she kept a boardinghouse with her sister for a while, but they couldn't make a go of it. They couldn't ever collect the money from the boarders. Then she went into Houston and got a job working as a seamstress in Munn's Department Store.

CLAIRE: Did you live with her in Houston?

HORACE: No. She left me back here with my grandparents. She took my sister with her. That's where she met Mr. Davenport.

CLAIRE: Who is that?

HORACE: The man she married.

CLAIRE: Why didn't you go and live with them then?

HORACE: Because Mr. Davenport didn't want me. He had to go to work when he was twelve and he thought that was good for a boy, so they left me here and I lived with my grandparents until they died and then I lived with my Aunt Virgie. She has been like a mother to me. I'm crazy about my Aunt Virgie.

CLAIRE: She's a lovely lady.

HORACE: I think so.

(*Pause.*)

CLAIRE: Funny thing it's so quiet all of a sudden, isn't it?

HORACE: Yes, it is.

CLAIRE: Everybody on this street has gone to bed but us.

HORACE: Not everybody. There is a gambling game over at Mr. Bobby's. That could go on all night.

CLAIRE: Do you like to gamble?

HORACE: Not a whole lot. I have an uncle that gambles all the time—my Uncle Albert. He's had farms and he's lost them all by gambling. He gambles every night, all night long. I'm a pretty serious person, I guess, Claire. I hope you don't think I'm too serious.

CLAIRE: No, I don't.

HORACE: But I sure want to amount to something. I'm ambitious. I don't really know what I'm ambitious about just yet, but I sure am ambitious. That's why I'm going to Houston to take a business course. I thought for a while of reading law in Mr. George Tyler's office, but his son is reading law there now, and anyway, I'm not sure I want to be a lawyer, even though my father was. (*Pause.*) We were so poor when my father died we didn't have enough money to put a tombstone on his grave. The first money I get ahead, I'm going to put a tombstone on his grave.

CLAIRE: That was the first thing I did, put a tombstone on my husband's grave. A big one too. As big as any they've got out there. Sissy said, "Have you gone crazy? You can't afford a big tombstone like that. You'll go to the poorhouse in a month if you keep on spending money like that." "Well, I can't help it," I said. "I may be going to the poorhouse, but he's going to have a fine, big tombstone." Do you have a picture of your father?

HORACE: Yes, we do.

CLAIRE: Well, that's a comfort. I don't have one of my husband. I wish I did for the children's sake.

HORACE: Do you have a picture of yourself?

CLAIRE: Yes, I do. I went down and had one taken a week after my husband died, so in case anything happened to me the children would at least have my picture to remember me by.

HORACE: May I have a picture of you to take with me to Houston?

CLAIRE: You certainly may. And may I have a picture of you to remember you by?

HORACE: Yes, you can. As soon as I have some taken.

CLAIRE: Molly says you have a beautiful voice.

HORACE: Oh, I don't know about that.

CLAIRE: Sing something for me. I love to hear people sing. I missed all of that by marrying so young. So many of the young men go around and serenade different girls at night. Have you ever done that?

HORACE: Once or twice. (*He sings "Sweet Alice, Ben Bolt."*)

CLAIRE: That's a very sad song.

HORACE: Yes, I guess it is.

CLAIRE: I always feel like crying when I hear that song.

HORACE: I'm sorry. I didn't mean to make you feel sad.

CLAIRE: It doesn't take a lot to make me feel sad these days. That's why I like you to come over. I always feel better after talking to you. I'll miss you while you're away in Houston.

HORACE: And I'll miss you. (*He goes to her and holds her.*)

CLAIRE: Are you going to forget all about me while you're in Houston?

HORACE: No.

CLAIRE: You promise me?

HORACE: I promise.

(MOLLY *comes out holding the empty candy box.*)

MOLLY: Buddy has his mouth so full of candy he almost choked to death.

CLAIRE: Is he all right now?

MOLLY: Yes. I wish he had choked. He's a hog.

CLAIRE: Now, you don't mean that.

MOLLY: I do too. He ate every last piece of that candy.

CLAIRE: We'll get you some tomorrow. Now go on back to bed.

MOLLY: When are you going to bed?

CLAIRE: Pretty soon.

MOLLY: I'm going to wait for you.

CLAIRE: Buddy is in bed.

MOLLY: But he's not asleep. He's whistling.

CLAIRE: Tell him to stop.

MOLLY: He won't listen to me. Anyway, he says he's whistling to keep Val away. He says if Val comes back here and hears him whistling, he'll think there is a man in the house and be scared and leave.

CLAIRE: Now you go tell Buddy not to worry. He's not coming back tonight.

MOLLY: Is he ever coming back?

CLAIRE: Yes, when he can behave like a gentleman.

MOLLY: Buddy says he heard Val say Uncle Ned dyes his hair. Is that true?

CLAIRE: No.

MOLLY: Why did he say it if it wasn't true?

CLAIRE: Because he's jealous of your Uncle Ned.

MOLLY: Why?

CLAIRE: Because Uncle Ned asked me to marry him and he thinks I might.

MOLLY: Please come to bed now, Mama.

CLAIRE: All right, darling. (*She takes* HORACE's *hand.*) Good night, Horace.

HORACE: Good night.

CLAIRE: Write to us.

HORACE: I will. Good night, Molly.

(HORACE *leaves.* CLAIRE *picks* MOLLY *up and holds her.*)

MOLLY: Why are you doing that?

CLAIRE: Because I love you.

MOLLY: Do you love Buddy too?

CLAIRE: Of course I love Buddy. (*She sings a snatch of* "*Sweet Alice, Ben Bolt.*")

MOLLY: That's a sad song, Mama. Don't sing that song. I don't like it.

CLAIRE: I don't either.

MOLLY: Sing me a happy song. Sing me "Good Night, Irene."

CLAIRE: All right—if I can remember it. (*She sings* "*Good Night, Irene.*")

(*She continues to sing as she goes offstage. The lights fade.*)

(*The lights come up right on the roominghouse area.* FELIX *and* ARCHIE *are there.*)

FELIX: I guess Spence is staying over at Little Bobby's until the game breaks up.

ARCHIE: I guess so.

FELIX: Maybe they'll even let him into the game.

ARCHIE: Oh, no—not that game. That's a serious game with very high stakes.

FELIX: Spence says his ambition is to become a professional gambler. Do you think he'll ever get to be one?

ARCHIE: I don't know.

FELIX: What do you want to become, Archie?

ARCHIE: Oh, hell. I don't know. Have a good time, I guess. (*Pause.*) What do you want to do?

FELIX: I don't know. Maybe we should go to business school in Houston like Horace.

ARCHIE: No. No.

FELIX: We have to do something.

ARCHIE: I've had jobs.

FELIX: Not many.

ARCHIE: And you've had jobs.

FELIX: Not many. I helped take the census one year.

ARCHIE: That was a job.

FELIX: I worked for two months over at the cotton gin during cotton season.

ARCHIE: And that was a job too.

FELIX: I hope to be rich one day, that's all I know.

ARCHIE: What are your plans for getting rich?

FELIX: Marry me a rich woman.

ARCHIE: Maybe you should set up to Claire.

FELIX: She's not rich.

ARCHIE: She has three houses. One she lives in and two she rents.

FELIX: You can't give houses away here.

ARCHIE: Three houses are better than nothing.

FELIX: Not for me. I'm talking about real rich. (*Pause.*) Do you think that's what old Horace has on his mind? Getting hold of those rent houses?

ARCHIE: I don't know. What the hell is Ed doing in my bed?

FELIX: He came home so drunk he didn't know what bed he was in.

(HORACE *enters.*)

HORACE: I thought you would all be asleep.

FELIX: We were, but Ed came home drunk and woke us up.

ARCHIE: Want to play some cards?

HORACE: Nope.

ARCHIE: Come on . . .

HORACE: No. I'm scared to. I only have enough money to last me the six weeks in Houston. I won't even be able to afford cigars or a newspaper. If I even lost a dollar, I would be in trouble.

ARCHIE: Felix said you were going to give him the money to take Claire to the dance. How were you going to do that if you have so little money?

HORACE: I don't know. It was crazy of me. I would have been in trouble if he'd taken me up on it.

FELIX: Maybe you'd win. Then you'd have a little extra.

HORACE: No.

ARCHIE: I'll loan you a dollar. If you lose it, you can pay me back when you get back from Houston and go back to work.

FELIX: Come on, Horace.

HORACE: All right, but if I lose this dollar that's the end of it.

FELIX: Dwight Lester came by here and wanted me to go serenading some of the gals in town this weekend. He wanted three fellows to go with him, and hire a guitar and a fiddle player to go around with us. I said no. No more serenading for me. It costs too much. Let the girls come here and serenade me. Last September we went serenading, and when we got to Eloise Dockery's house, I started singing and Old Man Dockery came out with a shotgun and said if we didn't shut up he'd blow our brains out.

ARCHIE: Do you think he meant it?

FELIX: We didn't wait to find out.

HORACE: How much does it cost to hire a guitar and a fiddle player?

FELIX: Plenty. More than I have. Why, are you thinking of serenading someone?

HORACE: Maybe.

FELIX: Who?

HORACE: Claire.

ARCHIE: Tonight?

HORACE: No, not tonight—when I get back from Houston.

(ARCHIE *shuffles the cards.*)

FELIX: Did you straighten Val out?

HORACE: He was gone by the time I got there.

ARCHIE: I think he's after her money.

HORACE: Whose money?

ARCHIE: Claire's.

HORACE: She doesn't have any money.

ARCHIE: She owns her house and two rent houses. That's more than Val has. (*He deals the cards.*)

HORACE: Did you ever know a man that dyed his hair?

ARCHIE: No.

FELIX: I knew a man once that did. The dye got stuck in his skin someway and turned his skin a blue gray.

ARCHIE: Who was that?

FELIX: I forget his name. Why did you ask that question, Horace?

HORACE: Because Val said the traveling man that calls on Claire dyes his hair. Claire says he doesn't.

FELIX: Val is a lot of hot air.

ARCHIE: What's the name of the traveling man?

HORACE: Ned.

ARCHIE: Ned what?

HORACE: I don't know. I only know Ned. He sold to my uncle. He don't have any gray hairs, come to think of it, and I think he's older than my Uncle Albert. My Uncle Albert already has some gray hairs.

ARCHIE: And he calls on Claire?

HORACE: Yep.

ARCHIE: I wonder why she lets an old man like that call on her.

HORACE: She gets lonely, she says.

ARCHIE: I talked to White Jenkins the other day. He said he was walking around the other night—he couldn't sleep, he said. He walked all over town trying to get sleepy.

FELIX: White is very nervous.

ARCHIE: He's taking medicine for it.

HORACE: For his nerves?

ARCHIE: Yes. He carries a little bottle of medicine around with him all the time and every time he gets nervous, he takes a swig from the bottle.

FELIX: I bet it's just whiskey.

ARCHIE: No, it's medicine. He got a prescription. He showed it to me. Anyway, he said the other night when he was walking around he seen Val come out of Claire's house at five o'clock, just before daybreak. (*Pause.*) He said he's seen him come out of there at all hours.

HORACE: Let's play cards if we're going to play.

FELIX: I wonder if he's ever seen old Horace come out of there at daybreak? (*He and* ARCHIE *laugh.*)

ARCHIE: Has he, Horace?

HORACE: Let's play cards.

FELIX: Old Horace is blushing.

(ARCHIE *and* FELIX *laugh again. This time* HORACE *joins them and they begin to play cards.* ED *stirs in his sleep.*)

ED (*muttering*): Roberta . . .

HORACE: Who's Roberta?

FELIX: I don't know. Who is Roberta, Archie?

ARCHIE: I never heard of her.

FELIX: Who's Roberta, Ed?

ED (*muttering*): Roberta . . . Roberta . . .

(*Pause.* ED *begins to snore.* HORACE, FELIX, *and* ARCHIE *continue playing cards.*)

ED (*muttering*): Roberta . . . Roberta . . .

FELIX: I never knew Ed to go out with a girl, did you? I thought he was too shy to go with a girl.

ARCHIE: He's too shy to go with a nice girl. I've known him to take out plenty of the other kind.

FELIX: I've heard a lot of nice girls say they wouldn't go out with him because he didn't respect women.

ED (*muttering*): Roberta . . . Roberta . . .

FELIX: Shut up, Ed. Roberta ain't here.

ARCHIE: I wonder if Roberta is a nice girl?

FELIX: And I wonder if he respects her.

(BUDDY *comes to the edge of the area.*)

BUDDY: Horace . . . (*Pause.*) Horace . . .

(HORACE *puts the cards down and goes to him.*)

HORACE: What do you want now, Buddy?

BUDDY: Val snuck back into the house. My mama doesn't

know me and Molly heard him. She thinks we're asleep. Come beat him up, Horace.

HORACE: It's none of my business, Buddy, if your mama wants him there.

BUDDY: She don't want him there, but she's scared to tell him to leave.

HORACE: How do you know?

BUDDY: She told me that. She's afraid he'll hit her.

HORACE: Now, he doesn't hit her, Buddy. That's just your imagination. She told me that. (*He goes outside.*) You had better go on home, Buddy.

(ED *rises from the couch and gives a wild, bloodcurdling scream.*)

BUDDY (*terrified*): What's that?

HORACE: It's one of the fellows in there.

BUDDY: What's the matter with him? Is somebody trying to kill him?

HORACE: He's drunk.

BUDDY: My God! I thought they were trying to kill him.

HORACE: He'll be all right.

ED (*calling out*): Roberta . . . Roberta . . .

BUDDY: Who is he calling?

HORACE: Roberta.

BUDDY: Who is Roberta?

HORACE: We don't know. You better go on home, Buddy.

BUDDY: You walk with me. I'm scared.

HORACE: You weren't scared to come over here.

BUDDY: But now I heard that drunk man hollering like someone was trying to kill him. I'm scared.

HORACE: All right. Come on.

(*They exit as the lights fade.*)

(*The lights are brought up down left on the yard area.* BUDDY *and* HORACE *enter.*)

HORACE: This is as far as I'm going.

BUDDY: Give me a nickel.

HORACE: Now, I gave you two nickels tonight.

BUDDY: This is for Molly—you only gave her one. It hurt her feelings when I told her you gave me two.

HORACE: All right. (*He gives him the nickel.*)

BUDDY: Do you think Uncle Ned dyes his hair?

HORACE: I don't know.

BUDDY: Val says he does. I think Val's a liar, don't you?

HORACE: I don't know.

(VAL *comes out of the house area.*)

BUDDY: Yonder comes Val. I told you he was in there. (*He calls out.*) Val, Horace is going to beat you up.

VAL: Yeah? I'm scared to death. (*He grabs* HORACE.) Look, I don't like being spied on.

HORACE: I'm not spying on you.

(*He throws* VAL'S *hands off.* VAL *pushes him and he pushes him back. They start to fight. It's a savage fight.*)

BUDDY (*yelling*): Mama . . . Molly . . . come watch . . . they're having a fight! Horace is going to kill Val! Kill him, Horace! Kill him!

(CLAIRE *and* MOLLY *enter from the house area.*)

CLAIRE: Stop it! Stop it! Val, have you gone crazy? Buddy, be careful!

(VAL *knocks* HORACE *out.*)

Go on home, Val.

VAL: That damn sneak was spying on us.

CLAIRE: Go on home, Val.

MOLLY: Is he dead, Mama?

CLAIRE: I don't think so.

(CLAIRE *bends over* HORACE. VAL *exits.*)

CLAIRE: Horace . . . Horace . . . (HORACE *opens his eyes.*) Are you all right?

HORACE: Yes. Where did he go? (*He slowly tries to get up.*)

CLAIRE: He went home. Now you go home too. And no more fighting. Do you promise me?

(HORACE *sits up.*)

Are you all right?

HORACE: I'll be all right.

CLAIRE: Buddy, did you bring him back over here? Buddy?

BUDDY: Molly, he gave you a nickel too.

CLAIRE: Buddy, I don't want you changing the subject on me. Did you go and get Horace and bring him here?

BUDDY: Well . . .

(HORACE *is on his feet now.*)

HORACE: I wasn't spying, you know. I don't spy on people. Buddy came over to the house to tell me he had come back, and I said it was none of my business and for him to go on home, but he was afraid to walk back by himself.

BUDDY: Because of this drunk man. He hollered like he was being stabbed to death and he hollered this lady's name. What was her name, Horace?

HORACE: Roberta.

BUDDY: Do you know who that is, Mama?

CLAIRE: No.

HORACE: I'll come back next weekend from Houston and take you to the dance.

CLAIRE: Thank you, but I've already been asked.

HORACE: Who asked you?

CLAIRE: Val.

HORACE: I thought he couldn't dance.

CLAIRE: He can't, but he's coming over before then and I'm going to teach him. Thank you anyway. And he asked me to marry him too.

HORACE: He did?

CLAIRE: Yes. Now I have two offers of marriage and I'm real confused about what to do.

MOLLY: Don't marry Val, Mama.

CLAIRE: Shh. Now, you mind your own business. Val is

rough and all, but to tell you the truth I like him better than Ned.

MOLLY: Why?

CLAIRE: Because he's nearer my own age, of course, but then he doesn't have a job. He says he's going to get one soon, but I've never known him to keep a job more than a week or two. What do you think I ought to do, Horace?

HORACE: I don't know. I swear I don't.

BUDDY: Don't marry Val.

CLAIRE: I'm asking Horace, not you.

BUDDY: I'll run away from home if you marry Val.

CLAIRE: Be quiet, Buddy, and go on back to bed. And you too, Molly.

MOLLY: I like Uncle Ned. We have a picture of Uncle Ned in there. Did you ever see what he looks like, Horace?

CLAIRE: Yes, Horace knows what he looks like, Molly. Now go on, both of you.

(*They start away.*)

CLAIRE: Say good night to Horace.

BUDDY: Good night.

MOLLY: Good night.

HORACE: Good night.

CLAIRE: Good night.

(*They go.*)

Sissy says Val is just after what I have. She says he'll marry me and get me to sell my houses, spend the money, and leave me flat. That's what Sissy says he'll do. Val says I'm the first girl he's ever asked to marry because I'm the first girl he's ever loved. Ned says he's determined to be married before he's forty and he'll be forty soon. I guess you're too young to think about marrying yet, aren't you?

HORACE: I think about it.

CLAIRE: Did you ever meet a girl you'd like to marry?

HORACE: I like you.

CLAIRE: You don't think I'm too old for you?

HORACE: No. My Aunt Virgie is six years older than my Uncle Doc.

CLAIRE: You told me that. And are they happily married?

HORACE: Oh, yes. I think so.

CLAIRE: They certainly seem congenial.

HORACE: But I couldn't consider marriage to anyone at present. . . .

CLAIRE: You couldn't?

HORACE: No. I couldn't. I have no job. I have no money. I would want to have a job and a little money saved before I married.

CLAIRE: After my husband died I swore I would never marry again. Maybe I won't. Maybe I won't marry anybody. I mean, why should I? I have a nice life. I can take care of myself and the children. I can have all the company I want. Sissy said my husband wanted me to marry again. He never said that to me, but Sissy said just before he died he called her into the room and he said, "I know I'm going to die and I want you to promise me one thing before I die. I want you to promise me you'll see to it that Claire marries again. Because I want my children to have a father as they're growing up." Do you believe he said that?

HORACE: I don't know.

CLAIRE: Sometimes I think he did, but then again I think he didn't. Sissy will tell you anything to get you to do what she wants, and she wants me to marry again, that's for sure. I said, "Sissy, worry about the others. You have three other sisters that have never married, and in my opinion, if they wait much longer, are in danger of becoming old maids. Nag them about marrying." "They're not twenty-five yet," Sissy says, "so I wouldn't worry about their becoming old maids." "You were married at fourteen," I said, "Mama was fifteen, and I was sixteen. What's wrong with them?" "They're waiting for rich husbands," she said. "So am I," I said. "Well, then marry Ned," she said. "He's rich." "How do you know what he's worth?" I said. "Well, I got eyes," she said. "He has a good job and is always buying you and the children presents." And he is, of course. He gave me the ring and a wristwatch, and the next time he comes, he said he wants me to go with him to the jewelry store and pick me out a diamond bar pin.

(MOLLY *comes out.*)

Have you gone crazy? It's four in the morning. Get on back to bed.

MOLLY: I can't find Uncle Ned's picture.

CLAIRE: What do you want with his picture?

MOLLY: I want to look at it.

CLAIRE: At four in the morning?

MOLLY: Where did you put it?

CLAIRE: My God, Molly, I don't know where I put it. It was on my dresser the last I remember.

MOLLY: It's not there now.

CLAIRE: I bet it is. I just bet you didn't see it, is all. You never can find anything.

MOLLY: I bet Val took it.

CLAIRE: Why would he take it?

MOLLY: Buddy said he did.

CLAIRE: Buddy is crazy. He blames Val for everything.

MOLLY: Here's the ring and the wristwatch he gave Mama.

CLAIRE: Where did you get those?

MOLLY: In your dresser. (*She shows them to* HORACE.) They're real diamonds, aren't they, Mama?

CLAIRE: Yes.

MOLLY: He said they cost a lot of money, didn't he, Mama?

CLAIRE: Yes.

MOLLY: How much?

CLAIRE: He didn't say exactly. Now, go put them back where you found them. If you lost them, I would die.

(BUDDY *comes out with the picture.*)

BUDDY: I found Uncle Ned's picture.

MOLLY: Where was it?

BUDDY: On Mama's dresser.

CLAIRE: See . . . I told you. Now get back to bed . . . both of you! And take the picture and the jewelry and put them back on my dresser. And in the future, if you please, don't touch my things without permission.

BUDDY: Let me show his picture to Horace first.

CLAIRE: My God, Buddy, he doesn't want to see his picture. How many times do I have to tell you a thing?

BUDDY: Do you want to see it, Horace? (HORACE *glances at it.*) Do you think he's a nice-looking fellow?

HORACE: Yes, I do.

BUDDY: Do you think he dyes his hair like Val says?

HORACE: I don't know, Buddy.

MOLLY: Val is a liar.

CLAIRE: Shh.

MOLLY: Buddy says he is.

CLAIRE: Don't call people liars. It isn't nice.

HORACE: Now go to bed, Buddy. Mind your mama.

MOLLY: Uncle Ned never sends us away. He just begs Mama to let us stay with them at all times.

CLAIRE: Well, Horace isn't your Uncle Ned. So go on to bed now, both of you, before I get mad.

(*They go.*)

CLAIRE: Sissy says they need a man's discipline, and I guess they do. Their daddy never could say no to them about a thing. He was always softhearted as far as they were concerned.

(HORACE *reaches out to her. They embrace and they kiss. She touches his face.*)

Horace, you have blood on your face.

HORACE: It doesn't matter. (*He reaches out to her again.*)

CLAIRE: I'll go and get some water and wash it off.

(*She starts away. He pulls her back to him.*)

HORACE: No, don't go.

CLAIRE: Well, give me your handkerchief and I'll wipe it off.

(*He takes out his handkerchief. She wipes the blood away.*)

HORACE: When I come back from Houston, I'm going to get together with some fellows and a guitar and a fiddle player, and we'll come over here one night and serenade you.

CLAIRE: Oh, that would be nice. I would like that. I've never had anyone serenade me in my whole life.

(ROGER *comes in. He has a bottle of whiskey.*)

ROGER: Oh, excuse me. I was looking for Val.

CLAIRE: Val's not here.

ROGER: Oh, excuse me. He told me he was coming over here.

CLAIRE: Well, he's not here.

ROGER: Was he here?

CLAIRE: Yes, but he's gone.

ROGER: Has he been gone long?

CLAIRE: Not too long.

ROGER: He asked me to loan him the money to buy a bottle of whiskey and I said I would, and then he asked if I would mind buying it and bringing it to him over here as he was coming back over here to see you and he wanted to give you a little present.

CLAIRE: He was here but he left.

ROGER: Oh, I'm sorry I was so late getting over here, but he told me to take my time and I got to talking to some friends where I went to get the whiskey. I had to get this fellow out of bed to sell me the whiskey and that made him mad as a hornet at first, being awakened out of a sound sleep and all. But then I told him the circumstances and all, and he was real nice about it. (*He hands her the bottle.*) I guess this is for you.

CLAIRE: Thank you.

ROGER: It's not the best whiskey in the world, but it is the best I could do this time of night. I think it's as good as the whiskey that fellow from Galveston brought you, though.

CLAIRE: I appreciate it, thank you.

ROGER: I meant to say earlier I'm not much of a dancer myself, but if you could stand it, I would like to take you to the dance next week myself.

CLAIRE: Thank you, but I've already been asked.

ROGER: Who asked you?

CLAIRE: Val.

ROGER: He did?

CLAIRE: Yes.

ROGER: When?

CLAIRE: Just now.

ROGER: He can't dance.

CLAIRE: I'm going to teach him.

(ROGER *reaches in his hip pocket and takes out a bottle.*)

ROGER: I bought myself a bottle the same time I bought yours. Can I offer anyone a drink?

CLAIRE: Not me. Thank you.

ROGER: Horace?

HORACE: No, thank you.

ROGER: Do you mind if I have one? I find it damp and cold out. (*He has a swig.*)

(MOLLY *comes out.*)

MOLLY: Mama . . .

CLAIRE: What?

MOLLY: Buddy has Uncle Ned's picture in bed with him.

CLAIRE: Has he gone crazy? Why is he doing something foolish like that?

MOLLY: I had it under my pillow and as I was falling asleep, he snuck over and took it and put it in his bed.

CLAIRE: What do you want me to do about it?

MOLLY: I want it under my pillow.

CLAIRE: Oh, my God!

(*She leaves.* MOLLY *goes after her.*)

ROGER: Val says he stays over here sometimes. You know, like a husband and wife. But Val is such a big liar, I don't know if he's telling the truth or not. Do you think he does?

HORACE: I don't know.

ROGER: He says he tells her he's going to marry her so she'll let him stay. But he says he don't have no intention of marrying nobody. I thought to myself, "She'd be a fool to marry you, a man that can't even buy a bottle of whiskey as a present." I think she's right pretty. Don't you?

HORACE: Yes, I do.

ROGER: And she comes from a lovely family, you know.

HORACE: I know she does.

ROGER: She has four sisters. One is married and three aren't. The married one is called Sissy. The unmarried ones are called Nadine, Lily Belle, and Clara Gertrude.

HORACE: Yes. I know them all.

ROGER: They are going to have a hard time getting married; they are all three plain. I understand they all went to live with an aunt in Nacogdoches, as no one here will ask them out. . . . (*Pause.*) Claire is the beauty. She's as pretty as any girl in town. Do you think she would go out with me if I asked her?

HORACE: I don't know.

ROGER: Val says she wouldn't. He says I'm not refined enough for her. "I may not be refined," I says, "but I have a job and I work steady. I don't have to borrow money to buy anyone a bottle of whiskey." Do you always bring a present when you come to see her?

HORACE: Yes, I do.

ROGER: What did you bring tonight?

HORACE: Candy.

ROGER: Do you think any of it's handy? I have a sweet tooth. I'd like a piece of candy.

HORACE: It's all gone.

ROGER: That's all right. What kind of candy was it?

HORACE: Assorted chocolates.

ROGER: I love chocolates of all kinds. (*Pause.*) I like hot tamales too. Do you like hot tamales?

HORACE: Yes, I do.

ROGER: That Mescan Eli sure makes good hot tamales. Don't you think so?

HORACE: Yes, I do.

ROGER: I think I heard you say you're going to business school?

HORACE: Yes, in Houston.

ROGER: I'd have a hard time in business school, even if I could afford it. I only went to the second grade in school. How far did you go?

HORACE: Sixth.

ROGER: Why did you quit?

HORACE: I had to go to work.

ROGER: Where did you work?

HORACE: All over. At a plantation store, over in a store in Glen Flora, then for my uncle here, and Mr. Jackson.

ROGER: That's quite a record. (*Pause.*) Do you prefer the light or dark meat of chicken?

HORACE: The light.

ROGER: I prefer the dark—drumsticks and second joints. (*Pause.*) My God, there's daylight beginning! You reckon she'll be back out?

HORACE: I don't know.

ROGER: I expect she'll be back out to say good night to you at least. (*Pause.*) Well, I'll say good night to you. I have to work tomorrow. Say good night to Claire for me. Tell her I'm sorry I had to leave before I could tell her good night myself.

(*He goes.* HORACE *cleans the sleeve of his jacket.* CLAIRE *comes outside.*)

CLAIRE: It's come to me just as clear what to do. I'm not going to marry anybody.

HORACE: You're not?

CLAIRE: No. I'm going to sell these three houses and move to Houston with the children and get me a duplex. We can live downstairs and rent out the upstairs. That way I'll always have some kind of an income. So don't be surprised if you get a call at your boardinghouse saying, "I'm here." (*Pause.*) Kiss me good night now and go home. I'm mortally tired and I know you must be. (*He kisses her.*) I'm so relieved, now it's come to me what to do. The kids almost had a fit when I told them I wasn't going to marry Ned. But I said, "Shoot, I'm not getting married just to please you." I have a right to lead my own life, don't you think?

HORACE: Yes, I do.

(*She kisses him again.*)

CLAIRE: Good night, Horace.

HORACE: Good night.

CLAIRE: Buddy and Molly say good night.

HORACE: Tell them good night for me.

CLAIRE: They sure like you.

HORACE: I like them.

CLAIRE: Next to Ned, they say they like you best of all the men that come to see me.

HORACE: Thank you.

CLAIRE: Here's my picture I promised you.

HORACE: Thank you very much. (*Pause.*) Claire?

CLAIRE: Yes. . . .

HORACE: I'm glad you're not marrying right away. I'm certainly glad about that.

CLAIRE: Are you? Well, I'm glad about it too. Good night.

HORACE: Good night.

(*She goes. He waits a beat and starts away as the lights fade.*)

(*The lights are brought up down right.* ARCHIE, FELIX, *and* SPENCE *are there.* ED *is still in bed.*)

SPENCE: Poker is a serious business. It's a science. I saw thousands of dollars pass hands tonight. Luck had nothing to do with it. Cool heads won. There were two gamblers there from Galveston. They never said a word to nobody all evening—just kept their eyes on the cards. Of course, everybody says they won by cheating.

ARCHIE: Do you think they cheated?

SPENCE: If they did, no one caught them at it.

ARCHIE: One of those gamblers was redheaded, and the other had black hair.

SPENCE: That's right.

(HORACE *enters. He has the picture of* CLAIRE.)

ARCHIE: We found out who Roberta was.

HORACE: Who is she?

ARCHIE: She's a twin. She has a twin sister named Alberta. Alberta and Roberta. They travel in a medicine show. Spence and Ed met them over at a barbecue outside of Ganado.

HORACE: What were they doing at Ganado?

SPENCE: I don't know. I didn't ask them. (*Pause.*) I went over to that gambling game at Little Bobby's. Your Uncle Albert was in it. He lost his shirt.

HORACE: It's not the first time.

SPENCE: But it might be the last. This time they got him for fifteen thousand dollars. He put up his house and the stock of his store . . . everything, just to stay in the game.

FELIX: Who took his money? Anyone from here?

SPENCE: No, those two gamblers from Galveston. Someone said they had been run out of Galveston for cheating. I don't know about that, but they've taken everything he has. (*Pause.*) Someone asked him if he was going to quit gambling now that he's lost everything. "The day I quit gambling," he says, "is the day I die."

ED (*muttering*): Roberta . . . Roberta . . .

SPENCE: You never can tell about old Ed, can you? I thought he was stuck on Alberta. Of course, it was hard to tell them apart. I thought Roberta was the one I had, but I could have been wrong. I told them they should wear signs so you could tell them apart. (*Pause.*) How was the widow?

HORACE: She was all right.

FELIX: Whose picture is that?

HORACE: Claire's.

FELIX (*taking it and reading*): "For Horace, lest he forget his friend Claire."

SPENCE: Lest he forget?

ARCHIE: That's what it says.

SPENCE: Lest he forget?

ARCHIE: Yes.

SPENCE: What happened to your face?

HORACE: I got into a fight.

SPENCE: Who with?

HORACE: Val.

SPENCE: Leave him alone. He cut a man once, you know, fighting over a woman. Cut him from ear to ear.

FELIX: Did the man die?

SPENCE: I don't think so.

(BUDDY *comes to the edge of the area.*)

BUDDY (*calling*): Horace . . .

(HORACE *goes to him.*)

HORACE: Yes, Buddy.

BUDDY: My mama says to stop by on the way to the station. She has something to tell you.

HORACE: All right, Buddy. Tell her I'm packing now. I'll be by in about an hour.

BUDDY: Yes Sir. How is that man now?

HORACE: What man?

BUDDY: The one that was hollering so.

HORACE: He's asleep.

BUDDY: Did you ever find out who Roberta was?

HORACE: Yes. It was a girl he met over in Ganado.

BUDDY: Is that right?

(*He goes.* HORACE *gets a suitcase and begins to pack.*)

SPENCE: I got someone to take your share of the rent while you're gone, Horace.

HORACE: Good.

FELIX: Do you think you're ever coming back, Horace?

HORACE: I don't know.

SPENCE: I have five dollars says he'll never come back. Any takers?

FELIX: You'll bet on anything.

ARCHIE: I'll bet you'll meet plenty of pretty widows in Houston, Horace.

HORACE: Think so?

FELIX: Is Claire the first widow you've gone with?

HORACE: Yes.

ARCHIE: She's the first widow anyone's gone with. There is no other widow here, is there?

FELIX: Not under fifty.

ED (*muttering*): Roberta . . . Roberta . . .

ARCHIE: Were those twins pretty?

SPENCE: Pretty enough.

FELIX: They all look alike in the dark.

(HORACE *continues packing.* ARCHIE *gets up.*)

ARCHIE: Let's go across the track and get a woman.

FELIX: I'm broke.

SPENCE: Don't you even have fifty cents? You can have any woman over there for fifty cents.

FELIX: I don't have a dime.

ARCHIE: How are you going to eat today?

FELIX: I don't know. I'll go over to my aunt's and see if she'll feed me.

SPENCE: Here, I'll loan you fifty cents. (*He hands it to him.*)

FELIX: Thanks. (*He takes it.*)

ARCHIE: We'd better wake up Ed. He'll be mad if he wakes up and finds we've gone without him.

SPENCE: He's drunk. He's not going to wake up.

ARCHIE: You want to come along, Horace?

HORACE: I don't have time. My train leaves at eight.

ARCHIE: Don't study too hard.

HORACE: I won't.

SPENCE: Good luck to you, Horace.

HORACE: Thanks.

FELIX: Send us a postcard.

HORACE: I will.

(*They go on.* HORACE *continues packing.*)

ED (*muttering*): Roberta . . . Roberta . . .

(*The lights fade.*)

(*The lights are brought up in the area of* CLAIRE'S *living room.* CLAIRE, BUDDY, *and* MOLLY *are in the area. The children are dressed for school.*)

MOLLY: Mama, I can't find my spelling book.

CLAIRE: Did you leave it in your room?

MOLLY: No.

CLAIRE: Are you sure?

MOLLY: Yes.

BUDDY: I'm going to school. (*He starts out.*)

CLAIRE: You wait for Molly, Buddy.

BUDDY: No, I'll be late. I don't want to be late.

MOLLY: Wait for me, Buddy.

BUDDY: Well, come on then.

MOLLY: I can't go without my spelling book.

CLAIRE (*looking around the room*): Here it is. Now, see? Kiss me goodbye.

(MOLLY *does so.*)

Buddy, kiss me goodbye.

(*He does so. She picks up around the room. She puts on the record of "Waltz Me Around Again, Willie," then turns it off.*

She goes out to the yard area. HORACE *comes in with a suit-case.*)

CLAIRE: Oh, hello, Horace. On your way?

HORACE: Yes.

CLAIRE: Thank you for coming by. I said to the children, "Horace is going to think I'm crazy, asking him to stop by on his way to the train," but I wanted to tell you myself that I changed my mind after you left. I looked at the children asleep and I thought, what if the duplex in Houston doesn't work out and I can't find a renter and all my money will be gone and what will become then of me and the children? I have to think of what will happen to them, you know, because if I don't, who will? So I woke them both up and we had a good long talk, and I decided then and there to marry Ned, for their sake. So I sent him a wire as to my decision to marry him and I asked him to come here next weekend. When I did that, I said to Buddy, "You go tell Horace now to come by here on the way to the train so I can tell him my decision . . . as I want him to hear it from nobody but me." Do you think I'm doing the right thing?

HORACE: I guess so.

CLAIRE: The children do. They couldn't wait to get to school and tell all their friends. They went over to Sissy's and woke her up to tell her. Anyway, right or wrong, we won't be here when you come home.

HORACE: You won't?

CLAIRE: No, because Ned wants us to live in his house in Galveston. So we'll move there after we're married. I don't know what will happen to his sister.

HORACE: Maybe she'll live on with you.

CLAIRE: Maybe so. Ned says she's sweet and easy to get along with and likes children as much as he does. If you're ever in Galveston, come to see us and have a meal with us.

HORACE: Thank you.

CLAIRE (*handing him a piece of paper*): I wrote out the address for you.

HORACE: Thank you.

CLAIRE: Ned says they have a lot of oleander in the front and backyard. I love them, don't you?

HORACE: Yes. My father's people all lived in Galveston.

CLAIRE: Did they?

HORACE: Yes, his father was sent there by the Confederate government. He was in charge of shipping cotton for the Confederacy.

CLAIRE: If you're going to be a traveling man, you and Ned will have a lot in common.

HORACE: Well, I'm not sure, of course, that I'll be a traveling man. It's just that when I finish my business course, I hope to get a job traveling.

CLAIRE: Well, if you do, I hope you will have great success at it. Ned says it pays very well, if you're good at it.

HORACE: I've heard that too.

CLAIRE: And I'm sure you'll be good at it. You have a very nice personality.

HORACE: Thank you.

(*The courthouse clock strikes eight.*)

I guess I'll have to go now, Claire.

CLAIRE: I know. I'd ask you to kiss me goodbye, but it's daylight and all the neighbors are watching.

HORACE: I understand.

CLAIRE: It's been very nice knowing you, and the children and I wish you a lot of luck.

HORACE: Good luck to you too. (*Pause.*) Claire, if I come into the house, could I kiss you goodbye?

CLAIRE: Sure.

(*She goes inside. He follows her and kisses her. A train whistle blows.*)

CLAIRE: There's your train. Hurry, or you'll miss it.

HORACE: So long, Claire.

CLAIRE: So long.

HORACE (*taking his suitcase*): Good luck.

CLAIRE: Good luck to you.

(*The train whistle blows again. He goes hurrying out. As he gets to the edge of the yard area, she calls.*)

CLAIRE: Good luck.

HORACE: Thank you. Good luck to you.

(*The train whistle blows again as he runs out of sight and she comes into the yard area. She waves a last farewell as the lights fade, and we never know if he sees her or not.*)

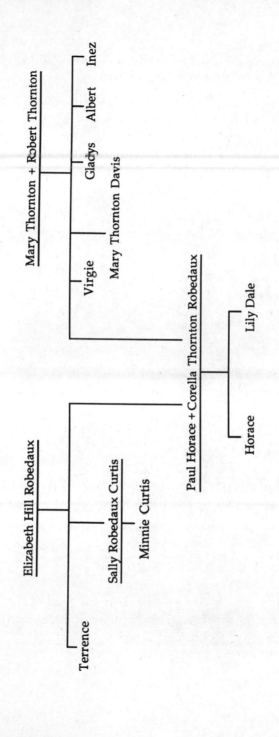